Eduard Fornés

DALÍ ILLUSTRATOR

Reproduction rights for illustrations in this book were granted by:

Christine Argillet, for Chants de Maldoror and books published by Pierre Argillet

Albaretto-Cristini, for Sacred Bible and images from the Albaretto collection

Daniel David, Les Heures Claires, Paris for Divine Comedy illustrations and lithographs

Thérese Lacroix ADPG, France for Dalí images

© Texts: Eduard Fornés

© Texts: Paul J. Karlstrom

© Foreword: Daniel David

© Introduction: Dr. A. Reynolds Morse

© Expert opinion: Robert K. Wittman

© Expert opinion: Alfredo Ghio

© Photography, the image owners

© 2016 of this edition: Les Heures Claires, Paris

Design: Estanis

ISBN 2-911386-20-5

Table of Contents

PROLOGUE
Eduard Fornés

All of my meetings with Dalí were memorable. But among the most memorable were those that took place in his home in Port Lligat where I first met him, the Dalí Museum in Figueres, the restaurant Duran in Figueres, the Meurice Hotel in Paris, the Ritz Hotel in Barcelona and the Castle of Púbol. My last recollection of Dalí was a sad one. That was when I was honored to accompany his cousin Montserrat Dalí to his funeral at Galatea Tower in Figueres.

Since meeting Dalí, I have worked on 20 publications (including this one) on the subject of Dalí, some written by the artist himself: *Babaouo*; *The Secret Life of Salvador Dalí*, the Opera-Poem *Etre Dieu*, and *Museum Works* by Josep Pla, illustrated by Dalí. Other publications included catalogs and studies by art critics and a range of other topics devoted exclusively to the subject of Dalí.

The exhibition *Dalí and His Books, Dalí the Writer, and Dalí the Illustrator*, which was proposed by Dalí himself, is without a doubt the event which best gave me a deeper understanding of the complexity of his life and work. This understanding was developed during my organization of 34 exhibitions based on the contents of the books, in 11 different countries over a 12-year period.

My memories have surfaced from time and oblivion, and although I have vivid recollections of most of the experiences, I am well aware (and now is a good time to admit) that unfortunately some wonderful details are probably lost, since I have never been in the habit of committing everything to notes and archiving them. However, since my meetings with Dalí were always memorable I am pleased to have retained substantial notes of my times with him.

Having said that, I would like to state that what I have allowed to appear in these pages are only those facts which can be proven through documentation. Because of the complexity of crossed interests that abound in the Dalínian world, I have enclosed, along with the text, illustrations of documents of important historical value. These documents should prove to be useful for authentication and provenance by collectors, galleries, auction houses, appraisers and academics.

I was pleased to have noted scholar Paul Karlstrom elect to take part in this project, and publish *The Dalí Enigma: Art, Ambition, and Abnormal Psychology* and *The Dalí Dilemma* for the first time in this book. These new writings should prove useful for academics as well as galleries, collectors and all who are interested in gaining greater insights about Salvador Dalí, his art and his world.

As a result of more than 20 years of research and access to the aforementioned documents, I can now report with clarity and certainty that I am confident in my findings reported in this book and am sure that they are quite accurate.

One of my reasons for writing this book was to add something to the understanding of the complex world of Dalí by drawing upon experiences I had during the years I worked with him. In addition, I limited myself to carefully researching the specific body of works in this book using the documentation provided by the editors who worked with Dalí in publishing them. Dalí published special editions rich in engravings and other graphic works. Many of these graphic works were signed by Dalí himself. While the basic subjects I am writing about are known, the information included herein provides archival documents from Dalí's publishers for the first time in any book. I did substantial research so that this book could very accurately add to the body of knowledge of the works presented herein. What I offer in these pages is only part of the complexity surrounding the enigma of Salvador Dalí.

In March 1991, I asked Dr. A. Reynolds Morse (President of the Salvador Dalí Foundation, St. Petersburg, Florida) for an introduction to my catalog about Dalí and the books, and especially about Dalí as illustrator. About a month later on April 24 he responded in a letter saying:

> "In reference to the "Dalí as Illustrator" book and your letter of March 20th, I will be happy to write its introduction, but I cannot promise just when it will be done."

In another paragraph of the same letter he wrote:

> "This way we will have the definitive book on Dalí as Illustrator and nobody can possibly publish a better or more complete one because we can be sure your edition is the definitive one..."

Two months later I received, as promised, the introduction from Dr. Morse. Receiving the letter stimulated me to establish the outline I would use to approach the project. Dr. Morse and I agreed this book needed to be an accurate, thoroughly documented historical treatise.

Many years have passed since I sold the company Distribucions d'Art Surrealista to the Gala Salvador Dalí Foundation and left behind this intense period of my life when I was so absorbed with the work and the personality of Dalí. I can now see that leaving that period was the only way I would ever have the time to work on this book and complete it.

Without the unfettered access I was granted to the considerable documentation belonging to the publishers of the artwork, I would not have been able to complete this book. I wish to thank Jean Estrade and Daniel David of Les Editions d'Art Les Heures Claires Paris, the Albaretto family of Torino, the Pierre Argillet family of France and the many private collectors and friends of Dalí who helped in bringing this book to fruition.

Eduard Fornés

DALÍ AS ILLUSTRATOR
Dr. A. Reynolds Morse

Among the many facets of Salvador Dalí's total genius is his little publicized ability as a versatile illustrator. No truly definitive list of his skills in this area is possible without some arbitrary definitions of what is meant by the general term "illustrator." Are his works created for various ballets illustrations? In what category do his seven oils belong which he made for the film, "Seven Wonders of the World?" or the works done for Shakespeare's MACBETH (1946) and MIDSUMMER NIGHT'S DREAM? Etc., etc.

Any book on Dalí's illustrations today cannot fail to recognize all the commissioned watercolours and gouaches which the artist produced especially for reproduction after 1963. These valid signed limited edition folios or suites were not strictly either books or illustrations, even though the original works were on specific topics such as CARMEN, the GATES OF PARIS, or based on MARQUIS DE SADE or such strangely assorted subjects as baseball, Chicago, The Plaza Hotel in New York and Honolulu, or the Costa Brava, etc. These various signed reproductions were generally sold separately, or laid into various sorts of "covers." But can they be honestly called illustrations? No, in the general sense of the word, as used here. Indeed, Mr. Field is planning a long needed catalog of the painter's prints, graphic reproductions or "separates" as they are variously called.

These are not insurmountable problems, however, but they do highlight the need today for honestly definitive books on various aspects of Salvador Dalí's skills in many areas. If we limit the subject to illustrations for books and do so in an authoritative and consistent manner, it is possible to show Dalí for the truly facile and brilliant artist we know him to be.

The rewards for pure scholarship in Dalí's case, however, are difficult to come by at this remove. Remember, there were no scholars and biographers keeping contemporaneous tabs on the mercurial spirit of this great artist, and he vocally preferred chaos and disorder to the rigors of what he called "morturial projects". He was a suspicious man, and he would say of well-meaning attempts to record his multi-faceted activities, "myself is no like dees project. Is only ok after y am dead!" And so here we are in 1992 putting together an ambitious attempt to show Dalí as an illustrator!

This ranges typically from his four totally different sets of illustrations for DON QUIXOTE to superb limited editions such as THE CASTLE OF OTRANTO (1964) or his boldest project that required half a decade to achieve – his illustrations for Dante, 1960. These were refused by the Rome State Press in 1954 on the curious grounds that it was inappropriate or indelicate for a sensational Spanish Surrealist to illustrate the work of Italy's greatest author!

The formats of Dalí's illustrated works run from small books such as his Benvenuto Cellini (1947) or THE HOUSE WITHOUT WINDOWS written by his friend Maurice Sandoz (1948) and six other novelettes by the same writer, on to large imposing formats measured in feet rather than inches, and some of which are almost too heavy for one librarian or collector to lift. In topical scope his illustrations are legion. Indeed one book he made early on for Gala and Paul Eluard is so intimately erotic it still has never been published.

"Dalí as Illustrator" thus remains a challenging subject as this ambitious attempt to show the fabulous scope of Dalí's imagination and the sureness of his draftsmanship will prove.

Today Dalí clearly belongs among the great illustrators of all time. This means placing a Spaniard in an internationally sacrosanct literary category. This talent, however, its variety, and the artist's grasp of his topics, many of which were preparatorily read aloud to him by Gala, triumphs over his popular image as the scandalous maker of improbable Dalínian myths, and a breaker of traditions in many fields.

Dalí, however, is never over-personalizingly destructive of his author, nor his selected texts. In fact, he revitalizes them, and raises them to new heights well above the level where our plebeian imaginations often tend to fumble for an acceptable visualization which is both apt, precise, and fully in line with imagined traditions and which it is the illustrator's role to immortalize in a fully visual but not overly personalized form. Thus Dalí always embellishes but NEVER overwhelms the text.

The artist can also be overwhelming when dealing with himself as an author. This is proven by his illustrations for his SECRET LIFE (1948). And to me it is significant that Dalí chose NOT to illustrate his own brilliant novel, HIDDEN FACES (1944), except for a frontispiece to which he was pressured, over our objections at the time, to add a fig leaf.

Cover of the book *THE HOUSE WITHOUT WINDOWS* by Maurice Sandoz, illustrated by Salvador Dalí.

Tracing Dalí's career as an illustrator from his youthful drawings for local Catalan writers' modest genre novels such as L'ONCLE VICENTS by Puig Pujades (1926) or BRUIXES DE LLERS (1924) to his watercolours done for the Rizzoli Bible so many decades later, is an extraordinary adventure in this Catalan's creativity. Without straining or profaning an author, Dalí never misses a key nuance that is fully creditable to the writer to whom the painter never fails to pay tribute by his special embellishments that prevent his illustrations from ever being either trite or too derivational.

The definitive book on Dalí as an illustrator has long been needed, especially as book collectors wake up to the fact that Dalí was a truly prescient artist who could not only add fresh immortality to our own imaginings so as to enhance the verbal picture – his precious image sacred not only to the author, but also to the reader – and quite spontaneously to Dalí's own unique genius – all at the same time.

Certainly many astute people may well ask why I have not referenced some of the overshadowingly great illustrators of the past, and tried to introduce Dalí into their august and classic ranks. The reason is that Dalí's freshness of outlook is entirely forward looking – not backward to his vaunted precursors. Thus, he set a totally new pace and a new standard for the whole genre. In fact even without Dalí's charisma and sans his art, his work as an illustrator alone would have brought him a well-deserved immortality, all his other brilliant attributes notwithstanding.

This volume is aimed at being a landmark book – and it is hoped a truly definitive one. It is also an international memorial tribute to Dalí as the friend and mentor of all of those involved in presenting it for the record.

It is well to remember that Dalí's illustrations are done in various medias. These range from pen and ink to etchings, at which he was very adept, and in the publications of which Pierre Argillet was perhaps the boldest and the best. He was deft both with watercolors and gouaches, as well as oils, although at this remove no one can be certain on who selected the medium, the artist or the publisher.

DALÍ AS ILLUSTRATOR will become even more formidable when it is realized this is but one facet of his remarkably inventive brain.

Cover of the novel *L'ONCLE VICENTS* by Puig Pujades, which contains illustrations taken from Dalí's drawings as a young man.

The tendency today is to overlook the need for truly definitive studies of each area of this distinguished Catalan's facile genius. This is because true scholarship is increasingly being made secondary to the profitable exploitation of Dalí's inherent sensationalism.

Both Albert Field and I feel honoured to be allowed to participate in what we hope is the first of many truly scholarly analyses and studies of the multi-faceted talents of Salvador Dalí. THE WORLD OF DALÍ is thus deeply indebted to Eduard Fornés for his willingness to work to publish what we hope is the definitive work on Dalí's illustrations.

That is opposed to the usually hurry-up exploitive books which put Dalí's sensationalism, myths and the publisher's quick personal gains ahead of the accuracy and completeness needed to firm up his real image as the art of history will eventually appraise it.

Dr. A. Reynolds Morse
May 25, 1991

Among the many facets of Salvador Dali's total genius is his little publicised ability as a versatile illustrator. No truly definitive list of his skills in this area is possible without some arbitrary definitions of what is meant by the general term "illustrator." Are his works created for various ballets illustrations? In what category do his seven oils belong which he made for the film, "Seven Wonders of the World?" or the works done for Shakespeare's MACBETH (1946) and MIDSUMMER NIGHTS DREAM? etc., etc.

Any book on Dali's illustrations today cannot fail to recognize all the commissioned watercolors and gouaches which the artist produced especially for reproduction after 1963. These valid signed limited edition folios or suites were not strictly either books or illustrations, even though the original works were on specific topics such as CARMEN, the GATES OF PARIS, or based on MARQUIS DE SADE or such strangely assorted subjects as baseball, Chicago, The Plaza Hotel in New York and Honolulu, or the Costa Brava, etc. These various signed reproductions were generally sold separately, or laid into various sorts of "covers." But can they be honestly called illustrations? No, in the general sense of the word, as used here. Indeed, Mr. Field is planning a long needed catalog of the painter's prints, graphics reproductions or "separates" as they are variously called.

These are not insurmountable problems, however, but they do highlight the need today for honestly definitive books on various aspects of Salvador Dali's skills in many areas. If we limit the subject to illustrations for books and do so in an authorative and consistent manner, it is possible to show Dali for the truly facile and brilliant artist we know him to be.

The rewards for pure scholarship in Dali's case, however, are difficult to come by at this remove. Remember, there were no

FAX TRANSMISSION
IMS Company
TODAY'S DATE 5/30/91

Eduard Fornés   A. Reynolds Morse
                       IMS COMPANY
FAX NUMBER 011-34-3231-1312   (216) 643-1815
                                   (216) 546-1069

scholars and biographers keeping contemporaneous tabs on the mercurial spirit of this great artist, and he vocally preferred chaos and disorder to the rigours of what he called "morturial projects." He was a suspicious man, and he would say of well-meaning attempts to record his multi-faceted activities, "myself is no like dees project. Is only OK after y am dead!" And so here we are in 1992 putting together an ambitious attempt to show Dali as an illustrator!

This ranges typically from his four totally different sets of illustrations for DON QUIXOTE to superb limited editions such as THE CASTLE OF OTRANTO (1964) or his boldest project that required half a decade to achieve - his illustrations for Dante, 1960. These were refused by the Rome State Press in 1954 on the curious grounds that it was inappropriate or indelicate for a sensational Spanish Surrealist to illustrate the work of Italy's greatest author!

The formats of Dali's illustrated works run from small books such as his Benvenuto Cellini (1947) or THE HOUSE WITHOUT WINDOWS written by his friend Maurice Sandoz (1948) and six other novelettes by the same writer, on to large imposing formats measured in feet rather than inches, and some of which are almost too heavy for one librarian or collector to lift. In topical scope his illustrations are legion. Indeed one book he made early on for Gala and Paul Eluard is so intimately erotic it still has never been published.

"Dali as Illustrator" thus remains a challenging subject as this ambitious attempt to show the fabulous scope of Dali's imagination and the sureness of his draftsmanship will prove.

Today Dali clearly belongs among the great illustrators of all time. This means placing a Spaniard in an internationally sacrosanct literary category. This talent, however, its variety, and the artist's grasp of his topics, many of which were

preparatorily read aloud to him by Gala, triumphs over his popular image as the scandalous maker of improbable Dalinian myths, and a breaker of traditions in many fields.

Dali, however, is never over-personalizingly destructive of his author, nor his selected texts. In fact, he revitalizes them, and raises them to new heights well above the level where our plebeian imaginations often tend to fumble for an acceptable visualization which is both apt, precise, and fully in line with imagined traditions and which it is the illustrator's role to immortalize in a fully visual but not overly personalized form. Thus Dali always embellishes but NEVER overwhelms the text.

The artist can also be overwhelming when dealing with himself as an author. This is proven by his illustrations for his SECRET LIFE (1943) and his subsequent FIFTY SECRETS OF MAGIC CRAFTSMANSHIP (1948). And to me it is significant that Dali chose NOT to illustrate his own brilliant novel, HIDDEN FACES (1944), except for a frontispiece to which he was pressured, over our objections at the time, to add a fig leaf.

Tracing Dali's career as an illustrator from his youthful drawings for local Catalan writers' modest genre novels such as L'ONCLE VICENTS by Puig Pujades, 1926 or BRUIXES DE LLERS (1924) to his watercolors done for the Rizzoli Bible so many decades later, is an extraordinary adventure in this Catalan's creativity. Without straining or profaning an author, Dali never misses a key nuance that is fully creditable to the writer to whom the painter never fails to pay tribute by his special embellishments that prevent his illustrations from ever being either trite or too derivational.

The definitive book on Dali as an illustrator has long been needed, especially as book collectors wake up to the fact that Dali was a truly prescient artist who could only add fresh immortality to our own imaginings so as to enhance the verbal

picture - his precious image sacred not only to the author, but also to the reader - and quite spontaneously to Dali's own unique genius - all at the same time.

Certainly many astute people may well ask why I have not referenced some of the overshadowingly great illustrators of the past, and tried to introduce Dali into their august and classic ranks. The reason is that Dali's freshness of outlook is entirely forward looking - not backward to his vaunted precursors. Thus, he set a totally new pace and a new standard for the whole genre. In fact even without Dali's charisma and sans his art, his work as an illustrator alone would have brought him a well-deserved immortality, all his other brilliant attributes notwithstanding.

This volume is aimed at being a landmark book - and it is hoped a truly definitive one. It is also an international memorial tribute to Dali as the friend and mentor of all of those involved in presenting it for the record.

It is well to remember that Dali's illustrations are done in various medias. These range from pen and ink to etchings, at which he was very adept, and in the publications, of which Pierre Argillet was perhaps the boldest and the best. He was deft both with watercolors and gouaches, as well as oils, although at this remove no one can be certain on who selected the medium, the artist or the publisher.

DALI AS ILLUSTRATOR will become even more formidable when it is realized this is but one facet of his remarkably inventive brain.

The tendency today is to overlook the need for truly definitive studies of each area of this distinguished Catalan's facile genius. This is because true scholarship is increasingly

Original text (pages 1-4) written by Dr. A Reynolds Morse including notes of Eduard Fornés being made secondary to the profitable exploitation of Dali's inherent sensationalism.

Both Albert Field and I feel honored to be allowed to participate in what we hope is the first of many truly scholarly analyses and studies of the multi-faceted talents of Salvador Dali. THE WORLD OF DALI is thus deeply indebted to Edward Fornes for his willingness to work to publish what we hope is the definitive work on Dali's illustrations.

That is opposed to the usually hurry-up exploitive books which put Dali's sensationalism, myths and the publisher's quick personal gains ahead of the accuracy and completeness needed to firm up his real image as the art of history will eventually appraise it.

A. Reynolds Morse, PhD

Dr. A. Reynolds Morse
May 25, 1991

Original text (page 5) written by Dr. A Reynolds Morse including notes of Eduard Fornés

FOREWORD
Daniel David

As director of Les Heures Claires, the publisher and copyright holder of Dalí's *Divine Comedy*, and the person who for many years worked side-by-side with its former director, Mr. Jean Estrade, I am grateful to Eduard Fornés for giving us the ability to publish this book. Over the years, I learned a great deal about the works of Dalí from our company's founder, Mr. Estrade, who worked very closely with Dalí during a time when Dalí was in complete control of all his faculties. I am sure Mr. Estrade and Dalí himself would have been equally pleased to see this book finally published.

Now the complete universe of those interested in having a greater understanding of Dalí: art historians, experts, academics, students, writers, biographers, researchers, museums, appraisers, authenticators, collectors and the general public as well will have access to this extremely thorough and scholarly work. On behalf of Les Heures Claires, I endorse this book as the definitive one for this part of Dalí's artwork. Importantly, the book offers new insights into Salvador Dalí by Eduard Fornés, someone who knew him well and worked side-by-side with him, and two well researched new writings about Dalí by the noted art scholar Dr. Paul Karlstrom.

As part of the process, I provided Eduard Fornés unlimited access to the archives of Les Heures Claires and my own archives dealing with Dalí and Jean Estrade. These included records, contracts, certificates and attestations by Dalí, Jean Estrade and myself, photographs, notes, written anecdotes, illustrations and artwork. As a result of the painstaking work of Eduard Fornés, we now have the most detailed and accurate information in existence regarding the group of artworks studied in this book. This includes *Les Chants de Maldoror*, *The Divine Comedy*, *28 Graphic Editions* published by Les Heures Claires with Dr. Giuseppe Albaretto, and the *Biblia Sacra*, commissioned by Albaretto and published by Rizzoli.

In reviewing the manuscript provided to me for this book that Eduard Fornés has worked on for more than 20 years, it became clear that Fornés left no stone unturned in fulfilling the confidence expressed by Dr. A. Reynolds Morse, founder of the Salvador Dalí Museum in St. Petersburg, Florida where he states in this book's introduction: "The tendency today is to overlook the need for truly definitive studies of each area of (Dalí's) facile genius. This is because true scholarship is increasingly being made secondary to the profitable exploitation of Dalí's inherent sensationalism." I am quite certain that Mr. Fornés held this statement uppermost in his mind as he contributed his extraordinary efforts and determination to bringing this book to completion.

To understand more about what is contained in the pages of this book, it is important that I comment briefly on Dalí. On the one hand, in his early artistic life, Dalí was scrupulous and meticulous in his standards of excellence and developed the masterpieces of graphic work which are the subject of this book. Dalí's unrelenting quest for perfection and fidelity in the illustrations he created for *The Divine Comedy* engravings revealed this to me firsthand.

On the other hand, he welcomed, embraced and fostered controversy. In his later life he produced many editions of graphic work which were quickly done and poorly documented, and as a result fostered numerous forgeries. This behavior opened the door for unscrupulous individuals to prey upon an unsuspecting public, which was unarmed because of the absence of reliable research and documentation resources.

The two catalogs of Dalí's graphic art that were published in the 1990s, the first by Michler and Lopsinger in 1993 and the second by Albert Field in 1996, made great strides in correcting this dilemma. However, considering the enormity of the task and the complexity of Dalí himself, much of the available information on the artwork was not fully documented.

This book now provides, for the first time, meticulously accurate research on such matters as *The Divine Comedy* and *Biblia Sacra* graphics and the annotations and numbering of these works. The 59 known variations of block signatures that are on *The Divine Comedy* engravings are presented along with identification of the canto illustrations on which they appear. Other sections provide a thorough and fascinating analysis of Dalí's authentic hand signatures in pencil, colored pencil and ink on these artworks, conducted by individuals who witnessed Dalí's signings, and experts in art authentication procedures and graphology.

Throughout the book Fornés illustrates documents from his own archives that vividly bring to life the man who was Salvador Dalí, his love for great literature, and the relationship between the two men. Dalí's editors and friends are discussed along with the people who were close to him and involved in his book projects. Another section reproduces for the first time, personal letters, certificates, attestations and other material from our own archives at Les Heures Claires and from the archives of others involved in illustrated book projects and editions of graphics. These documents shed a clear light on Dalí's unwavering commitment to these projects and the diligence and faithfulness to detail of the people who worked with him to bring them to fruition.

In 2014 Enciclopèdia Catalana, in order to commemorate the 25th anniversary of Salvador Dalí's death, published a deluxe edition of *A thousand and one nights* with color reproductions in the original size of some of the 50 watercolors which Dalí painted. This edition of 999 numbered examples included a text by the art critic Ricard Mas about Dalí's illustrations in *A thousand and one nights*, and a text by Eduard Fornés about this book *Dalí illustrator* and about the relationship between Dalí and the Albaretto family

I wish to thank Eduard Fornés for his scholarship, his determination and his unflagging commitment to making this exceptional resource available to the world. Les Heures Claires is proud to be the publisher and to further continue our historic lineage of great fine art publications with the long-awaited completion and publication of this book.

Daniel David

THE DALÍ ENIGMA:
ART, AMBITION, AND ABNORMAL PSYCHOLOGY

Paul J. Karlstrom, Ph. D

Salvador Dalí is among the best-known figures in 20th-century art, but he is also one of the most problematic. For this he has not only his considerable talent as a draftsman to thank, but also his seemingly insatiable need and penchant for calling attention to himself. In an age of avant-garde "outsiders," Dalí skillfully played both sides of the modernist divide. In fact, despite his early association with André Breton and his fellow Surrealists in Paris, Dalí and his art were, on the surface, fundamentally conservative and traditional. True to his nature, he perversely positioned himself against the modernism of his Parisian colleagues. As a result, although the young Spaniard from Catalonia was initially embraced by Breton as the most imaginative of the Surrealists, he was ultimately banished from the movement.

For viewers less familiar with modern art history, Dalí's superficially transgressive imagery was both exciting and accessible. The soft watches and burning giraffes, not to mention the shocking sexual imagery, were much easier to appreciate than the abstractions of Kandinsky or Mondrian, or even the cubist distortions of Picasso. The technical virtuosity – Dalí's skill at creating an illusion of reality, subject notwithstanding – in itself denoted "good art" for many. Even his critics still acknowledge that Dalí was a master draftsman, among the best of his generation. But ability with the medium, no matter how impressive, is not enough. According to Dawn Ades, Dalí himself was aware of that, his technique being the servant of his ideas.[1]

The renowned intellectual historian Peter Gay, in his award-winning book on modernism, described Dalí dismissively: "As eager to astonish the public with his pronouncements as with his bizarre, often distasteful Surrealist canvases, he gave the back of his hand to all his modernist competitors."[2] The artist's proclaimed objective was "to rescue painting from the void of modern art."[3] With statements like this, Dalí was taking on his natural colleagues while pandering to the bourgeois taste of an uninformed and tradition-bound public. It is difficult to account for this self-destructive position, which isolated him – and not in a

The Surrealist group in Paris, 1930

Top Row: Paul Éluard, Jean (Hans) Arp, Yves Tanguy, Rene Crevel
Bottom Row: Tristan Tzara, André Breton, Salvador Dalí, Max Ernst, Man Ray

1. Dawn Ades, *Dalí* (London and New York: Thames & Hudson, 1982 and 1985). Dalí's pragmatic attitude towards technical virtuosity is emphasized here (see for example 6, 101-103) and elsewhere in her writing on the artist. Ades is the leading authority on Dalí, and this World of Art series paperback is the most thorough and art-historically informed study readily available. Dalí wrote that "My whole ambition in the pictorial domain is to materialize the images of concrete irrationality with the most imperialist fury of precision." *The Conquest of the Irrational* (1935), quoted in Ades, 126.

2. Peter Gay, *Modernism: The Lure of Heresy, From Baudelaire to Beckett and Beyond*. New York, W.W. Norton & Company, 2008, 16.

3. Gay, 16. Dawn Ades cautions against the over or exclusive use of Freudian psychoanalysis to explain Dalí and his art and prudently informs the reader that she is "not qualified to undertake fully the type of psychological/sociological analysis that Dalí's work seems to beg." (Ades, 6). In the end, however, she returns constantly to that approach, and she draws upon Freudian and related ideas when discussing his imagery. There really is no other choice with an artist who strategically and consistently employed in his paintings symbols both personal and drawn from Freud, a practice which appears to have begun even before his association with the Surrealists.

Dalí drawing a lithographic plate of the portrait of Freud. (photo A. Matabosch)

4. See William S. Rubin, *Dada, Surrealism, and Their Heritage*, New York: The Museum of Modern Art, 1968, 109-113. Rubin quotes a letter from Freud to Stefan Zweig the day after he and Dalí paid a visit to the famous founder of psychoanalysis in 1939. Dalí did a sketch of Freud and commented that his subject's cranium was reminiscent of a snail. Freud wrote that"...until now I have been inclined to regard the Surrealists, who have apparently adopted me as their patron saint, as complete fools.... That young Spaniard, with his candid fanatical eyes and his undeniable technical mastery, has changed my estimate. It would indeed be very interesting to investigate analytically how he came to create that picture." (212).

5. *L'Ane pourri, Le Surrealisme au Service de la Revolution* (Paris), vol.1, no.1, 1930, 9. Quoted in Rubin, 109.

6. Andre Breton, *The First Dalí Exhibition*, in *What is Surrealism?* translated by David Gascoyne (London, 1936), 27-30.

7. Breton in *Entretiens* 1913-1952 (Paris, 1952), 159. Quoted in Rubin, 107.

8. Rubin, 111. Later Rubin compares the "miniature dimensions" of these works as "ideal for an image projected by imagination, analogous as they are to the 'screen' of the mind's eye...located just inside the forehead" (113). He credits Meyer Schapiro for that interesting observation, derived from the works of Paul Klee, about the location and size of the "screen" of the imagination (195, note 96).

particularly original way –from the flow of modern art. He chose the worn-out techniques of 19th-century academic painting (based on the Renaissance) as the proper technical basis for all art. His modernism was in the bizarre subjects and irrational juxtapositions of imagery he favored, both calculated to attract an admiring audience. Over the years, his flamboyant life-style and behavior – finally more than his paintings and other art – accounted for his burgeoning fame. In this he actively compounded the problems that came to surround his reputation as an artist.

Most writing about Dalí has focused on the psychological aspects of his art (including his objects and poetry) and, indeed, the ritualized acting out of his own fears and sexual obsessions. Derived from and, in circular self-reinforcement, contributing to his personal "aberrant" psychology, Dalí's creative life was governed by what he called his "paranoiac-critical method," an example of the influential ideas of Sigmund Freud.[4] Much is made of this by way of explanation for the contradictions and flamboyant perversities – often self-destructive – which contribute to the Dalí "enigma." The artist's own statements seem to encourage this general view: "I believe that the moment is near when by a procedure of active paranoiac thought, it will be possible... to systematize confusion and contribute to the total discrediting of the world of reality."[5] And, as evidence of the young Spaniard's early good standing with the Surrealists, André Breton wrote, "It is perhaps with Dalí that all the great mental windows are opening."[6] Embraced by Breton at a moment (1929) of crisis in the Surrealist movement between abstract automatism and the emerging narrative direction of Yves Tanguy and René Magritte, Dalí for several years was the newcomer who, in Breton's words, "incarnated the Surrealist spirit [and] whose genius made it shine."[7]

The fact that Dalí was eventually banished by Breton takes nothing away from the positive, perhaps refreshing, impact his illusionistic dream paintings and possibly even his imaginative Freudian imagery had on the look of modernist art during his early association with the Surrealists. William Rubin, writing in his catalog for the important Museum of Modern Art exhibition on Dada and Surrealism, gives Dalí his full due as a serious and gifted contributor to the movement. He describes the first mature works of 1929 as "a series of brilliant small pictures whose hallucinatory intensity he was never to surpass."[8] It is clear that, for Rubin and others seeking to sort out the conflicting parts of Dalí's art career and place him within the broader context, the slick academic verisimilitude that marked the artist's technical skill was an effective and legitimate tool in the modernist project of upsetting ideas of what constitutes reality. This same painterly skill was, and remained, an attractive feature of

Dalí's pictures for a large and appreciative audience. However, this popular appeal rankled art critics and historians, bringing severely harsh appraisal, even dismissal, of the later work – that is, until Dalí's newly appreciated influence upon Post-modernist and Pop art polished his faded reputation as a modernist provocateur.

It is precisely Dalí's transgressive projects, outrageous behavior, and shameless self-promotion that seem to fit comfortably with much of the art of the 1960s and 1970s. Dalí, among other things, can be easily recognized as a performance artist who builds the entire spectacle around himself. The self-reference and compulsive "confessionalism" of much recent art can also be traced back to Salvador Dalí, notably in the work and theatrical self-presentation of Andy Warhol and Jeff Koons (not to mention Matthew Barney, Damian Hirst, Andreas Serrano, even Cindy Sherman, all of whom in their different ways echo Dalí's stratagems), who connect themselves to Dalí without apology. The blurring of boundaries in art that characterizes an important and liberating aspect of modernism can be seen as part of Dalí territory. But the attendant and bogus process of democratization (think of the 15 minutes of fame bestowed by Warhol on all of us and which has helped to produce our contemporary world of "reality" entertainment) is also part of the legacy.

It is, in fact, more than a little ironic that Dalí, given his fundamental academic conservatism and reverence for the past as a measure of artistic importance, would have lent his talents and ideas to what amounts to a removal of the distinctions between high and low art. Dalí's motives, as is the case with many contemporary individuals, seemed increasingly to be directed toward the acquisition of popular attention and acclaim. If fame was his primary goal, for a time he was wildly successful – at first for his astounding ability to create illusion with paint and later for the calculated sensationalism that became his trademark in collaboration with his wife and muse, Gala.[9] For Dalí, always in the public eye, fame morphed into notoriety. But that seems less problematic now, with the solidly established art historical position of Warhol's elitist popular culture. The Factory, Velvet Underground, Studio 54, and the multiple "poster" portraits of, among others, Marilyn Monroe and Mao Tse-tung, are icons of the second half of the 20th century. In their way, Dalí's accessible Surrealism and transgressive public persona participate in the same ethos.

Interestingly, it may be as much the photographic quality of Dalí's paintings as other, perhaps less superficial, art considerations that begin to suggest Dalí's specific position in art history. Certainly it provides an apparent link to much recent art, whether in the proliferation of

9. Gala's central role in Dalí's life, from the time of their meeting in 1929 in Cadaqués and civil wedding in Paris in 1934 to her death in 1982, is recognized and well documented. Gala (Elena Ivanovna Diakonova) was, at the time of her meeting with Dalí, married to Surrealist poet Paul Éluard, with whom she had a child and a "modern" open marriage. After an affair with another leading Surrealist, Max Ernst, she was won over by Dalí and soon took over the job of wife, muse, model, and business manager. Although Dalí said Gala introduced him to "normal love," just what that means is still unclear.

contemporary realism or the pushing of photography to tour-de-force extremes of scale and manipulation that provides a kind of common meeting ground between public taste/admiration and artistic ends. Dalí deserves credit for helping to create an aesthetic of fame that is undeniably a part of contemporary life and a great deal of creative endeavor. Above all, sex and nudity carry the challenge directly to a polite middle-class with its ideas of appropriate subjects for art – the long history of the (mainly female) nude notwithstanding. What distinguishes Dalí's masterful use of realist means are his unexpected – often shocking – juxtapositions, with typically disturbing and revealing (and in Dalí's case, irrational) imagery. In this he brings to mind the creepy, over-the-top sexually perverse staged photographic works of Joel-Peter Witkin.

Dalí's ego and ambition to establish his position as the greatest artist of modern times further clouded his always fragile self-critical faculty, and he took strategic steps to remedy that perceived lack of full appreciation. Scale provided one tool. Among his late period works are monumental compositions – such as *The Sacrament of the Last Supper*, a popular work with visitors to Washington's National Gallery of Art – that ironically sacrifice the compelling hermetic and fantastic qualities that brought him fame in the beginning.[10] Much of the charm and power of Dalí's early surrealist works is in the claustrophobic, and at the same time emotionally expansive, landscape space that conjures a complete and utterly new imaginative world. In contrast, the religious themes that he turned to, especially the large-scale compositions, fail in that respect. What we are drawn to is the meticulous treatment of these obsessively depicted and rendered modern-era icons of Freudian anxiety. Not surprisingly, illustrated books such as *The Divine Comedy* and *Sacra Biblia* preserve in the best drawings, partly through intimacy of scale, the compressed energy that Romanesque depictions of death and damnation unleash as the viewer is drawn into their restricted space. In so doing, these and related works continue to look back to and provide reminders of one of Dalí's strongest periods.

But, alas for his reputation as a serious artist, Dalí insisted on presenting himself within the context of mental illness. Despite the attention it brought him, perhaps his famous paranoia should have been directed back at himself. In any event, he came to be known as a madman, and the cultivation of this image was accelerated with his first trip to the United States in 1934. It also seemed closely aligned with his desire to gain access to the fashionable, and wealthy, quarters of American society. Dalí was encouraged to go to the States by his patron Caresse Crosby and, despite his fears of the ocean crossing, he was "finally overcome by those purveyors of upper middle-class American affluence."[11] In a very

10. Dalí's grand *Sacrament of the Last Supper* (1955), measuring 65 x 105 inches, is a testament to the artist's popularity and the long reach of his ambition. It was donated to the National Gallery of Art, Washington, D.C., in 1963 by collector Chester Dale, a major patron of NGA whose portrait by Dalí also hangs in the museum. There could not be a bigger discrepancy in scale and subject than that between this grandiose religious statement and a small "cabinet" painting such as *Persistence of Memory*.

11. Dickran Tashjian, *A Boatload of Madmen: Surrealism and the American Avant-Garde 1920-1950* (New York: Thames and Hudson, 1995), 51. Dalí patrons Caresse Crosby and her socialite poet husband, Harry, were avant-garde book publishers. Caresse continued Black Sun Press in Paris after Harry's suicide. They also had a residence in New York where the Dalís were frequent guests.

real way, Dalí was seduced and further corrupted by America, or rather by what he imagined he needed to do to assure his success there. As art historian Dickran Tashjian describes the situation, the Surrealists by 1930 were already suspicious of Dalí's bizarre imagery and behavior as "commercial pandering."[12] In New York he was being inaccurately described by the press as the leader of Surrealism. But the main attraction seems to have been that his painting was purportedly the work of a "madman." Again, in the words of Tashjian, "Dalí might not have gained such ready entry into the world of high fashion if he had kept out of the public eye. The American public, willing to view the modern artist as 'crazy' ever since the 1913 Armory Show, was all the more willing to be seduced by the handsome Dalí, as photogenic as a Latin lover on the Hollywood screen."[13]

Peter Gay is among those who find Dalí's place as an artist less than secure, and he credits George Orwell's early appraisal for getting it right: "The two qualities that Dalí unquestionably possesses are a gift for drawing and an atrocious egoism." Gay further observed that "without the first he never would have been able to gratify the second."[14] But in a strange way, Dalí's offensive ego and relentless self-promotion, to the point of creating and exploiting what amounted to an aesthetic of mental illness, fits comfortably in the post-modern era. Critic Robert Hughes expressed the Dalí-Warhol continuum in an interesting and provocative way:

> "The cultural moment of the mid-sixties favored a cultural void. Television was producing an affectless culture. It was no longer necessary for an artist to act crazy, like Salvador Dalí. Other people could act crazy for you: that's what the Warhol Factory was all about. By the end of the sixties craziness was becoming normal, and half of America seemed to be immersed in some tedious and noisy form of self-expression."[15]

These observations are less than flattering to either subject. However, there are more generous treatments that appear in recent years as the focus of critical thinking has shifted. Warhol has emerged as one of the great creative figures of the 20th century, a judgment that requires not only acknowledgment of the obvious lineage going back to Marcel Duchamp, but also recognition of Dalí as among the other predecessors.

But even in the earlier period, there were admirers of the imaginative scope of the work and apologists for the commercial self-promotion. Among the most interesting of these is a fellow artist, a Dadaist and peripheral Surrealist himself, the American transplant to Paris, Man Ray. In his 1963 autobiography, *Self Portrait*, Ray served up a sympathetic, and informative, profile:

12. Tashjian, 50.

13. Tashjian, 51.

14. Gay, 149.

15. Robert Hughes, *The Rise of Andy Warhol* in the New York Review of Books (February 18, 1982), 6-10. Anthologized in Steven Henry Madoff (ed.), *Pop Art: A Critical History* (Berkeley and Los Angeles: University of California Press, 1997) 375-384.

"He knew that he could outrage the sensibilities of the Surrealists by his apology of fascism and later by his adoption of religious themes. Since he saw eye to eye with the group, it may have been a form of masochism on his part... I hold no brief against him if his extra-pictorial activities enabled him to sell his paintings. The world is full of unscrupulous businessmen publicizing more harmful products at much greater expense–I'd have to quarrel with the whole world."[16]

As it happened, Dalí wrote his own self-portrait, which focused on his childhood and early career up to his 1934 departure for New York. This first visit to the United States was for his exhibition at the Julien Levy Gallery, an event marking the advent of Dalí's spectacular American fame. Published in 1942, *The Secret Life of Salvador Dalí* is, in contrast to Man Ray's later memoir, entirely unreliable as a document of historical fact. On the other hand, as self-revelation and a dramatic (if exaggerated) exposure of personal obsession and desire, it provides considerable insight into his art. As a psychological self-portrait, the book gives us much more than a strictly factual account ever could, and it is surpassed in this respect only by the art itself. It is best to approach Dalí's fictionalized memoir as self-promotion. And even more frustrating, in terms of coming to a satisfactory interpretive understanding, is the degree to which Dalí uses autobiographical fabrication to underpin his personal surrealist goals. To what extent can we attribute Dalí's imagery to personal psychology and, by way of nullifying the personal, how much of it is a modernist agenda of simply illustrating Freudian theory? At the very least, we are reminded that Dalí lends himself to multiple interpretations, none of which preclude the others.

Love, sex, religion, and politics typically intermingle in the life stories of most interesting people. And in Dalí's case these come together in connection with four important individuals through his relationships to them: his mother and father, the poet Federico García Lorca, and Gala – his wife, muse, and general support system. A brief introduction to each will indicate the complex forces that formed Dalí and will also set the stage for a first-hand account from Eduard Fornés.

Dalí's mother, Felipa Domènech y Farrés, was described by Dalí as affectionate and nurturing, but she died when he was in his early 20s, just at the time he met Gala. She was a devout Catholic, and her son's religiosity, seen especially in his later "mystical" work, may in part be attributed to her early influence. In contrast, his father, Don Salvador y Cusí, was a figure of parental disapproval and, later, of imagined competition. He also appears to have fed his son's extreme anxieties with

16. Man Ray, *Self Portrait* (Boston and Toronto: Little, Brown and Company, 1963), 246-247.

horror stories of disease and other sexual hazards.[17] Dalí swore that he never had sex with anyone, and he feared being "unmasked" as impotent. Two paintings – *William Tell* (1930) and *William Tell and Gradiva* (1931) – illustrate Dalí's deeply disturbing problems with his father. William Tell represents his father and Gradiva is Gala. The latter painting is a pictorial response to his father's disapproval and rejection of Gala, which Dalí may well have attributed to Don Salvador's sexual desire for her. It may not be going too far to suggest that, beyond the unsavory father image (if that is indeed what is represented), Dalí's tortured fantasies and profound sense of personal inadequacies are also present here. They surely are in other Freudian surrealist works such as *The Great Masturbator* (1929) in which a young woman is about to attempt oral sex on an injured man, whose penis hangs limply, failing to register any sign of arousal. The project seems doomed. The point is made even clearer in *Vertigo* (1930), in which a female seated between the legs of a standing male figure covering his face with his hand is stabbed in the lower chest by the woman about to perform oral sex. His genitals are poised at her mouth. And, again, as in *The Great Masturbator*, the man (Dalí?) is both modestly equipped and limp. The two sources of the artist's personal sexual insecurities, size and impotency, are clearly depicted. These and other works, whatever additional symbolism may share the pictorial space, are surely self-portraits of extreme sexual anxiety. In fact, this feature is so prevalent in Dalí's *oeuvre* that it constitutes a major *leit-motif*, essential to an understanding of his art. Of the many interpretations offered by various writers, the psychological explication, whether strictly Freudian or not, invariably takes a central place.

The poet García Lorca.

It seems likely that Dalí's relationship with Gala was largely asexual, except in the various and repeated rituals that they substituted for actual intercourse (Gala had her string of young men friends who filled her sexual needs). Dalí's surprising practice – acknowledged and observed – of masturbating during the theatrical spectacles he created in rented palaces with androgynous young men and women, also rented, and presumably in the beginning with Gala's encouragement as a collaborator, may have been the extent of their conjugal erotic life. On the other hand, Dalí gratefully claimed that Gala "saved" him by introducing him to "normal" sex. (See note 9)

A much more hopeful relationship, in terms of the possibility of Dalí's finding a physical connection, might have been his youthful friendship with Federico Garcia Lorca. Despite spending summers together at Dalí's family home at Cadaqués, the two never, or so it seems, became physical lovers. On the other hand, Lorca wrote *Ode to Salvador Dalí* as an open and eager expression of his love. But Dalí claimed not to reciprocate, or at least physically express a response to, Lorca's great attraction for

17. Dawn Ades provides in her first chapter a brief but useful account of Dalí's early, formative years, early education, and the considerable influence of his Catalan environment. Although his mother is barely mentioned, it seems likely that she as well as his father played some role in forming him. However, the father is presented as a sexually negative and destructive force, a powerful source for his son's extreme sexual anxiety and dysfunction-and therefore a figure of great importance in connection with Dalí's personal iconography. Not much is written about mother and sister, Anna Maria (who was among his first models), in terms of any appreciable influence. Freud would certainly have taken a closer look.

Cover of the first edition of *The Secret Life of Salvador Dalí* by Salvador Dalí

18. The 2008 film *Little Ashes* (Paul Morrison, director), is based directly on the story of Dalí, Lorca, and Buñuel. With Robert Pattinson (Dalí), Javier Beltran (Lorca), Matthew McNultry (Buñuel), and Arly Jover (Gala), it actually serves as a useful introduction, albeit a romanticized one, to its subject. Dalí's voyeuristic tendencies are depicted in the scene where Lorca has sex with the woman in love with him, as a surrogate for his own love, Dalí, who watches the coupling in his room. Years later the artist wrote "I am totally happy if I can be present at a successful act of sodomy. For me, everything that matters happens via the eye."

19. Salvador Dalí, *The Secret Life of Salvador Dalí* (New York: Dover Publications, Inc., 1993; republication of Dial Press edition of 1942), 360.

20. Amanda Lear increasingly stood in for Gala as she aged, and, at her request, looked after Dalí following her death in 1982. In 1965 Lear took the "muse baton" from another Dalí protégé and "extreme makeover," Ultra Violet (Isabelle Collin Dufresne), who had left him in 1964 to join Andy Warhol's retinue. She in turn was dethroned as the main Warhol Factory "super star" by the younger Viva. This pattern of surrounding themselves with attractive and exotic creatures and using them as living art material provides a further link between Warhol and Dalí, no doubt at least a part of what Warhol had in mind when citing Dalí as an influence on him and the entire Pop art phenomenon.

him.[18] Instead it seems that Dalí focused most of his sexuality on his art, where it became distorted beyond recognition in the bizarre imagery and iconography of his surrealist paintings.

The unresolved friendship with Lorca played out in other revealing ways. Both men were part of the coterie of fellow students in Madrid where Dalí was attending the School of Fine Arts of San Fernando. Dalí, Lorca, and Luis Buñuel, residents of the Residencia de Estudiantes, constituted the core of an intellectual artistic avant-garde, the youthful promise for future Spanish culture. Each collaborated with one another according to their talents. Dalí assisted Buñuel with two of his films, the most famous of which was *Un Chien Andalou* (1929), followed a year later by *L'Age d'Or*. Both were among the most important examples of Surrealist filmmaking, the first dealing with the theme of the unconscious as a source for creative insight and the second, revolutionary politics. Dalí also designed sets and costumes for Lorca's play *Mariana Pineda*. But there was a problem in these endeavors, given the left-wing and anti-Catholic sentiments of their authors. Dalí was apolitical (he believed art in general and Surrealism in particular could, maybe should, transcend politics) in a group that was generally very liberal and cared about political positions. But worse than his inability to feel passionately about social causes, Dalí was mainly opportunistic. His sympathies, if not active support, tended to lean to the right.

Even with the assassination of Lorca by Franco's Falangist forces, Dalí remained neutral – uninterested and uncommitted. "The Spanish Civil War changed none of my ideas. On the contrary, it endowed their evolution with a decisive rigor... there was going to be rediscovered nothing less than the authentic Catholic tradition peculiar to Spain... I believed neither in the Communist revolution nor in the national Socialist revolution... I believed only in the supreme reality of tradition."[19] Nonetheless, his perceived Nazi sympathies and certainly his support and defense of Franco, entirely self-serving, caused his banishment from the Surrealist group and contributed to the loss of virtually all his potential friends in a left-leaning international artist community. Except for the companionship of Gala, and after her death, the transsexual entertainer Amanda Lear,[20] Dalí spent his late years virtually alone and largely isolated first at the Port Lligat house near Cadaqués and finally as an invalid at Púbol where Gala was buried.

For all his apolitical posturing, upon his return to Catalonia in 1948 Dalí became an "ardent supporter" of Franco. There is even a photograph of him presenting to Franco an equestrian portrait of his granddaughter.

Judging from the photograph it is a dreadful painting, and if that was a hidden message from Dalí to Franco we might excuse this complicity. But the sad fact is, despite the circumstances of Lorca's assassination for his liberal political ideas, Dalí seemed to have no reservation about currying favor with the last vestiges of Spanish fascism. This, more than anything else, may be the most disappointing aspect of the fascinating and, at its high points, extraordinarily creative Dalí saga.

In the end, however, we may wonder if Dalí had adopted an alternative path, happier and more "normal," what would have been the source for his bizarre imagery and behavior? Without the striking imaginative products of his over-the-top Freudian exhibitionism, both in his painting and in his life, he would be left only with his technical prowess. A magician he was, to be sure, but an academic one of which there were many others almost as skilled. There would have been no Salvador Dalí for a still-admiring, or at least curious, public to be titillated and shocked by, to puzzle over, and wonder about – or for the critics and historians to find, at last, a meaningful place for in the history of art. That effort appears to be ongoing, though Dalí's efforts seem to have presented more obstacles than assistance. Whether or not Dalí will find the appropriate historical niche, he will remain among the most singularly fascinating, outlandish, transgressive – and still enigmatic – figures in modern art.

THE DALÍ DILEMMA
Paul J. Karlstrom Ph.D.

It was a great, great honor for me to meet Salvador Dalí. This was very important for me as a publisher, and we made amazing works together. Since meeting him I have been involved with all his exhibitions; it was a very important part of my life. ...I started my contact with this extraordinary artist in 1977, and it lasted until 1985. It was always a surprise with Dalí because of his different "faces": he was involved in movies, books, painting, sculpture, jewelry, and also scientific research. He was truly an amazing person.[1]

Eduard Fornés, 2009

As the years go by it becomes increasingly difficult to find and talk with individuals who had direct personal contact with Salvador Dalí. This is especially the case with his early years and the critical Surrealist period. In this regard we should be grateful for accounts from artist associates such as Dada/Surrealist Man Ray, who devoted several descriptive and insightful pages of his autobiography to Dalí whom he was commissioned to photograph by art dealer Julien Levy on the occasion of his first New York gallery exhibition. But, unfortunately, Man Ray is no longer around to answer our questions. Dalí's own writings, of which there was a surprising amount, are considered unreliable as factual biography. The artist seemed determined to hide behind the legend of the Divine Dalí. Therein resides the dilemma, and the enigma.

So, the memories of those who worked with him during the later years of his career are especially welcome, providing in some cases a largely disinterested if not entirely objective picture of this colorful and controversial artist. This is certainly the case with Eduard Fornés, a fellow Catalan whose professional relationship with Dalí, starting in 1977, provided an unusual opportunity to observe other areas of his life as well. The long association began with Fornés approaching Dalí on behalf of his employer, Labor Editions, to agree to appear in an artist series. This was the beginning of an active and productive professional relationship, seemingly without serious conflict, always a possibility when working with Dalí. Fornés subsequently published a number of Dalí-related books and evidently earned the artist's provisional confidence. That was the basis of their relationship, but Eduard was also an interested and attentive observer of the work – not necessarily the individual – he so admired. Furthermore, there were important points of contact between the two, especially their deep attachment to Catalonia. Dalí believed the center of the earth was Catalonia, according to his last secretary, Robert Descharnes. "Do you suppose

1. This essay is based upon conversations and interviews with Fornés—in addition to some of his writings—conducted by the author.

there are landscapes suitable for painting all over the earth, just because the earth is round? A round face isn't all noses, is it? There are very few [worthy] landscapes."[2] But to fully appreciate the edifying divide between them, one should first listen to Eduard's account of his great life transformation from the Catholic priest to secular humanitarian advocate for the people. This of course is about Fornés, not Dalí. But Eduard's journey provides a kind of political and social alternative context for Dalí's exclusively self-focused life.

The contrast between these two Catalans, by chance creatively associated, is nothing less than a study in character. While this essay is not specifically devoted to that ethical abstraction, there really is no other way to characterize the divergent – occasionally diametrically opposed – values embodied by Dalí and his collaborator. Let us allow Eduard's words to make the point:[3]

> "I was born in Barcelona. I studied philosophy and theology for seven years. In 1965 I was ordained as a Catholic priest who took care of his parishioners, not a priest in a monastery. … I spent five years at the Church of Sacred Heart in Sabadell, where newly arriving immigrants are concentrated near Barcelona. Conditions were really inhuman and services were lacking. Being a priest at that time [I thought] was a privilege. I wanted to be a symbol of the Church among the people, to give [through my actions] testimony to what the Gospels said. Normally the state would provide priests with payments as they would other state officials – I renounced this payment.

> In 1968 I was invited to a workers union party in the countryside. I was pleased because I wanted to be accepted as one of them. Coming back from the party the police were waiting for us. They were going to use force against the workers, so I opened the doors of the church and let the people in for their protection. …But during the night the police, armed with AK-47s, directed spotlights on the church. At one point I went outside in my cassock to call an ambulance for a pregnant woman – I remember her name, Pilar, to this day – who had miscarried due to the beatings. The next morning, the police were able to enter the church with the permission of the bishop. All inside were arrested. The Spanish government under Franco used the Church to control the population, the problem being that one part of the Church was against him, and all secret meetings were held in the Church.

> One day the police arrested me in the street; they handcuffed and beat me. I lost my memory for two days. Some months later I went to a closed door trial in Madrid. They wanted to give me two years in prison, but my lawyers provided such a good defense that I thought they were going to give me a medal… instead they reduced my sentence to six months. The experience in prison was very hard,

2. Dalí quote from Dalí with Louis Pauwels, *Les passions selon Dalí* (Paris, 1968).

3. From this point onward, unless otherwise indicated, the Fornés statements are taken from my interviews and his written accounts. The quotes were selected and edited to present the subject's relationship to Dalí in his own words.

and when I got out I couldn't continue to collaborate with my bishop. They told us [the priests involved] that we were going to be treated as political enemies…. Several Basque priests were on death row. A fellow prisoner who was released was able to conceal a letter which I had written from the confinement of my cell about the situation. The letter reached its intended destination, the Bishop of Lyon, (France) with whom I shared a close friendship. He visited the Cardinal Jean-Marie Villot, secretary of state to Pope Paul VI. The Vatican contacted Franco's administration to ask for an open trial. The subsequent trial, made open to the public, guaranteed us a fair hearing. Shortly thereafter, I was released along with two other Catalan priests."

The ultimate result of this experience, and Fornés' disenchantment with the Catholic Church as an effective servant of the people, was his secular radicalization. He escaped to France where he sought the counsel of the Bishop Alfred Ancel who told him, "I'm thinking I can help you be a useful member of society."[4] Eduard remained several years in France before returning to Spain in 1971 after Franco extended a general amnesty.

Eduard Fornés returned with the aim of serving Catalans, no longer as a priest, but a secular advocate and harsh critic of fascism. This was to be his new career. One important change was that he became more politically active, always with the interests of Catalonia and its people foremost in his mind. In 1975 he was appointed General Secretary of the Christian Democratic Party with the responsibility of directing the campaign and voter registration efforts for the first democratic election following the Franco Falangist regime. After the election, Fornés abandoned politics and returned to publishing. But his goal in the various publishing endeavors remained consistent. "I lived in a time and place, the circumstances of which determined specific deeds. I have lived some years under the Franco dictatorship, with a necessity to fight for major liberties and the respect for human rights." This marks one of the great divides, ordinarily unbridgeable, between politically-engaged Eduard and the self-described apolitical Dalí who apparently supported Franco.

It was his work in publishing that led him to Dalí and defined their relationship. Again, Fornés should tell that story himself, thereby introducing the personal and professional connection that accounts for our interest in him and his important presence in this book.

> "When I was in Paris I knew Dalí's name and his famous works, but I wasn't involved–he was better known in Paris and the U.S. than in Spain. However, my work at Labor Editions included making a list of artists as subjects for books: Toulouse-Lautrec, Goya - perhaps also Dalí.
>
> At this point I began to get interested in art. I met some artists. I became interested in the art market after I became involved with Dalí."

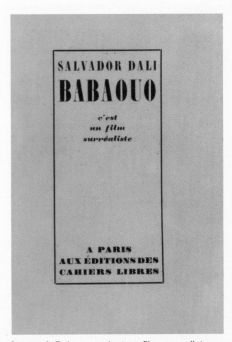

Cover of: *Babaouo, c'est un film surrealiste*. Authors: Salvador Dalí; Esteban Riambau Published in 1932 by Editions des Cahiers Libres, Paris in an edition of 623.

4. Fornés writes in a letter to the author (3 August 2009) of the extensive correspondence he maintained over the years with Bishop Ancel and recalls that when he told him that he was considering leaving the priesthood, his answer was only that he wanted to "*help me to be a loyal and useful person for society.*" The point is that Fornés continued to hold and act upon deeply felt spiritual beliefs.

After their first meeting at which Dalí's secretary at the time, Enrique Sabater, asked him for a new edition of the book *Babaouo*. Dalí and Fornés worked together on 19 publications – for some of which Dalí contributed original drawings – over a 10-year period. The first one was with Labor Editions and also with the company Dasa Editions NV and the other editions by the publishing company Editorial Mediterrània founded by Eduard Fornés. Within this latter publishing company, a subdivision was begun which specialized exclusively in Dalí's works, including postcards, posters, and other such reproductions. This subdivision, entitled Distribucions d'Art Surrealista, also owned the book shop within the Museu Dalí in Figueres. "The different materials we published, 1,500 books, gave me the feeling of participating in a collective action in the construction of our cultural identity. I believe this has made a useful contribution to Catalan culture, ...I sold the related Company Distribucions d'Art Surrealista in 1995 to the Gala-Salvador Dalí Foundation and with the proceeds created the Committee for the Rights of the People, a foundation dedicated to the promotion and enrichment of Catalan culture, history, and education." The Committee was made up of high-level people from Catalonia, among them the former president of the University of Barcelona, the Bishop of Barcelona, and the president of the Association of Physicians – 12 or 15 in all. These people and other leaders became Eduard's supporters and colleagues in his philanthropic projects, for which he received numerous honors for public service and promotion of Catalonia.

Catalonia's President Mr. Jordi Pujol, receiving the board of the Fundacío pels Drets Collectius dels Pobles.

At this point, it becomes clear that Dalí and this publisher were at a considerable distance from one another in goals and motivations. This apparent discrepancy is among the more interesting aspects of the unlikely Dalí-Fornés relationship. And it clearly troubles Eduard that his involvement with the artist might be misunderstood as participating in the more extreme and scandalous behavior of the Dalí-Gala entourage:

> "I never felt myself one of them. Moreover, I had a critical opinion of many of the things that I observed, both his marriage as well as the people I met in his environment. In the text that I wrote for Dalí Illustrator, I avoided any excess of praise for Dalí and limited myself to discussing the publications and exhibitions that I had the occasion to organize, though it is necessary to mention the people that I met and describe their actions, of which I am often critical." [5]

Eduard tends to err on the side of diplomacy, typically withholding judgment even where he clearly disapproves. In the interviews, he largely avoids the exhibitionistic bacchanals and public sexual activities for which Dalí was once notorious (from our contemporary perspective, at least in some circles, most were relatively tame). But he does reveal just enough personal information to provide some insight into the unusual marital and domestic arrangements of

5. Fornés letter to author (3 August 2009).

Salvador and Gala. Although he avoids saying much, at least directly, about their conjugal lives and practices, a subject of considerable curiosity, now and then a window briefly opens. For example:

> "In 1979 – mid-December – the major Dalí retrospective exhibition opened in Beaubourg [Paris] at the Centre Pompidou. The day of the opening there was a strike of the people who worked at the museum, and Dalí was refused entry. He was very disappointed. ...No, no, no. He didn't have any sympathy for the strike. Since it was impossible for him to attend the opening, he also refused the official dinner in his honor hosted by the French Minister of Culture."

Eduard offered his opinion that "Gala filled a key role in the life of Dalí.[6] Without Gala, Dalí would most certainly not have dared to take such radical and ground breaking personal and artistic positions." Sprinkled throughout the Fornés interviews are picturesque and occasionally ribald descriptions, providing the color that one would expect given the subject. Especially bizarre was Fornés' description of the staging instructions for Dalí's opera *Être Dieu*, which grew out of an idea that Lorca and he had when they were students in Madrid, and which after his friend's assassination, he vowed to realize before he died. As described by Eduard, the opera as planned presents in full Surrealist regalia "the creation of the world that Dalí reinvents from his obsessions and his own myths." Among the more striking features were to be flaming giraffes on a burning New York Fifth Avenue.

One of the more elaborate Dalínian settings was the castle of Pierre Argillet, a printer and one of Dalí's leading patrons. During Dalí's many visits to Vaux-le-Penil, on the Seine outside Paris near Fontainebleau, Argillet would film ceaselessly, often without the subjects – including Dalí himself – being aware of the camera. Argillet's ongoing project was to make a documentary movie about Dalí, a copy of which, according to Fornés, still exists.

> "In this castle there are 37 rooms. I attended several dinners and even slept there in one of the cold, damp rooms of this medieval ramshackle monstrosity. Some rooms are decorated by Dalí himself. In several rest rooms there are special bidets – just the bidets – and the arrangement is such that men can look at the women as they wash themselves."

This single detail serves to suggest that Dalí's voyeuristic imagination was not only given free rein by his patron, but was also incorporated into the décor of Argillet's eccentric residence. Fornés provides a description of Dalí's French memorial at castle Vaux-le-Penil, a predictably unconventional affair held on 24 June 1989 (he died on January 23). Along with elaborate performances in the garden all afternoon and evening, there were men sporting antlers and models in paper costumes. There were 500 people (50 from Barcelona) eating

Cover of the catalog of the Dalí retrospective at the Museum of Modern Art - the Beaubourg in Paris.

Castle of Vaux-le-Penil, where Pierre Argillet lived until his death.

6. Although he does not say it, the implication of Fornés' story is that Dalí and Gala had a completely open marriage, as she had with her previous husband, the Surrealist poet Paul Éluard. While married to Éluard, Gala carried on an open affair with Max Ernst followed by her liaison with Dalí. The further implication is that Dalí encouraged Gala's extramarital activities to provide for her well-known sexual needs, which for one reason or another he was not equipped or inclined to satisfy. To a certain extent this remains speculative, but Dalí claims in his various writings that he never had sex with a woman before Gala. The question remains did he have intercourse with her. Eduard Fornés wisely avoids such questions.

lobsters, drinking expensive French champagne – dancing. There was even a *papier maché* elephant with long ostrich legs which rose with a hot air balloon. It is clear from Eduard's accounts that Argillet was a generous and imaginative host, albeit shamelessly catering to the hedonistic (not to mention voyeuristic and exhibitionist) impulses of the Dalí disciples and camp followers. Dalí surely would have approved.

But as for Argillet's professional integrity, that would seem to be all but annihilated by the accusation that he convinced Dalí to sign blank sheets of paper, thereby – whatever his intentions – effectively corrupting the artist. According to Eduard, "The first person who proposed to Dalí to sign white, blank sheets – was Pierre." This unethical (but not unknown in France) practice, virtually inviting forgery, dealt a major blow to the credibility of Dalí in the art market that in recent years has reached crisis levels. The problems are thereby compounded, with questions inherent in the art extended to the authenticity of many of the works themselves. Dalí has provided enough confusion in terms of his actual artistic identity and intentions without the complication of possibly widespread forgeries. Unfortunately this is a major factor in the larger Dalí dilemma, one to which the artist cheerfully contributed.[7] It is a situation that a principled person such as Eduard Fornés could never condone.

Another revealing area in this professional relationship was Catholicism and religious belief, also a matter of authenticity. In a discussion of the late religious imagery, often featuring Gala, I asked the former priest if he could comment on the sincerity of Dalí's return to the Church. He answered thoughtfully in an interesting and nuanced way:

> "The Sacra Biblia, Divine Comedy, Apocalypse of St. John – there are many religious works, illustrated books. And the question is, as Dalí made so many artworks on religion, did he believe in God? My conclusion is, provisionally – yes. But, we cannot conclusively say whether Dalí believed or not. There is a contradiction between the way he lived his life and his professed faith. So I cannot give a final opinion."

Despite the possible influence of early maternal influence reappearing, Dawn Ades would seem to disagree with Fornés regarding the significance of the later religious subjects as expressions of renewed faith. She interprets this change of subject matter, along with the introduction of scientific symbols into the work, as Dalí's "strategy to reintroduce metaphysics into physics."[8] However, the ultimate goal of Dalí's religious mysticism was to establish communication with God through the study and depiction of natural forces and scientific principles. In other words, physics for him provided a means to approach the concept of divinity. If that was the case, Dalí's religious belief remained intact, if not canonical.

7. There are numerous accounts of Dalí boasting that the signing of blank sheets, hundreds at a time, provided him the best hourly rate he ever received. This alone deeply undermined Dalí's image as a serious artist fully dedicated to, and protective of, his work. His motives can only be explained, generously, by naivete, reduced mental capacity - or, more likely, simple greed.

8. Ades, 178.

Dalí not only claimed to be religious, when it was convenient he even adopted a faux political posture. Fornés talks of the May 1968 student rebellion in Paris, during which students from the Sorbonne tracked Dalí down in the Hotel Meurice where they asked him for a painting as a contribution to support their "revolution." He told them to come back the next day and then overnight produced a 16-page document, printed by Argillet, entitled *My Cultural Revolution*.

He wrote the brochure as if it was *his* revolution, but he wrote with some irony. Instead of a painting or money, he presented the students 20,000 copies of the brochure describing his art ideas. After Dalí proclaimed himself a Catholic – Apostolic and Roman – he announced that he was against bourgeois culture and would support the revolution with his paranoiac-critical method. But it wasn't for the students, it was about Dalí.

It seems as if his contribution to the students, as Dalí insisted was true for his art in general, was a gift of the irrational. In the end, religion and politics – and presumably everything else – were useful only as far as they served Dalí's personal ends. This was entirely opposed to the position of Fornés who, with some reluctance, described Dalí as an "opportunist" who, above all, "needed to be the center of attention. His insane behavior was mainly a means to attract attention. Dalí was from the beginning, when he was a student in Madrid, to the end, a narcissist."

Cover of the catalog of the exhibition *Dalí i els Llibres* (Dalí and His Books).

Eduard Fornés worked with Dalí for 10 years on the publishing of his books and 34 exhibitions that he organized with works of art around his own *Dalí and His Books* (first in Catalan, *Dalí i els Llibres*, 1981). He claims that Dalí had a strong work ethic. Other writers describe Dalí and Gala as enjoying a quiet and peaceful life in their initially small cottage in the fishing village of Port Lligat, with Salvador painting every day except Sunday, all day long. This picture of domestic tranquility is difficult to reconcile with the life of sensationalist antics in Paris and New York, but apparently this was something they sought. Fornés surely had some opportunity to observe this other, less well-known, side of the Dalí coin as well as its obverse in the Argillet mansion and other elaborate venues on both sides of the Atlantic. By his own admission, Fornés was seldom alone with Dalí, and it may well have been the case that suspicious parties with personal vested interests in the artist and his work were monitoring such contacts. The exceptions were meetings between the two at the Hotel Ritz in Barcelona and the Meurice in Paris. However, Fornés was in a position to observe Dalí at work – his drawing facility and his commitment to the act of creating striking and compelling imagery. This is of no small consequence when it comes to questions about Dalí's attention to the production of his work, particularly the graphics in his later declining years.

Dalí was very professional. He wanted to see every step of creating the book. For example, for *The Divine Comedy* he followed all the processes, and he gave his approval each time the printer Jacquet finished one of the images. He gave his permission, his "okay," for moving on to the wood engravings. The same for the *Biblia Sacra*: Salvador followed the entire process, all the different steps, to realize this illustrated book. Dalí was always involved in his work.

However, this presents a difficulty when one considers Dalí's acquiescent collaboration with Argillet in signing the blank sheets and thereby opening the door to forgery. This extreme contradiction seems to be at the heart of the Dalí dilemma, and it suggests that the problem will not be solved and the differences reconciled any time soon, if at all.

It may be that an observation by Dickran Tashjian is as close as we will get to understanding the enigmatic and often perverse art career and art of Salvador Dalí. His behavior and choices were irrational, in keeping with his method. He refused to be held accountable. And he cultivated the image of madness.

Torre Galetea, where Dalí lived until his death, is located next to the Figueres Dalí Theatre-Museum.

If Dalí was insane, then he could be dismissed as a lunatic who had duped the art world. If he was not insane, then he was a charlatan. In either case, Surrealism was discredited. But the ambiguity would not go away, and so Dalí remained at the center of attention as a not-mad madman. From the point of view of public relations, keeping matters in a state of irresolution was the best way for Dalí to generate interest. [9]

This almost certainly gets the Dalí question right, and is at least partly the answer. Dalí was undoubtedly a genius in several respects. Perhaps one is the intuitive understanding that if you keep people puzzled and confused, keep them guessing and wondering, then you will hold their attention. In that regard, if indeed it was a strategy, Dalí would seem to have succeeded admirably. In this he may well have pointed the direction for at least a few of the luminaries of post-modern art.

As for the question of relative contributions to Catalonia, the Teatre-Museu Dalí in Figueres, the home in Port Lligat, and Gala's castle in Púbol are important attractions that contribute to the image of Catalonia as a prominent center for artistic accomplishment. Still, that focus is entirely on Dalí. On the other hand, Eduard Fornés, through his civic activism, publishing career, and above all his foundation, has served more directly the Catalan people and the broader idea of a unique cultural identity. His life seems to have been devoted to what he calls Catalan nationalism. It is interesting that the two came together, with different but contextually related objectives, to promote and honor − through a creative collaboration − the land that formed and defined them. But in their individual ways they represent − beyond the accident of a brief but productive professional association − two sides of the Catalan character. In the end, it is Dalí's art and his extravagant, transgressive life, with its accompanying image, that make of the comparison a useful source of insight into the phenomenon that is Salvador Dalí.

9. Dickran Tashjian, *A Boatload of Madmen: Surrealism and the American Avant-Garde, 1920-1950* (New York: Thames and Hudson, 1995), 53-54.

Paul J. Karlstrom, Ph. D. / Author biography

Author Paul J. Karlstrom received his B.A. in English literature from Stanford and his M.A. and Ph.D. in art history from UCLA. Former West Coast Regional Director of the Smithsonian Institution's Archives of American Art for thirty years, he conducted more than two hundred oral history interviews with artists and art world figures in the western region. His 1980/81 interviews with Ed Ruscha are considered essential and have been published and cited frequently. He now maintains this long art world association through independent interviews and writing about art and artists.

Among his many publications are (editor) *On the Edge of America: California Modernist Art, 1900-1950* (UC Press, 1996) and (consulting editor/contributor) *Asian American Art: A History, 1850-1970* (Stanford, 2008). He has contributed essays to numerous books and journals, including *Reading California: Art, Image, and Identity, 1900-2000*, and the *Encyclopedia of American Art before 1914*. His "Eros in the Studio" first appeared in Cándida-Smith (ed.), *Art and the Performance of Memory* (Routledge, 2002). He has also contributed chapters to definitive studies of artists Diego Rivera, Jacob Lawrence, and Hassel Smith. His biography of the legendary modernist art historian and founding UC Berkeley museum director Peter Selz—*Peter Selz: Sketches of a Life in Art*—was published by UC Press in 2012.

Karlstrom lives in San Francisco with his wife, Ann. Their current joint project is a biography of the pioneering San Francisco art dealer Ruth Braunstein whose gallery was among the first in the United States to feature avant-garde ceramics. She introduced artists such as Peter Voulkos, Richard Shaw, and Edward Kienholz. Karlstrom's interest in Salvador Dalí dates back to his undergraduate years.

DALÍ ILLUSTRATOR

Eduard Fornés

HOW I MET DALÍ

You are about to enter a world where nothing is as it seems. Time disintegrates, men become three-headed and six-legged demigods, women turn into diabolical heavenly muses; and spectators turn from innocent lambs into greedy crows of painting, ready to pay whatever to get a piece of this controversial earthly figure known as Dalí. You know when you enter, but never know when you leave this surreal and unique universe of undoubtedly one of the greatest and arguably most influential artists of modern times - a dreamlike, extraordinary world of no return. Before you realize it, it is too late. You are possessed: the clocks are melting, your multiform eyes are those of a fly that capture everything, that see everything as you move on the swaying rump of a heavy golden elephant with a human face - a Dalínian Universe where time only obeys the laws, without rules, of ants entering and leaving ubiquitously. It is the incomparable world of Dalí, contradictory and fascinating; the vast universe of this Catalan, who is famous throughout the world and who is perhaps the most transcendental, original and versatile painter of all time, whom I finally had the opportunity to personally meet so long ago in 1977.

I was production director of Editorial Labor, a book publishing company located on Calàbria Street in Barcelona. I was manager of Talleres Gráficos Iberoamericanos y Encuadernaciones Sociedad Anónima, ESA (Iberoamerican Graphic and Binding Workshop Corporation, ESA). One of the book collections of Editorial Labor was entitled *Pocket Art Labor* and I had long wished to undertake a significant project with Dalí and wanted to include a book about his work in this collection. In an attempt to contact Dalí, I phoned Dalí's house at Port Lligat in Cadaqués. I was told that in order to speak with Dalí I should first contact his secretary, Mr. Enrique Sabater, and was given his phone number and address that was the Casa de Ses Brises in Llafranc-Wild Coast. I wasted no time in dialing the number. We arranged to meet, and a few days later, I drove my Renault 5 straight to Calella de Palafrugell, a charming village on the Costa Brava. I rang the bell at the garden gate. Under the gaze of a rotating camera that recorded my every move, the gate automatically opened to a large villa. I drove into the garden, where a butler (who I was to learn was named Germán) awaited me with pomp and circumstance, opened the car door and brought me into the villa. In the living room,

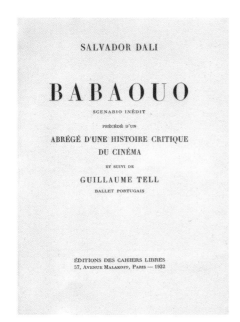

Introduction page of the first edition of *Babaouo*, Paris 1932.

with my feet sunk into a very thick carpet, I looked around at a number of paintings and small golden sculptures of Dalí. While gazing at all that surrounded me, I was astonished to see Concha, Sabater's wife, appear in a bikini and tell me that I should put on a swimming suit and meet at the pool. I was wearing a suit and tie, holding the portfolio that contained the draft contract under my arm and obviously not wearing swimwear. Before I could even gather my thoughts, I was shown to the changing rooms at the pool which contained many swim suits to choose from. After a bit, I left for the pool side garden dressed in a 'Meyba' with my portfolio under my arm. Sabater was on the telephone, with some kind of a phone apparatus artfully wrapped and plugged into a pine tree (wireless or mobile phones did not yet exist).

After explaining to Sabater the purpose of my visit, he suggested discussing the topic after lunch. I told him that I did not wish to impose, but he insisted and almost without realizing it, I was sitting at a table, in swim trunks, eating an excellent fish. According to the diligent Germán, the elegantly dressed butler, the fish had just been caught. The combination of the freshness of the fish and the wonderful preparation was spectacular.

I was finally able to explain the reason for my visit, to which Mr. Sabater responded almost immediately: "Mr. Dalí asks for $50,000 to discuss this book." I could not believe it. It was a pocket edition! The title of the collection made this quite clear, *Pocket Art Labor*. "Well, no problem, in that case, we will produce a different book," said Sabater. During the after-lunch chat, Sabater explained that Dalí wanted to reprint the book *Babaouo*, which Éditions des Cahiers Libres on Malakoff Avenue in Paris had published in 1932 under the title *Babaouo, c'est un film surrealiste*. It was a limited edition book bearing a justification page which read as follows; Printed July 12, 1932; 3 copies on imperial Japan paper, numbered from 1-3; 20 copies on Holande Van Gelder, numbered from 4-23; 600 copies on vélin Outheninchalandre, numbered 24 to 623.

BABAOUO

We made a contract to print a collector's edition of the book with seven illustrations by Dalí. The next year (1978), we completed our work and published the Spanish-French bilingual edition with seven illustrations by Dalí. These illustrations, which were not a part of the 1932 edition, were based on wood engravings that Dalí made for a collector's edition for the Centre Culturel de Paris.

They were reproduced in a publication called Volume 44 of *Maldoror, (Ediciones Liberales)* (Maldoror, the Liberal Editions). Dalí created a new collage for the cover, which is seen at the right.

Before the book was printed, I went to Port Lligat to meet Dalí in order to get his approval. When I arrived at Dalí's villa in Port Lligat, I was greeted by his wife, Gala, in a beautiful waiting room with a large fireplace. When she entered, she showed me an envelope containing a black bordered card which had been sent by Raymond Roussel to Dalí on November 4, 1932, thanking him for sending him a dedicated copy of *Babaouo*. I asked Gala if I could borrow the card to make a copy and include it in the book we were going to publish. She told me that she "was fed up with things disappearing and nobody giving them back." Her response caught me so by surprise that I became completely unnerved and quite visibly upset. My reaction seemed to strike a positive chord in her and resulted in having her lend me the card with the envelope in spite of her initial reaction. Only because of that was I able to insert a reproduction of it in the book.

Cover of the 1978 Edition of *Babaouo*, published by Editorial Labor, Barcelona.

The Editorial Labor Spanish-French bilingual edition produced by Fornés included seven illustrations by Dalí, a collage on the cover, and a colored copper frontispiece all of which were done exclusively for this edition.

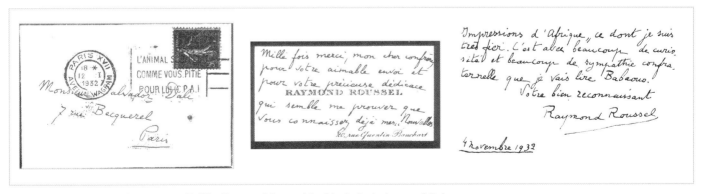

Thank you card and envelope sent to Dalí by Raymond Roussel for his dedicated copy of *Babaouo*.

In the fall of 1978, we presented *Babaouo* in the Dome Room of the Dalí Museum in Figueres. During the opening, using a black marker, Dalí hand-signed many books that I gave away to guests and journalists. I kept two, which I still have to this day.

That day, Salvador Dalí was in great form and still possessed complete control of his surroundings and the media. That control later began to disappear because of the onset of significant health problems. After the onset of his health problems, he started wishing to go unnoticed so that he not be seen as less energetic and vibrant than in former times.

I was very pleased when he told me how great an idea he thought it was to make a copy of Raymond Roussel's card for the book. I might add, I did not disappoint his beloved Gala since I promptly returned the card as soon as I possibly could. This was the first of 20 books, including this one, that I was to publish for and about Dalí.

Page of *Babaouo* signed and dated by Dalí on the day the book was presented in the Dome Room of the Theater-Museum of Figures.

THE RETROSPECTIVE EXHIBITION
AT THE CENTRE POMPIDOU IN PARIS

In mid-December 1979, I travelled to Paris and stayed at the Hotel Meurice in a first floor bedroom next to where Gala and Dalí had their suite.

On December 18, 1979, the exhibition of Dalí's retrospective at the Beaubourg (the Museum of Modern Art in Paris) was inaugurated. It was the same day that a workers' strike began that resulted in Dalí not being able to attend the opening of his own retrospective at one of the world's greatest museums. Dalí became extremely upset! He was so upset that he refused to attend the dinner that the French Minister of Culture had organized in his honor that evening. This was typical of the behavior Dalí would regularly engage in.

Gala filled a key role in the life of Dalí. Without Gala, it is my view from knowing both of them that Dalí might not have taken as many radical and ground breaking personal and artistic positions as he did. She was a very aloof person, distrustful towards those who wanted to get close to her dear Dalí, who was so highly sensitive and so easily disturbed. But she was also able to do a complete about-face and seemed to completely open up if there was some indescribable and unexplainable detail about the person with whom she was dealing that caused her to do so. As a result, she often became impulsive, unstoppable and unpredictable. The 'detail' that caused a sudden change of attitude could sometimes be a simple gift or perhaps her realization that she could make a profit from this person. Frivolous and malicious at times, Gala had no interest in others. The personal contacts I had with her and Dalí led me to unequivocally conclude that they were people who were focused only on themselves; in short, they were extremely selfish. In their world, everything should and did revolve around them.

Gala in her residence in Púbol.
(Photo by Marc Lacroix)

During a lengthy conversation I had with Gala that morning, she repeatedly asked me if I was a journalist, as though somehow by repeatedly asking, my answer might change. Of course it did not. She expressed a kind of contempt for Catalans whom she harshly criticized for having, in her view, not recognized the value of Dalí's work, even though it was well known in Catalonia that Dalí enjoyed not only great international recognition, but also already possessed a reputation as one of the most important painters of the 20th century. She strangely attributed Dalí's fame, in great part, to herself and acknowledged that she had been 'méchant' (naughty) with Dalí. But nonetheless, according to her it was thanks to her (and I think that she was in some part actually right) that many paintings undertaken by Dalí would not have been completed had it not been for her intervention. "One day," she said. "I told him I would not feed him until he finished the painting he was working on." I am sure she was quite serious.

Despite the difficulties and the adverse circumstances of the opening, the exhibition in Paris was a great success and had spectacular media coverage. Dalí and Gala had planned to leave for America a few days later, but Dalí, in the beginning phases of failing health, decided reluctantly to leave Paris and return with Gala directly to Port Lligat instead.

One of the ways I helped Dalí was to be responsible for the cataloguing of each of the works that were included in the exhibition, including their descriptions and values. In addition, I was responsible for receiving and cataloging all of the works that came from the private collection of Dalí, as well as all of the works that came from an exhibition that was held in Geneva.

It was also my responsibility to bring the cataloged information to the President of Catalonia, Jordi Pujol, in Barcelona. During my visit with the president, I strongly suggested that Dalí be awarded the Gold Medal of the Generalitat of Catalonia, a huge honor in our country. I am pleased that my suggestion was acted upon. In March 1982, I had a feeling of great joy and satisfaction when I attended the ceremony where the Gold Medal was ceremoniously awarded to Dalí in the Dalí Theatre Museum in Figueres.

THE GOLD MEDAL

On November 5, 1981, the President of Catalonia, following a proposal by the Minister of Culture, the Honorable Mr. Max Cahner, signed the decree whereby it was ratified that Salvador Dalí would be granted the Gold Medal of the Generalitat of Catalonia. The decree stated that: "Dalí was one of the paradigmatic art geniuses of the twentieth century." It then continued on with an analysis of his work and its impact on the international art world, and ended by affirming his roots as a Catalan painter: "Dalí's work is, consciously or unconsciously, always a work that conveys unmistakable Catalan roots, which is reflected in multiple symbols selected from his land and that remain within the framework of the horizon – so beloved by the artist – and within the blue of the Mediterranean of the Empordà of Port Lligat."

During the ratification ceremony, it was stated that the Catalan government publicly expressed the admiration of the people of Catalonia for his work and thus granted him the Gold Medal. The decree also stated that, despite the fact that his work was granted universal heritage status, it "must remain, above all, the property of the Catalan people."

The Gold Medal was formally awarded at the Dalí Theatre Museum in Figueres on March 22, 1982 by the President of Catalonia, the Honorable Jordi Pujol. In attendance at the ceremony was a large group of many of the most prominent people of Catalonia. The poet J.V. Foix was asked to present the Gold Medal to his friend Dalí. Foix was a person whom Dalí had always greatly admired. Between the years 1932 and 1936, Dalí wrote 38 letters to J.V. Foix. It was the culmination of the Surrealist movement, a movement where it can be said with certainty that Dalí was one of the most important players in its earliest stages of evolution and development. Foix, while on the board of directors of the newspaper *La Publicitat*, found a true correspondent in Dalí. Dalí, drawing on his Surrealist core, would keep Foix promptly informed of the many exceptional, extraordinary and unusual activities that were happening in the world of art, literature and politics at that time.

Rafael Santos Torroella was a poet, art critic and important scholar of Surrealism as well as a connoisseur of Foix and Dalí. He wrote a significant series of articles about Dalí's letters. These articles, inspired by Dalí, were

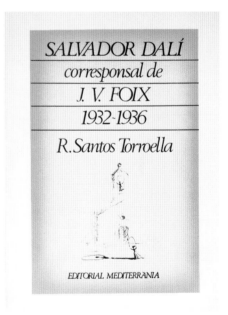

Cover of the book *Salvador Dalí corresponsal de J.V. Foix*.
Author: Rafael Santos Torroella
Publisher: Editorial Mediterrània

JAUME MIRAVITLLES

El ritme de la Revolució

EDICIONS «DOCUMENTS»
BARCELONA · 1933

Pages from the book *The Pace of Revolution* depicting one of his so-called "Putrefactos" (Rotten) drawings.

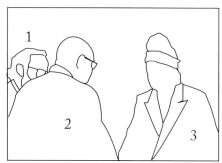

published in the Catalan newspaper *La Publicitat*. Editorial Mediterrània started a new Dalí collection of monographs under the name *Collection Port Lligat* with *Salvador Dalí corresponsal de J. V. Foix, 1932-1936* being the first title to be published. This first book covered the biographical and historical importance of this interesting, original and prolific period of Dalí.

Whenever he made a public appearance, Dalí loved to make a grand entrance. When he made his entrance into the museum where everyone expectantly waited, Wagner's music was playing loudly through the speakers of the museum and two attendants entered behind him holding up his oil painting *El camino del enigma* (The Enigma Track). The crowd broke into spontaneous uproar and applause.

While we observed the scene in amazement, the Count Güell de Sentmenat (seated next to me) and I heard Dalí whispering in J.V. Foix's ear: "My friend, we are doing a rotten act." It was in this way that the artist returned to the highlights of his youth in the Residencia de Estudiantes in Madrid, 1925-1926, where he and the poet García Lorca called everything that was thought to be outdated, unchanging, pathetic or sentimental, 'rotten'. In the correspondence between Dalí, Lorca and José Bello there were found several drawings of the so-called 'rotting' period. These drawings were created in the same ironic tone as the ones that illustrate the book by Jaume Miravitlles, *El ritme de la Revolució* (The Pace of Revolution).

At the Gold Medal award event, I introduced Dalí to Count Güell of Sentmenat, who was the son of Gaudi's patron (see key at left).

1. Eduard Fornés
2. Count Güell of Sentmenat
3. Salvador Dalí

48

MUSEUM WORKS
OR THE TRAIL OF THE RED POPPY

In 1979, I was approached by Sabater on behalf of Dalí to publish a book about Dalí with lithographs and original drawings by Dalí and text by Josep Pla. After discussions between myself and the Board of Directors of Editorial Labor, we agreed to publish the book provided that it would be published in Catalan and adhere to a very high set of standards. The title of the book was to be *Obres de Museu* (Museum Works) with the writings of Josep Pla.

The book was published just as we had imagined it, with two dry point engravings, printed in two ink colors *à la poupée,* hand-signed by Dalí, and with 20 of his lithographs. The total edition was 415 examples, of which 315 were signed by Dalí and Pla, and the other 100 signed only by Josep Pla. The edition was completed on April 23, 1980 on Sant Jordi's Day, the Catalan National Book Day.

Sabater asked me to number the sheets of the justification pages. A few days later he returned them signed by Dalí except for 100 or so. He told me that Dalí had grown tired of signing them and had told him: "You better get Pla to sign, he will die before I will." In fact, it was so. Pla died on Sant Jordi's Day in 1981 and Dalí in January 1989. Fortunately, Pla signed the complete edition. That was to be my last major book project with Editorial Labor, since after it was completed I decided to leave Editorial Labor and form my own book publishing company, Editorial Mediterrània, on October 20, 1980.

Dalí drew the letters of the title of *Obres de Museu* (Museum Works) and painted a red poppy. A little red trickle dripped down and I spontaneously told him not to worry, explaining that at the time of producing the engraving, I would make sure that the drip was erased. Dalí stared at me and said: "Who are you to correct an original work of Dalí?" He added: "This red drip is the most important part of this work, it is what gives greatness to the red poppy." I felt so embarrassed that I do not remember what I answered. I must have apologized, but I can assure you that in the first edition, as well as in the edition without the artworks which we produced one year later for Caixa Catalonia (they commissioned 150,000 copies in Catalan and 100,000 in Spanish as a gift to their customers for Sant Jordi's Day in 1981), I always reproduced the red poppy with that famous drip exactly as Dalí demanded.

Deluxe edition *Obres de Museu,* by Josep Pla and Salvador Dalí 1980 published by copy right of DASA editions.

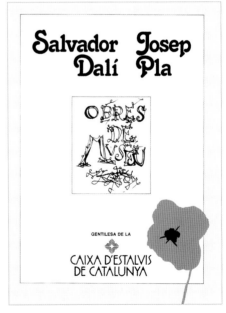

Title page of the regular edition *Obres de Museu* 1981 published by Editorial Mediterrània with the dripping red poppy.

THE JEWELS OF DALÍ

Jaume Miravitlles (known as 'the Met'), a politician and writer from Figueres, had a long and close personal relationship with Dalí. During one of the meetings I had with him, we spoke at great length about that relationship. During that meeting, he showed me a rare early photograph of him and Dalí from 1919 when they were 15 and attending secondary school in Figueres. I learned at that same meeting that Dalí and Miravitlles had published *Studium,* the monthly magazine of the school. From January to June of 1919, the young Dalí wrote a section entitled *Los grandes maestros de la pintura* (The Great Masters of Painting) which was a series of articles about the masters; Goya, El Greco, Dürer, Leonardo, Velázquez and Michelangelo. For me, this was an important discovery of the rare and early writing of the young Dalí.

Dalí at his villa in Port Lligat with his friend, Miravitlles. (Photo by Carles Fontseré)

Beginning in about 1944, Miravitlles, who lived in the United States for about 22 years, and Dalí would often meet in New York at the bar of the Hotel Saint Regis where they would talk for hours.

The friendship that started in their childhood was lifelong. It was a friendship that culminated with Dalí appointing Miravitlles as vice-president of the Public Services Foundation of the Dalí Theater-Museum when the Dalí Museum in Figueres opened. This was typical of how Dalí trusted, treasured and rewarded his lifelong friends.

In August 1980, Miravitlles excitedly called me telling me that it was urgent we meet in the next few days. He told me that while in New York, he and Dalí had just met with the Argentinian jeweller, Carlos Alemany, who collaborated with Dalí in the 1950s and the 1960s to make 39 gold and diamond jewels designed by Dalí. This highly unusual work had been commissioned by the wealthy businessman, Owen Robertson Cheatham, for his private foundation. Miravitlles was very excited about what had just happened. Mr. Cheatham had been dead for 10 years and his daughter, Celeste, had contacted Miravitlles through one of her sons, who stated that his mother had decided to sell the jewelry collection, and importantly, his grandfather in his final wishes requested that the watercolor drawings that Dalí created for the jewelry should become part of the permanent collection of the Dalí Museum. Miravitlles told me that they were selling the jewelry only for the value of the cost of the gold and precious stones.

Dalí's letter appointing Miravitlles as Patron and Vice-President of the Public Services Foundation of the Dalí Theater-Museum.

If the Dalí Museum were to purchase the collection, the 24 watercolor drawings that Dalí had done to design these jewels would be offered as a gift to the museum!

On September 23, I wrote a detailed report to the General Director of Culture, Mr. Albert Manent, who encouraged me to move forward and keep him informed of the conditions of the purchase. As a result of my report, I received a letter from the mayor of Figueres, stating that it was the explicit desire of Dalí that the jewelry was to be part of the collection of the Museum of Figueres (which has annually been the most visited museum in Spain after the Prado).

The following October 20, I met with Celeste to discuss the purchase of the jewelry. The meeting took place on Madison Avenue in New York and was attended by Celeste, the jeweler Carlos Alemany, and Ms. Ilse Meckauer. We agreed to a price of $4 million, to be secured by a deposit of 5 percent of the total amount within two weeks. Celeste dedicated a book about the jewels and the watercolor drawings to me. I made a series of calls, including one to the ex-president of Catalonia, Josep Tarradellas, who also spoke with the general director of La Caixa to let him know. However, soon thereafter, I learned with shock and great disappointment that, in spite of the letter I received, the situation had changed and they were not, at that time, interested in purchasing the jewelry collection and watercolor drawings of Dalí.

I can still remember watching the telex dated December 29, 1980 being sent, signed by Jaume Miravitlles and myself, giving our support to Rafael Estevans, grandson of Mr. Cheatham, who was also receiving letters from the Department of Culture. He wanted to follow his grandfather's wish to have the jewelry become part of the collection of the Museum of Figueres.

```
telex from barcelona/spain

mr. edward m. sills esq.
53 hollywood court
 rockville centre, new york 11570
 u s a
------------------------------------

started information campaign in cataluña to recuperate
dali colection jewels for showing in figueras dali museum.
in the next days you will receive letters of cultural and
official institutions to hold the efforts of cheatham grandson
rafael estevans.

 your sincerely

 eduard fornes/jaume miravitlles
 pelayo,42-2-1
 barcelona/1
--------------
spain
54691 franc e
 tgrmas1  bna
```

Telex sent to Rafael Estevans, signed by Miravitlles and myself on December 29, 1980.

At the end of October, Captain Peter Moore, a former secretary of Dalí, and an Arabic sheik purchased the jewelry on behalf of the company Tag Oeuvres d'Art SA of Geneva. A few months later it was sold for more than double their price to the Japanese businessman, Mr. Nasao Nanguku. He exhibited them soon after, along with some oil paintings by Dalí, at the Minani Art Museum in Tokyo (which I was able to visit years later).

On January 7, 1981, I sent a letter to the Secretary of the Presidency of the Generalitat, Mr. Lluís Prenafeta. In it I reproached him, as a representative of the Catalan government, for their lack of interest in wishing to preserve such an important heritage for Catalonia. They had passed up the gems of Dalí.

In that letter I also informed Generalitat Prenafeta that the following week, Dalí, Gala and Sabater would be traveling to Port Franc of Geneva, where all the works that had been in the exhibition at the Centre Pompidou would be arriving. I added that it would be a good time for a representative of the president to attend in order to be with Dalí and to offer him whatever he needed. Dalí was now sick and would be concerned about securing the future of his vast collection.

History would finally tell us that it would be the Spanish Ministry of Culture, a part of the federal government of Spain, which would be more active in preserving Dalí's legacy for Spain. The Ministry of Culture would inexorably take sole possession of the Dalí Collection and Dalí's heritage in art. As a result, all of the paintings in the Museum of Figueres are owned by the federal government, and when they travel to international exhibitions, the literature is precise and firm: "Property of the Museum Reina Sofia, on deposit at the Theatre Museum Dalí in Figueres."

As for the jewelry, it must be said that in recent years, the Dalí Foundation has made a major effort to recover more and more work by the painter. In 1999, they inevitably and finally purchased the exclusive jewelry collection for the permanent collection of the Gala-Salvador Dalí Foundation Museum in Figueres. Currently, there is a room dedicated to these jewels and they can be viewed, together with the drawings, at the Dalí Museum in Figueres.

THE SECRET LIFE OF SALVADOR DALÍ

Salvador Dalí published his fascinating fantasy autobiography (written in his one-of-a-kind unique and surreal manner) *Secret Life* in 1942 with Dial Press of New York. He finished writing this book in 1941 during a stay at the house of Caresse Crosby in Hampton Manor, Virginia. In the book, Dalí brings to light many of the myths surrounding him through the product of his fertile and brilliant imagination, expressed in the many purely fictional stories contained in the book.

At the beginning of 1981, Sabater asked Dalí for permission from DASA (Dalí-Sabater) to publish the first edition of *La vida secreta* (The Secret Life) in Catalan. We also were to publish it in Spanish as well. Later, in 1994, it was published by Poseidon in Buenos Aires.

Gala and Dalí at the house of Caresse Crosby in Hampton Manor, Virginia, 1941.

I wrote the introductory text for both the Catalan and Spanish editions, which were signed by DASA Editions S.A. In this text, I took the Catalan position in my writing that: "The collective conscience of the country should be capable of integrating all its men, without the opposition of the dust of ridiculing anecdotes or the scalpel of orthodox puritans." I later quote a fragment of an article Dalí had published in Liturgical Arts in May 1952, during the time when his mysticism period was most evident, where he says: "To believe in nothing inevitably leads you to non-objective and non-figurative paintings. If one believes in nothing one ends by painting nothing or almost nothing," he concluded. I end by saying: " 'The Secret Life of Salvador Dalí' allows the reader to definitively discover Dalí the man, this real person from whom emerged the abundance of hallucinatory creation, which is his work."

DASA Editions published *The Secret Life of Dalí* in German in 1983 and in Greek in 1985. In 1988, my company Editorial Mediterrània published the book in English. This book was commissioned by my dear friend Dr. A. Reynolds Morse, president of the Dalí Foundation in the United States.

Cover of the edition of *The Secret Life of Salvador Dalí* written by Salvador Dalí and published by Editorial Mediterrània in 1988 for the Dalí Foundation in St. Petersburg, Florida.

Professor Joaquim Molas wrote a text about *The Secret Life of Salvador Dalí* which he used to give a teaching conference in Vancouver, British Columbia. This is a text of incredible beauty and depth, and one in which he defines *The Secret Life* for what it is: a poem of love.

THE EXHIBITION: DALÍ AND HIS BOOKS; DALÍ, THE WRITER AND DALÍ, THE ILLUSTRATOR

Dalí and His Books

In the Spring of 1982, Dalí was staying at the Ritz Hotel in Barcelona. While he was there, I went to see him with a project I was very excited about. The project was to create a catalog of his work in three volumes: Volume I, *The Catalan Era before Surrealism*; Volume II, *The Surrealist Period, the Stay in Paris*; and Volume III, *The Post-Surrealism Period to Present Date*.

In our discussions, I told Dalí that I had been working on the project with Daniel Abadie from the Centre Pompidou of Paris (The Beaubourg). Mr. Abadie was responsible for the catalog of the Dalí retrospective, at the Beaubourg. I also told Dalí that I had the full support of Dr. A. Reynolds Morse, and that I had many discussions with Dr. Morse about the publishing of the volumes. As Dr. Morse and Dalí were very close, I was sure that this would be helpful in my endeavor. I explained that the catalogs would be in Catalan, English and French. Dalí became very excited and enthusiastic about the project and began to bombard me with questions until he finally stopped and said: "And why do you want to complicate your life so much? Don't you realize that even I do not know everything I have done?" To which he almost immediately added: "Do you know that I was born to be a writer?"

I thought he was pulling my leg, but he noticed my reaction and suddenly said: "Don't you believe me? When I was at the Student's Residence in Madrid with García Lorca, I felt better writing than painting." Dalí then began to list the books he had published during his Surrealist period, the articles in *Minotaure*, in *Surrealisme au service de la révolution*, and he proceeded to tell me that I should take on the project of having him become known as a writer. He told me that if I would do so, he would give me a huge bibliography of his published writings. What a surprise and what joy!

I approached the work with great dedication and energy, and for an important work, it was the fastest to go from idea and inception to publication that I have ever worked on. This book is at the other end of the spectrum and took the longest time to go from inception to publication. I was to find that this has great advantages when it comes to producing a scholarly work.

The following June, the President of the Catalan Government, Jordi Pujol, opened the first exhibition of *Dalí i els llibres; Dalí escriptor i Dalí illustrador*

Opening of the *Dalí and His Books* exhibition at the Real Capilla of Santa Ágata of Barcelona. Eduard Fornés (in white) standing next to the Honorable Jordi Pujol, president of the Government of Catalonia.

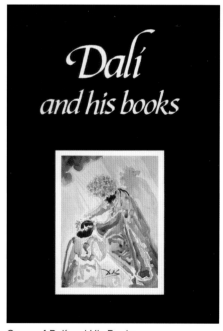

Cover of *Dalí and His Books* authored by Eduard Fornés and published by Editorial Mediterrània.

(Dalí and His Books: Dalí, the Writer and Dalí, the Illustrator) at Saint Agatha's Royal Chapel. It was during that same month that Gala died and in honor of her, an enlarged photo of Gala with a large bouquet of flowers was placed at the entrance - a touching detail, under the circumstances. The exhibition toured various cities in Catalonia, and from July 27 to August 26, 1982, where it was exhibited under the dome of the Dalí Museum in Figueres.

However, everything was done much too quickly and there was not enough time for preparation. The catalog, for instance, had errors and even some gaps, which in later editions of Spanish, French, Italian, German, Swedish, Slovak, English and Japanese were corrected as we expanded and improved the information. However, it must be said that the Minister of Culture, Max

DALÍ AND HIS BOOKS: Dalí, the writer and Dalí, the illustrator

Date	Location	City	Country
1982 – June	St Agatha Chapel	Barcelona	Spain
1982 – July-August	Theatre Museum Dalí	Figueres	Spain
1982 – September	Popular Library	Olot	Spain
1982 – September	House - Culture	Girona	Spain
1982 – October	Institute	Lleida	Spain
1982 – November	Parliament	Torino	Italy
1982 – December	Library	Tarragona	Spain
1982 – December	Cultural Centre	Terrassa	Spain
1983 – January	Botiller Palace	Tortosa	Spain
1984 – March	Bagatti Palace	Milano	Italy
1984 – November	Fine Arts Museum	Nîmes	France
1985 – March	Tour Fromage	Aosta	Italy
1985 – May	Caixa Catalunya	Madrid	Spain
1986 – May	Tel Aviv Museum	Tel Aviv	Israel
1987 – September	Kobe Shimbum	Kobe	Japan
1987 – November	Nagoya	Nagoya	Japan
1988 – January	Shimonoseki	Shimonoseki	Japan
1988 – March	Kanazawa	Kanazawa	Japan
1988 – April	Yokohama	Yokohama	Japan
1989 – May	Moderna Art Museo	Stockholm	Sweden
1991 – March	City Hall S. Gilles	Brussels	Belgium
1992 – March	Museum Fine Arts	Bratislava	Slovakia
1992 – April	Museum Fine Arts	Hilina	Slovakia
1992 – April	Museum of Modern Art	Berno	Czechoslovakia
1992 – April	Museum	Prostejov	Czechoslovakia
1992 – May	The Mall	Amberes	Belgium
1992 – June	Adornes Hall	Bruges	Belgium
1992 – August	City Hall	Luxemburg	Luxemburg
1992 – November	Maximilian Park	Hamm	Germany
1993 – February	Sistere Restaurant	Sta Coloma	Spain
1993 – June	Sant Pere del Bosc	Lloret de Mar	Spain
1993 – September	Karstadt	Nüremberg	Germany
1994 – March	Int. Golf Course	Caldes Montbui	Spain
1994 – September	Karstadt	Karlsruhe	Germany

Cahner, always gave his full support. This was a great learning experience for me, and through it, I determined to always slow a project down and take the proper amount of time so that the work could be completed as accurately as is humanly possible. For example, the book you are now reading has been painstakingly prepared, and as a result, has taken more than 22 years to come to fruition!

In spite of the inadequacies of the catalog, I was pleased to see in the report of the councillor of the Department of Culture of the Generalitat of Catalonia for the year 1982, the statement that: "...the exhibitions of 'Dalí and His Books' had the largest total attendance of any exhibition in Catalonia."

The centenary of Dalí's birth was held in 2004. During that year I was able to visit the exhibition, *Dalí, una vida de llibre* (Dalí, a life of books), which was held at the Biblioteca de Catalunya (Library of Catalonia). During my visit, I could not help but think that I had been a pioneer in that first exhibition, *Dalí and His Books: Dalí, the Writer and Dalí, the Illustrator.* I once again remembered when Dalí stared at me and said: "Do you know that I was born to be a writer?" Then to my scepticism: "Don't you believe me?"

Exhibition of *Dalí and His Books*, at the Museum of Tel Aviv (Israel).

Summer Afternoons

Dalí's interest in using me as his instrument to have himself known as a writer and illustrator of books allowed me to discover many unpublished texts that Dalí had written at a very young age. What joy to find myself unexpectedly holding and reading chapters from an early manuscript, a novel by Dalí, entitled *Tardes d'estiu* (Summer Afternoons), which was owned by his sister, Anna Maria. This unpublished novel was eventually purchased by the painter Joan Abelló who turned part of his home in Mollet del Valles into a Dalí museum as a testament to his admiration, honor and love for our great Catalan master.

When I published the first catalog for the exhibition *Dalí and His Books* in 1982, I also published previously unpublished sections of this novel which were written by Dalí when he was 16. He started to write it in 1920 but left it unfinished. No one, not his sister, not even Dalí himself in his memoirs, had ever mentioned this rare and poignant text from his youth where he speaks openly about his relationship with his first love, Carme Roget.

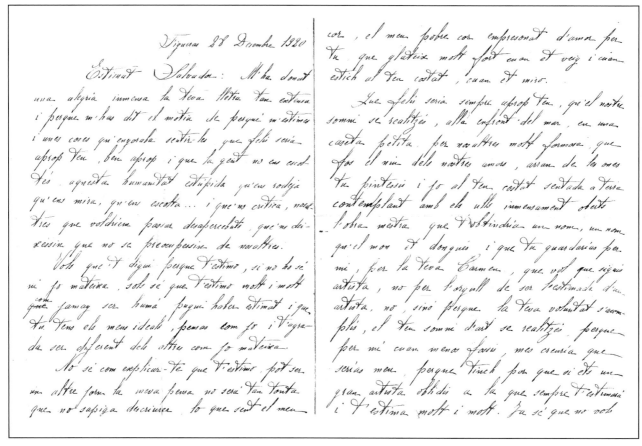

Unfinished love letter written by Carme Roget in 1920.

Roget was the daughter of a baker in Figueres, and in the unfinished text it seemed as though there couldn't have been a better place for them to meet. They met in the drawing class of Dalí's teacher, Professor Núñez. Up until the time Dalí left for the Escuela de Bellas Artes San Fernando (San Fernando School of Fine Arts) in Madrid, Dalí had an adolescent (most likely platonic) love affair with Carme. This love affair led to a series of letters, some of which I was able to recover through my friend Jaume Miravitlles "the Met."

In the novel, Luís, the protagonist, a young painter suffering from tuberculosis, is an orphan whose parents have died from the disease. In the novel, Luís is obsessed with seeking light and color in his paintings and through them expressing his repressed love for Isabel (Carme Roget). In this novel, Dalí reveals his grave fear of death. For the young Dalí, fiction became reality in the next year, 1921, when his mother died. Dalí was lovingly nurtured by his mother and was very attached to her. He openly and often professed his love for her. Whether it was the death of his mother or not, this fear of death was to stay with Dalí as an anguish that would accompany him throughout his entire life.

Carme Roget, Dalí's fellow student from his adolescent year in Figueres.

In 1985, at Editorial Mediterrània, I personally directed and edited a collection of Dalí books called *Collecció Port Lligat* (Port Lligat Collection). The second book in this series was an adaptation of the doctoral thesis on the literary works of Dalí done by the Dutch Professor Annemieke van de Pas. This doctoral thesis was presented at the University of the Sorbonne in Paris. In his thesis, Professor van de Pas explores the early writings of Dalí. He describes *Tardes d'estiu* (Summer Afternoons) as a story where Dalí intermingles his feelings about nature, his feelings of distress and his fear of death. The novel ends with an anarchistic and emotional speech by one of the characters that blends the romantic nature of man with the anxieties of contemporary society.

Focusing on part of the exhibition *Dalí and His Books*, I point out that *Dalí and His Books* contained many completely unknown original manuscripts and a series of articles published in journals and books, all of which were written by Dalí. The third part of the exhibition, *Dalí Illustrator*, contained approximately 350 engravings and lithographs from 30 different illustrated books, which were shown in frames and exhibited in chronological order. The illustrated books without the lithographs and engravings were exhibited in glass cases along with various documents and manuscripts that were a part of the literary and illustrative works that were a part of *Dalí and His Books*. My mind was already churning with what an important and enormous project a book on *Dalí Illustrator* would be. I did not know how big the challenge would be until I faced the enormous work which was to become this book.

Salvador Dalí's sister, Anna Maria.

Text about Velázquez written by Dalí, which was published in *Studium* - the school magazine of Figueres.

Two covers of the *Dalí News*,
New York - 1947.

Dalí as Writer

The Professor Joaquim Molas points out that to understand Dalí as a writer, it is not only important, but absolutely necessary to study Dalí's early years prior to his moving to the Student's Residence in Madrid. During those years, his capacity for learning and his education, along with his great love for reading, left an indelible mark on the developing Dalí - a mark that would remain with him throughout his life. The following three elements were to leave this dramatic and very important mark on who Dalí would become. They were: (1) the group L'Amic de les Arts (The Friends of the Arts); (2) the enormous influence of his teacher Núñez, the great freethinker; (3) the importance of the light and landscape of Cadaqués, the Empordà, etc., where Dalí grew up. These influences are all constant references that need to be considered as a whole in order to fully appreciate their impact on Dalí, his art and his writing. When considering them together it becomes clear that they are obsessively an integral part of his painting as well as his writing.

Dalí wrote articles on the subject *Los grandes maestros de la pintura* (The Great Masters of Painting), which were published in *Studium*, the magazine of his high school in Figueres. The group that made up the editorial board of the magazine, Dalí, Joan Xirau, Jaume Miravitlles, Ramon Reig and Joan Turró were very tight-knit. They maintained close and meaningful relationships with each other throughout their entire lives.

During 1919 and 1920, Dalí regularly wrote in his native Catalan in notebooks that he used as a personal diary. One of the earliest writings in those published notebooks, which he titled *Mis impresiones y recuerdos íntimos* (My Impressions and Intimate Memories), was edited by Dr. A. Reynolds Morse. In 1994, the Centre of Dalínian Studies of the Gala-Salvador Dalí Foundation in Figueres published seven recovered notebooks (of 11 which are believed to be his adolescent diary) along with *Summer Afternoons,* his unfinished novel, which also dates from Dalí's adolescent years.

For more than a decade, Dalí worked tirelessly for the magazine *Els amics de les arts* for which he wrote 23 articles. He also wrote for the magazines *Nova revista, Gaceta ilustrada, Gaseta de les Arts, La revista, Helix,* and *La Hora* as well as for the newspapers *Mirador* and *La Publicitat*. It is remarkable that Dalí, so well known for his paintings, wrote and published so many articles and yet is little known as a writer.

Eduard Fornés (facing) at the opening of the
Dalí and His Books exhibition at the
Theatre-Museum Dalí in Figueres – July 1982.

Dalí and His Books exhibition in Kobe (Japan) September 1987.

Eduard Fornés (far right) at the opening of the *Dalí and His Books* exhibition in Bratislava (Slovakia) in April 1992.

Cover of the *Hidden Faces*, New York 1944.

Cover of the Spanish edition *Rostros ocultos*, Barcelona 1952.

Illustration by Dalí which was used for the cover of the *Minotaure*, Paris 1936.

During the years he was with the Surrealist group in Paris, he wrote five books: *La femme visible,* Éditions Surréalistes, Paris (1930); *L'amour et la mémoire,* Éditions Surréalistes, Paris (1931); *Babaouo,* Éditions des Cahiers Libres, Paris (1932); *La conquête de l'irrationnel,* Éditions Surréalistes, Paris (1935); and *La Metamorphose de Narcisse,* Julien Levy Gallery, New York (1937). During this same time he also wrote in the journals *La révolution surréaliste, Le Minotaure, Cahiers d'Art, Le Surrealisme au service de la révolution,* etc. - important French avant-garde publications.

However, it was in the United States that he came to publish his first great book, *The Secret Life of Salvador Dalí,* by Salvador Dalí, Dial Press, New York. Two years later he completed and published his novel *Hidden Faces* Dial Press, New York. He continued to work with numerous magazines and he and his friend Miravitlles published two volumes of the *Dalí News, Monarch of the Dailies,* which was not only important for its literary content but also included an extensive and rich universe of illustrations.

The list below of the most important and significant books published about Dalí was published in 2004 on the centenary of his birth, and is also contained in his complete works:

1944   *Hidden Faces,* Dial Press, New York
1948   *Fifty Secrets of Magic Craftsmanship,* Dial Press, New York
1951   *Manifeste Mystique,* Robert J. Godet, Paris
1956   *Le cocus du vieil Art Moderne,* Fasquelle, Paris
1957   *Histoire d'un grand livre*, *Don Quichotte,* illustrated by Dalí, Joseph Forêt, Paris
1963   *Le mythe tragique de l'Angelus de Millet,* Jean Jacques Pauvert, Paris
1964   *Journal d'un Génie,* La Table Ronde, Paris
1966   *Lettre ouverte à Salvador Dalí,* Albin Michel, Paris
1967   *Hommage à Messonier,* Hôtel Meurice, Paris
1968   *Ma révolution culturelle,* Salvador Dalí, Paris
1968   *Les Passions Selon Dalí,* Salvador Dalí and Louis Pauwels, Denoël , Paris
1971   *In Procès diffamation,* Belfond, Paris
1973   *Comment on devient Dalí,* Salvador Dalí and André Parinaud, Robert Laffont, Paris

Other articles that are noteworthy to mention are the articles that were in magazines such as *Art News* and several unusual books that Dalí wrote including *Les diners de Gala,* Drager, Paris and *Les vins de Gala,* Drager, Paris, as well as his writing the text for the setting of opéra poeme *Être Dieu,* Distribucions d'Art Surrealista, Barcelona.

This selection of published writings by Dalí was presented and displayed at the exhibition *Dalí and His Books.* This exhibition was the first of its kind. It revealed, for the first time, this little known dimension of Dalí as a prolific and talented writer with an important place in the history of both Catalan and Spanish literature.

Dalí as Illustrator

The exhibitions, *Dalí the Writer* and *Dalí the Illustrator*, lay the foundation as to why Dalí is considered to be such a great illustrator of important literature. There can be no question however, that *Dalí the Illustrator* is more important since it is as an artist that Dalí's genius truly bloomed.

During his life, Dalí created original artwork illustrations for over 100 illustrated books. The complete list is contained in the bibliography. But the artworks by Dalí which illustrate *Les Chants de Maldoror, The Divine Comedy,* and *The Bible* are, amongst all of the 100 illustrated books, clearly the most important and powerful Dalí ever created.

The aim of this book, as suggested in the Introduction by Dr. A. Reynolds Morse, is to create a landmark book which would be the definitive reference on the illustrations of Dalí. It was my goal to delve as deeply as possible into Dalí as illustrator. As a result, I have made every effort to provide a thorough study and cataloging of the engravings of the aforementioned three master works that he illustrated. These three: *Les Chants de Maldoror* by the Count of Lautréamont, *The Divine Comedy* by Dante Alighieri and *The Bible* are fundamental artistic landmarks, all of which took many years to complete in order to arrive at their final impressive result. They are without question Dalí's most significant works as an illustrator of great books.

They were the most viewed and most talked about, and considered the most attractive art works in the exhibition *Dalí and His Books: Dalí, the Writer and Dalí, the Illustrator*. They not only attracted the most interest but also the most surprise among the visitors. After putting this exhibition together, it is my firm belief that these three works of illustration are without parallel anywhere in the world of art.

There was enormous media coverage of the 34 presentations. The exhibitions generated hundreds of essays, articles, columns, reports and reviews worldwide.

Pamphlet to introduce the visitors to the exhibition of *400 Works of Salvador Dalí 1914-1983*.

400 WORKS OF SALVADOR DALI (1914 - 1983)

In 1983, the remarkable exhibition *400 Obres de Salvador Dalí* (400 Works of Salvador Dalí) was organized by the Department of Culture of the Generalitat of Catalonia in conjunction with Javier Solana, the minister of culture of the Ministry of Culture in Madrid. The exhibition was organized under the auspices of Mr. Alfredo Pérez de Armiñán (general director of Fine Arts of the Government of Madrid) and Mr. Max Cahner (minister of culture of the Generalitat of Catalonia), in Barcelona on August 13, 1982. It was also agreed that it would be a joint project with expenses to be shared equally by the government of Catalonia and the federal Ministry of Culture. This was an important commitment on the part of the Catalan government as its financial resources are significantly less than those of the Spanish federal government.

To support their painter, Salvador Dalí, there was a need to make great efforts in both financial and human resources in order to properly demonstrate the international importance of Dalí in Spain. While Dalí had already achieved spectacular and unprecedented importance internationally, at this point the artistic recognition of Dalí in Spain was not at that same level. This extraordinary exhibition opened at the Spanish Museum of Contemporary Art in Madrid and was then moved to the Royal Palace of Pedralbes in Barcelona.

On the day of the opening in Madrid, I arrived a few hours prior to the arrival of their Majesties, the King and Queen of Spain, who were to inaugurate the exhibition. Police, accompanied by dogs trained to find explosives, were tirelessly roaming and inspecting the entire area while waiting for King Don Juan Carlos I's arrival at noon. Suddenly during the preview, I noticed that the *Portrait of Gala with two lamb chops balanced on her shoulder,* painted on a tiny wood panel (6.9 cm. x 8.8 cm.) with a velvet backing, had come out of its frame. I could not believe it! It was on the floor. Without hesitating, I picked it up, took it to the cloakroom and securely placed it with my things. I then quickly left the museum to purchase some proper adhesive. Returning to the museum, I carefully secured the masterpiece back in its original frame and without anyone noticing its absence, the picture was once again perfectly in its place.

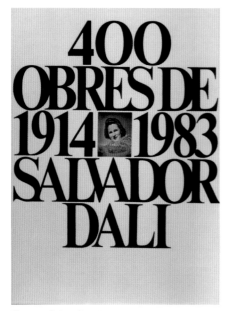

Cover of the Catalan catalogue for the *400 obres de Salvador Dalí (1914-1983)* exhibition.

The opening had a happy ending with a cocktail party for all of us who worked so hard in mounting this extraordinary exhibition. It was indeed a privilege that the cocktail party was presided over by their Majesties, the King and Queen of Spain.

The following year, the exhibition had its second opening at the Royal Palace of Pedralbes in Barcelona. Because of my friendship with Dr. A. Reynolds Morse, president of The Salvador Dalí Foundation in St.

Petersburg, Florida, I was able to arrange a loan of three extraordinary oil paintings for this exhibition from the St. Petersburg museum: "*La cistella de pa* (The basket of bread), 1926; *Pa català, Natura morta amb un rellotge tou* (Catalan bread, still life with soft clock), 1932, and *Eco morfológico* (Morphologic echo), 1936. This was a difficult accomplishment not only because of the high cost of packaging, transportation, insurance, etc., but also because the bylaws of the Salvador Dalí Foundation in St. Petersburg did not allow works in its collection to go out on loan. However the trustees of the Foundation, presided over by Dr. Morse, held a special meeting and agreed to make an exception. I can never thank Reyn (as he was known to his friends) enough for making that dream come true.

Corpus Hypercubicus

For the exhibition in Barcelona, I wanted something unique, different and original. No matter the cost, we had to get something which would make history in Dalí's native Catalonia. With the authorization of Mr. Max Cahner, I made contact with the Museum of Modern Art in New York (MOMA) to find out whether or not they would loan us the approximately 6-and-a-half by 4-foot masterpiece, *Crucifixión* or *Corpus Hypercubicus*. I was pleased to be successful in my discussions, but the conditions for the loan were very difficult. The artwork would have to be packaged in an airtight box, travel first class by air and always be accompanied by a curator from MOMA and two security guards on the flights. Upon arrival in Barcelona it would then be subjected to a rigorous examination to check whether any changes in humidity had stretched the canvas or had cracked the surface of any of the oil paint. This was only the beginning - there was also a long list of numerous additional conditions spelled out in painstaking detail. Max Cahner, the minister of culture, despite the high cost and significant difficulties, courageously undertook the responsibility and the loan was arranged. Fortunately for Spain and its citizens, Max Cahner understood the importance of this unique pictorial presence, so he made sure no efforts were spared.

When *Crucifixión* or *Corpus Hypercubicus* arrived at the airport in Barcelona, 'Mossos d'Esquadra,' a body of the Catalan police force, paid official tribute to the oil painting of Dalí as if it were an official visit from a head of state. The spectacular photographs of this deployment at the airport with all of its paraphernalia appeared in all of the media.

One of our responsibilities at Editorial Mediterrània in preparing the catalog in Catalan was to review the two volumes of the original catalog in Spanish. I asked Professor Rafael Santos Torroella to thoroughly check the catalog which had been written in Spanish for the exhibition in Madrid. We had a huge surprise. The Madrid exhibition catalog was riddled with

The Basket of Bread, 1926 The Salvador Dalí Foundation, St. Petersburg, Florida.

Back cover of the pamphlet to introduce the visitors to the exhibition of *400 Works of Salvador Dalí 1914-1983*.

errors. While it is not unusual for first editions of art catalogs to have mistakes, it is quite possible that this catalog set a record for mistakes in any catalog for an exhibition of such importance. For example, the catalog you are now reading has taken more than 22 years to complete so that it could be as close to perfection as humanly possible. Since it was my 20th and likely final book on or about Dalí, I decided to spare no effort and leave no stone unturned as a tribute to my friend and fellow Catalan, the great master Salvador Dalí.

From left to right: Mr. Max Cahner, minister of culture of the Government of Catalonia, Mr. Javier Solana, minister of culture of the Spanish Government, Mr. Jordi Pujol, president of the Government of Catalonia and Eduard Fornés, consultant for the *400 works of Dalí* exhibition, in front of the paintings on loan from the Dalí Museum of St. Petersburg.

Some of the errors in the Madrid catalog are actually quite humorous. The book written by Dalí in his Surrealist period, *La femme visible* (The Visible Woman) was translated as the opposite The Invisible Woman! When commenting on Dalí's famous interview with Sigmund Freud, there is an interesting episode in which Julien Green writes in his diary: "Freud spoke of Dalí as a Christian speaks of the Gospel" (translated from the French); however, 'Christian' (*Chrétien* in French) suffered a curious translation into Spanish and it appeared in the catalog as 'Cretino' (Cretin in English), thus appearing in the catalog as "Dalí spoke to Freud as a Cretin would speak of the Gospel." In 1936, an exhibition of Surrealist objects was held that included Dalí's *Aphrodisiac Tuxedo*, a tuxedo covered with glasses and peppermints that according to Dalí had aphrodisiac effects. The translation of *Veston aphrodisiaque* (Aphrodisiac suit) in the catalog of Madrid was *Bastón afrodisíaco* (Aphrodisiac baton). There were literally hundreds of errors of this kind. I did not know whether to laugh or cry. Professor Rafael Santos Torroella rightly published a very terse article exposing the enormous number of errors in the Spanish edition of the catalog of the exhibition *400 obras de Salvador Dalí, 1914–1983 (*400 Works by Salvador Dalí, 1914–1983*)* in the newspaper *La Vanguardia*.

The Little Story of Dalí, Editorial Mediterrània 1983.

For the exhibition, we also published a book for children, *The Little Story of Dalí*, which has been translated into foreign languages and has sold more than one million copies. We published this book so that the children who were taken by their parents to view the exhibition would have a written and illustrated reference, and could thus not only have a better experience of the exhibition but also learn something about the life and work of Dalí. I wrote the small volume myself and asked Pilarín Bayés, the great illustrator of children's books, to make the drawings for the book. This book was to be the first in a series of children's books on the subjects of artists and writers. It is still the number one seller in the collection of these short stories, which now has nearly 300 titles including stories on Miró, Picasso, Toulouse Lautrec, Goya, Gaudí, Subirachs, and also stories on musicians, poets, Nobel Prizes winners, etc. But *The Little Story of Dalí*, 25 years after its first edition, is still the best seller and has been published in more than 10 languages including Japanese and Korean.

DISTRIBUCIONS D'ART SURREALISTA

On February 17, 1983, Editorial Mediterrània set up a new company, Distribucions d'art Surrealista. We purchased the very beautiful and active bookstore and gift shop called Librería Surrealista of Teatre Museu Dalí in Figueres, Spain, which was designed and created by Salvador Dalí himself.

We acquired the rights from Dalí to 600 illustrations for the purpose of reproducing these images. One of our projects was the publishing of tarot cards that were painted by Dalí in a mixed media technique of collage and watercolor. Along with the card game, we published a book in both Spanish and English editions, *The Tarot of Salvador Dalí*, which explained each of the 69 illustrations by Dalí.

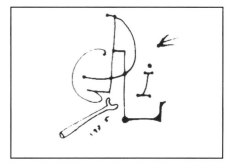

Logo of Distribucions d'Art Surrealista.

Distribucions d'Art Surrealista acquired other important agreements, such as the medals of *The Seven Days of the Creation of the World*, and the opéra-poema *Être Dieu*. *Être Dieu* is an opera starring Dalí himself in which he appears as God. It was clearly one of the most surreal and hilarious episodes in his life.

Distribucions d'Art Surrealista produced postcards, picture cards, posters, books, etc., giving Librería Surrealista the kind of character that I knew Dalí wanted. As a result, thousands upon thousands of yearly visitors to the museum had the opportunity to buy good reproductions of his works of all kinds and good quality souvenirs.

Advertising created by Dalí for the medals of *The Seven Days of Creation of the World*.

Surrealist Bookstore, next to the Theatre-Museum of Dalí in Figueres.

OPÉRA ÊTRE DIEU

In 1983, well-known Spanish television personality Jesús Hermida phoned me and asked me to meet him at the Hotel Princesa Sofía in Barcelona regarding a rare and little-known work by Dalí. This work was Dalí's complete presentation of an opera, including a painting created for the opera by Dalí. Even though I had a close relationship with Dalí and had written many books about him, this little-known fact was unknown, even to me. It is undoubtedly one of the most eccentric and, I dare say for Dalí, one of the most surreal chapters in his life. In all my dealings with Dalí, I discovered that his work had an extraordinary ability to present new and amazing surprises, so I quickly agreed to the meeting with enthusiasm and curiosity. I was excited that I might make another new discovery in Dalí's work, and so it would be again. Hermida was accompanied by an entrepreneur, Oriol Regàs. They told me about a contract that Dalí had made with Bocaccio Records in 1972 for Dalí to create paintings for the opéra-poema *Être Dieu*. An opera! This took me by complete surprise. I remembered indeed that in 1974, opéra poema *Être Dieu*, with music by Igor Wakhévitch and libretto by the well-known writer Manuel Vázquez Montalbán, was recorded at the Pathé Marconi studios in Paris. Hermida and Regàs were fully aware of my chronic obsession for everything Dalí, and proceeded to make an excellent presentation to sell me the rights to this opera which were owned by the Spanish Phonographic Company in Madrid. At that point, I had no idea exactly what Dalí had done for the opera, but my appetite was thoroughly whetted and I had no choice but to learn more.

Self-Portrait, 1972, for the cover of the LP's of the opéra-poema *Être Dieu*.

The following week I traveled to Madrid to visit the offices of the Spanish Phonographic Company, where I was left alone (obviously not by accident) in their waiting room sitting in front of a 4-foot by 3-foot Dalí painting titled *Autorretrato* (Self Portrait), 1972. This canvas was painted expressly for the cover of the album of the opéra-poema *Être Dieu*. It is a remarkable profile self-portrait, where in place of Dalí's ear is a collage of Marilyn Monroe superimposed over the face of Mao Tse Tung. Breathtaking and unique! Suddenly, as I was sitting in front of the painting, I heard a recording of the voice of Dalí, shouting through the loudspeakers: "*Être Dieu! Être Dieu!*" (To be God! To be God!) together with other hilarious selections from the opera. What a shock! I was ecstatic. There was now no way that I intended to let such a powerful, shocking Surrealist and Dalínian work escape.

Dalí painting his *Self-Portrait*, 1972 with Marilyn Monroe and Mao Tse Tung.

SER DIOS

·HAPENINGS EN 6 DIAS·
SIN MENSAJE

CERRADURA —

SER DIOS . SER DIOS . SER DIOS . SER DIOS . SER DIOS . SER DIOS . SER DIOS . SER DIOS . ect.
GRITAN LOS POPS ENCERRADOS COMO RATAS EN LA JAULAS DE LA LOCURA INMINENTE. LA MUSICA DE
FONDO QUE NO PUEDE NI DEBE SER OTRA QUE LA DEL CREPUSCULO DE LOS DIOSES DE RICARDO
WAGNER DECRECE COMO LA PROPIA PALABRA CREPUSCULO INDICA MIENTRAS EL ESTRUENDO
MAS VIOLENTO QUE NUNCA SE ABRA REGISTRADO EN TODA LA HISTORIA DE LA MUSICA PARA, EN
SECO PARA OIR LA VOZ DE QUE SE SOSPECHARA ES LA DE SALVADOR DALI QUE ANUNCIA
EL SIGUIENTE FLAX . NOUS VENONS D'APRENDRE A L'INSTAN LE DECES DE
FEDERIC NITCHE . HOSPITALISSE A PLUSIEUR REPRISSES APRES SA BROLLE AVEC WAGNER
PRECURSEUR DU ROMANTISME HITLERIEN . LA DERNIERE HEURU UNE PARTITURE MUSICALE INACHEVE DA ETE
SE OYE LA VOZ EN CATALAN DE FRANCISCO PUJOLS QUE DICE . JA LA BALLEM!
SIGMUND FREUD REPON AUSSI EN CATALAN. JA LA BALLEM ET DE MEME
TOUJOURS EN CATALAN QUAQUE AVEC UN ACCENT INPERTEPTIBLEMENT
ALLEMAND LA VOIX DE CARLOS MARX QUE DIT A SON TOUR: JA LA
BALLEM! EN EFET A CE MOMENT COMENCE LE TOUR CYCLISTE DE FRANCE
QUI FINIT AUSSI TOT PAR LA MORT DE TOUS LES PARTICIPANS, CE QUI DONE LIEU AUX
PLAINTES ESTRIDENTES DE TOTES LES EPOSSES DE TOUS LES TRICOTS JAUNES LES
QUELLES HABILLES PREMATIREMENT EN NONES SE RASEMBLENT DANS UNE
SARDANES LA MUSIQUE DE LA QUELLE DEBRA SI POSIBLE COMPORTER UN SOLO DE
TENORA DANS LE QUEL LE TEME DE L'ARLESIENE DE BISSET SOIT INCONFUNDIBLE
A FAIN D'ARRACHER LA SUIVANTE EXCLAMATION DES EGUTEURS'' CET LE COMBLE! CE QUE DE

SERA PRONONCE APRES LA NOTE FINALE. PAR LE PROPRE SALVADOR DALI LUI MEME

SUIVENT LES 6 APENIGS DE LA CREATION . CELLE DU REGNE ANIMAL
SERA COMENTE SUR LE THI POUR UN SPIKUER SPORTIF CELEBRE

LE SETIEME JOUR PAS DE REPOS. LA DOIT SE POSE L'IDEE GENIALLE
QUE MOI ET TOUS NOUS ATENDONS DE VOTRE UMBLE SERVITEUR

SALVADOR DALI

Port-Lligat Septembre 1971

Salvador Dalí's manuscript for the plot of opéra-poema *Être Dieu*

Back in Barcelona, I remembered that in the prologue of the novel *Hidden Faces* (1944) Dalí wrote: "In 1927, on a spring day, sitting in the sun on the terrace of the café Regina in Madrid, the much missed poet Federico García Lorca and I both had the idea of a new opera. Indeed, opera was one of our passions, because only by this means could all existing lyric genres merge into a perfect and triumphant unity, to the maximum of its greatness and needed stridency, which should allow us to express all the ideological, colossal, sticky, viscous and absolute confusion of our times. The day (in London) that I received the news of the death of Lorca, a victim of blind history, I told myself that I should do the opera alone. I persevere in my strong commitment to make this project one day, at the time of my full maturity, and my audience knows – as well as expects – that I do just about everything I say and promise."

Dalí signature and seal for the sleeve of the LP's of *Être Dieu*.

In 1972, 45 years later, Dalí began his contacts with Oriol Regàs, the owner of Bocaccio Records, for the recording of opéra-poema *Être Dieu*, an opéra-poema in six parts. For me it all worked out perfectly as we made the purchase. As a result, Distribucions d'Art Surrealista (and myself ecstatic with the project of such a unique work) became the owners of nearly 90 kilograms of original tapes, including the publishing rights, the original manuscripts of Dalí, and the fantastic oil painting made for the album cover in 1983.

During a meeting between Dalí, Regàs and Vázquez Montalbán that took place at the Hotel Meurice in Paris, they discussed this project of Dalí creating the opera. One of the photographs taken during that meeting is illustrated here. During that meeting, Dalí produced manuscripts suggesting ideas for the libretto of the opera. Contained in my archives (with utmost care) is an original document from Montalbán, where the creator of Carvallo speaks of his collaboration with Dalí. Montalbán writes: "When it was proposed that I write the libretto for a rock opera about Dalí, sung by Dalí and based on an original idea by Dalí I thought it was time to settle all matters with this merchant of stupidity who at the same time was one of the most evocative plastic poets of the century... Dalí wanted to sell to the world the idea that he was God and I can provide evidence that the only correction he made to my original script was to replace the title 'If Dalí was God' by the categorical affirmation 'To be God'..." The text by Montalbán concludes that: "I wanted to handle him as if he were an old actor in the service of his own character. He did not always let himself go. And definitively, when he does let go, he does not do anything other than to accept a game that he is perfectly aware of, and because of that, he never gets out of it; like the Catholics or the Marxists we never abandon a logic that ultimately defines us."

Dalí discussing the opéra-poema with Vázquez Montalbán and Oriol Regàs at the Meurice Hotel in Paris.

Igor Wakhévitch interpreting the percussion music of *Être Dieu*.

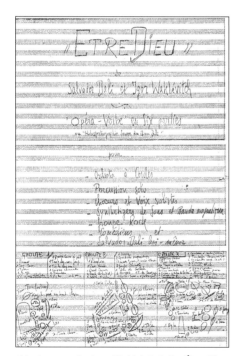

Music score by Igor Wakhévitch for *Être Dieu*.

Dalí's wish was that the music should be composed by Krzysztof Penderecki, the young composer from Krakow, who had success with the opera *The Devils of Loudun*. Dalí's outline for the creation of the libretto was very simple and started from the seven days of the creation of the world which, as Dalí saw it, was the final statement of the anti-matter. It was so short that the description of the sixth day read: "*Il ne passe rien*" (Nothing happens). Vázquez Montalbán compiled a 22-page booklet which Dalí approved in a meeting at the Hotel Meurice in Paris with Regàs and Montalbán. However, despite that fact, at the time of the recording he refused to follow it, using the simple argument that: "Dalí is God, and God never repeats anything." Dalí embodied the role of God in the opera. In fact, we eventually published it in a collector's edition in Distribucions d'Art Surrealista in 1985. New editions were eventually published on CD at a later date. The music, which was essentially percussion, was composed by Igor Wakhévitch and performed by the polyphonic orchestra of Paris, with Boris de Vinogradow conducting.

Être Dieu plot

Dalí applied what he refers to as his 'paranoiac-critical method' in creating this opera. Although initially it may seem to be created without apparent meaning in a Dalínean manner, opéra-poema *Être Dieu* keeps, deep-down, an implacable Surrealist logic which is almost overwhelming. "*The world was a paradise destined to be mystified by man*" (Dalí androgen). And so we witness the creation of the world that Dalí reinvents from his obsessions and his own myths, Marilyn Monroe, Mao Tse Tung, the Marx Brothers, the general secretary of the United Nations (with the United Nations being a brothel!), Gilles de Rais, Joan of Arc, Anne of Brittany, all singing in opéra-poema *Être Dieu*, while giraffes parade along Fifth Avenue through a burning New York City.

Humanity calls Dalí to establish a new order. And Dalí answers: "White! I want you white! To get to the creation of man, since its origin cannot be the same as that of an animal, because he must be born as a God". Dalí (God) rests: "I will take a nap. But if you are God – You will not be Dalí..."

In the second part, Dalí wakes up and explains his dreams: He is against democracy, He is against the death penalty and therefore against abortion. He is Catholic, Apostolic and Roman ... and He adds: "From the point of view of imagination, I must say that creation is zero. The only wonderful thing is the human being."

In the final act of the opera, Dalí runs the risk of being executed for having gone too far in exploding our imagination. As it turns out in this final act, he is not God, but only Dalí and regretting his pride is saved by an angel. He again submerges us into the mystery of his last hope, Gala, while at the same time giving us a glimpse of his Roman Catholic origins, being saved by an angel and not being executed, but forgiven by God for confessing his sin of pride.

THE BOOKS BY DALÍ AND ON DALÍ

Dalí's bibliography contains literally hundreds of references. He may well be the 20th century painter with the largest number of publications written about him. It is fascinating to realize that in addition to all that has been written about him by others, he himself has written an extraordinary number of articles as well as several books. He has also created illustrations for more than 100 books. These hundred books, which in the context of Dalí's total work are often ignored, are truly gems not only because of their imagery, but also because of their importance in both the worlds of art and of literature. This is precisely the place where Dalí combined his two great artistic passions: writing and painting. There are numerous writings about many aspects of Dalí's life, work and the myriad dimensions of his personality. However, many of these works have not been carried out with rigor and an adequate knowledge of his complex character. They are, unfortunately, often excessively concerned with his many weaknesses and enormous fragility.

Of the books about Dalí in different languages and various editions I have been involved in, four of them have sections written by Dalí himself. Three of the four are: *Babaouo* (1978), *The Secret Life of Salvador Dalí*, by Salvador Dalí (1981), and the opera-poem *Être Dieu* (1985) (however it was Vázquez Montalbán who did the writing of the libretto from texts and conversations with Dalí). The fourth is *Les morts et moi* (The Dead and Me) (1991).

However, when considering which are the best published works on Dalí, there is no doubt that for the reader, the real fan of Dalí, these are the real gems: *Salvador Dalí, corresponsal de J. V. Foix 1932-1936*, (1986) of Professor Rafael Santos Torroella. This work was the beginning of a collection that continued a year later with: *Salvador Dalí, l'obra literària* (Salvador Dalí, the literary work) (1989); the aforementioned thesis of Anamieke van de Pas; and *200 dedicatorias de Salvador Dalí* (200 dedications of Salvador Dalí) (1990), which provides great insights into the extraordinary range of the different signatures of Dalí. There is no other artist in the history of art who even remotely approaches Dalí in the complexity, range and inconsistency in the way he signed his name. Like the famous saying "the only thing constant about time is change", it is true to say that the only

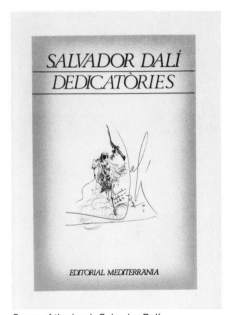

Cover of the book *Salvador Dalí, Dedications* from the collection Port Lligat of Editorial Mediterrània, 1990.

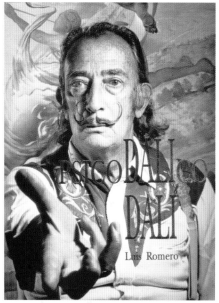

Torero al·lucinogen, (Hallucinogenic Bullfighter)
Luis Romero, Editorial Mediterrània, 1990.

PsicoDÁLIco DALÍ, Luis Romero, Editorial
Mediterrània 1991.

thing constant about Dalí's signatures are their enormous variations and inconsistencies. I was fortunate when editing *200 dedications of Salvador Dalí* to be able to compile 200 authentic signatures of Dalí, including drawings in signature style, from the archives of Dalí's close friends. The variety of signatures and forms of dedications of the artist are without a doubt the most extensive and diverse that any famous painter has ever used. However, they are only a fraction of the many unique and different ways that Dalí expressed himself through his signature. There is no science of graphology which could possibly determine that all of these signatures came from the same hand. In his painting as well as in his writing this is the true and unique genius of Dalí. He could not be contained, restrained, restricted or defined. As he put it in the opera: *"Dalí is God."*

But speaking of remarkable books, it would be incorrect not to mention *Todo Dalí en un rostro, (1975)* written by Luís Romero, who had a close relationship with Dalí. This great volume has a central theme revolving around the painting, *The Hallucinogenic Toreador* by Dalí. In 1988, Editorial Mediterrània published a small Catalan-English bilingual book entitled *Torero al·lucinògen,* written by Romero, based on the archives of Romero, relating to the documents that he had regarding this unique and captivating work of Dalí. *The Hallucinogenic Toreador* is magnificently on permanent exhibit at the Salvador Dalí Foundation, St. Petersburg, Florida. In 1991, we published *PsicoDALíco DALÍ*, also written by Romero. At the time, we believed it to be the most complete biography of Dalí yet written and it remains today one of the most thorough and best documented biographies of Dalí in existence.

However, it would be unfair to conclude a discussion on the books by and about Dalí without mentioning *Les morts et moi* (The Dead and Me),(1991). This book is one of the most exciting, fascinating and little-known texts written by Dalí.

Les Morts Et Moi

Title page for
Les morts et moi
by Fonsterè, Molas.

In 1991, we bought an original and until then little-known manuscript by Dalí from the artist and writer, Mr. Carles Fontserè. Fontserè was a fascinating character who was exiled after the Spanish Civil War, a friend of Dalí, a skilled photographer and also known as a designer for Mexico's comic character and film star Cantinflas. Peculiarly amongst all these other things, he was also considered to be a distinguished gravedigger!

The manuscript was written in New York in 1952. It consisted of 6 numbered straw colored sheets of 43-cm. by 33.5-cm. paper. They were folded in half and had the watermark "Mead Bond / USA." We published the original manuscript for *Les morts et moi* (The Dead and Me) in facsimile including the original corrections and additions by Dalí, which he must have been working on in parallel to the manuscript itself.

We published a collector's edition of 275 numbered examples of the manuscript signed by Joaquim Molas, the author of this study, and also signed by Fontserè, the photographer who made the photographs of Dalí in the privacy of Port Lligat. We included reproductions of these rare and special photographs in each of the six facsimile pages of the manuscript.

In the introduction of *Les morts et moi*, Joaquim Molas writes: "Altogether, the chronological inventory becomes a 'small homeland,' at once historical and personal. There are for example, two 'fathers,' the biological, with whom he had sustained a very complex relationship, and the theoretical, Sigmund Freud, who died in exile in London. From Freud he learned many things which he was to use as resources for this book. There were also the people he met through Freud: the Zweig couple and

The artist and writer Carles Fontserè, friend of Dalí.

The Catalan literature Professor, Joaquim Molas, scholar of the works of Dalí.

the Kleists who, for different reasons, committed suicide together. Then a princess, Baba Faucigny-Lucinge, who according to *Secret Life* 'was indisputably a woman who possessed a most precise sense of Parisian elegance' and who, like the Counts of Noailles or The Beaumonts, entertained one of the most brilliant gatherings of people in a Proustian* salon of the 30s. And with the Princess was, Misia Godebska, who was at the center of another salon where 'the juiciest gossip of Paris was cooked,' and finally the circle of the painter Sert and his second wife, the Georgian Princess Roussy Mdivani, who was shortly to die like a dehydrated flower. A group that was, according to Josep Pla, alive and riotous, that included among others, Alexis, the brother of the Princess, married for a time to Barbara Hutton. Alexis was killed and smashed to pieces in the company of a Baroness von Thyssen in the Albons passage on the road from Palamós to Figueres. Also, close to this decadent and fascinating 'happy world,' were the artists who admired it or who at the least frequented it. The decorator Jean-Michel Franckand who committed suicide, the painter Christian Bérand, the actor Louis Jouvet and the writer Gertrude Stein, who gave name to a lost generation. With them we find the dissidents: Robert Desnos, Antonin Artaud, Paul Éluard, the first surrealist cross-overs. Finally with an insidious programmatic intention, Dalí put among the defunct, two great French movements that revolve around the two wars; Surrealism, where he was one of its leading protagonists until Breton expelled him, and Existentialism where he was a real antagonist."

In January 1989, Dalí died in his hometown of Figueres. After his death, the world of Dalí had to face yet another obstacle in a way that he could never have imagined while he was alive; his will was changed. An ugly manipulation, clearly motivated by greed and political reasons only known at the time by those who perpetrated it. This led me to publish the book *Les contradiccions del cas Dalí* (The contradictions of the Dalí case) (1989). This book is a compilation of important genuine documents concerning Dalí, which are contained in my personal archives. The book consists of 50 documents including the constitution of the Gala-Dalí Foundation, statutes, donation legal deeds, letters, reports, notarial deeds of the meetings of the Trustees of the Foundation, inventories of books, contracts, lawsuits, etc.

The director of the newspaper *Avui* asked for, and was granted permission to distribute, 60,000 copies of this volume. Dr. A. Reynolds Morse himself sent me a praiseworthy letter of congratulations in which he stated that this volume contained the greatest documentation he had ever seen gathered on Dalí.

Les contradiccions del cas Dalí

EDUARD FORNÉS

Llibres de l'AVUI

Cover of the copy *Les contradiccions del cas Dalí (The Contradictions in the Case of Dalí),* which the newspaper «AVUI» gave their subscribers, Barcelona 1989.

* Pertaining to the aristocratic world described by the French novelist Marcel Proust (1877-1920).

In any event, Dalí's death aroused old interests and new promises about this controversial and fascinating figure who may only be described in essence as a totally ambiguous icon of the contemporary art world. He remained enigmatic until his final day. Dalí's father had warned his son of a fate which partially came true in the following statement "In the end you will die bankrupt and alone" - and that is how Dalí died. Some mysteries about his life and work are still to be unveiled, still unresolved - unanswered questions that perhaps no one can answer. However, we cannot close our eyes to the unfathomable depth of his paintings without somehow detecting some hidden meaning, powerfully revealed through symbols and objects. I must stress the importance of Dalí's roots - the umbilical cord that binds him to his land of the Empordà, Cadaqués, and the light of the Mediterranean Sea.

Invitation for the Opening of *Sant Narcís, Dalí i les mosques* exhibition.

Having said that, many wonder at times why one of the leit-motifs that Dalí tirelessly repeated in his works was 'flies.' In many of his most important paintings flies are there - at least one fly. The annual celebration of the City of Girona is held on the day of Sant Narcís, its patron saint, which presides over the Cathedral of Girona. The legend says that when the Napoleonic troops occupied the city, the tomb of the saint was desecrated and many large flies came out from inside and attacked the army of Napoleon, who had to retreat. In Girona, in 1986, we held an exhibition with a catalog titled *Sant Narcís, Dalí i les mosques* (Saint Narcís, Dalí and the flies) where various works in which Dalí painted flies were exhibited, including *El asno podrido* (The Rotten Donkey) in 1928 or *Cenicitas* (Little Ashes) in 1927 and the oil painting *El Torero Alucinógeno* (The Hallucinogenic Toreador) 1968-1970, or *El sueño de Cristóbal Colón 1958-1959* (The Dream of Christopher Columbus 1958-1959).

Among the texts of the catalog is one by Dr. A. Reynolds Morse entitled *The Flies of Dalí* and another of which I am the author called *Dalí and Surrealism.* Morse writes in his text: "There, in the lower left side of the large oil, Dalí depicts St. Narcís who was Bishop of Girona from 304 to 307. Dalí told us that the Bishop was murdered 'by gentiles' and that the site of his tomb was revealed to Charlemagne who founded the See of Girona in 786. The grave of the saint was inside the church-fortress of St. Fèlix, which was named after the Bishop's deacon Sant Feliu. It was from this tomb that large, stinging horse flies emerged in October, 1285, on September 24, 1653 and in May 1648. On each occasion, the flies attacked the horses of the invading French with such violence that the city of Girona was saved."

Cover of the catalog for the *Sant Narcís Dalí i les mosques* exhibition.

Dalí et Dieu, un rendezvous manqué?
(Dalí and God, a missed appointment?)

In 1984, the exhibition of Dalí (*Dalí and His Books: Dalí, the Writer and Dalí, the Illustrator*) was opened at the Museum of Fine Arts in Nîmes (France). At that time, Bernard Durand, who was fascinated by Dalí and an avid collector of his writings,

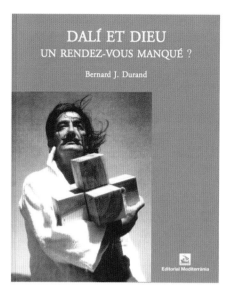

Book by Bernard Durand, *Dalí and God, a Missed Appointment?*, published by Editorial Mediterrània, 2008.

Invitation to the presentation of *Dalí and God, a Missed Appointment?*

Presentation of the book by Bernard Durand (second from left) at the Ateneu Barcelonés. With the author are: Father Costabella (second from right), Playá Masset (far right) and the publisher, Eduard Fornés (far left).

books and illustrations, was the counselor of culture for Nîmes. The exhibition marked the beginning of a friendship between Dalí and Durand that lasted until Dalí's death in 1989. Durand always wondered how Dalí perceived transcendence and what feelings of faith he might have experienced. In 2007, he called to inform me that he had finished his study on the relationship of Dalí and God, a subject I was also curious about. We met a few days later and agreed to publish his study. He asked me to write the foreword for the book introducing his thesis.

In his book, Durand writes that Dalí's spontaneous answer to a journalist's question in 1970: "What would you be if you hadn't been a painter?" was: "I'm going to surprise you, I think I would have been a priest." An incredible reply which contrasts with the image of the dandy, the clown, or the iconoclastic Surrealist transmitted with complacency by the media and, on many occasions, with his own consent. Obviously this remark has some roots in Dalí's insatiable need to provoke, but at the same time it allows a glimpse of the hidden Dalí behind appearances. The Dalí fascinated by the great mystics, tormented by death, worried about the beyond.

Durand's book reveals Dalí through the different stages of his life: the child; the adolescent, divided between a practicing Catholic mother and a freethinking and atheist father; the student who frees himself from the student residence in Madrid; the youngster who arrives in Paris to enter the extravagant world of Surrealism; the Dalí with Gala and his deviant sexuality; and finally the older Dalí, who does a complete turn-about to exhibit an ostentatious: "I am a Roman Catholic." The author analyzes the writings, lectures, interviews, witnesses, all his broad religious work, and leaves the initial question unanswered, so that each of us may generate our own answer with an uncertain final verdict.

The book *Dalí y Dios, ¿Un encuentro que no fue?* (Dalí and God, a Missed Appointment?) was presented on September 15, 2008 at the Ateneu Hall in Barcelona where in 1950 Dalí had given a lecture titled, *Why was I Sacrilegious, Why am I Mystical.* Now, some five decades later, this packed conference room was hearing about and discussing Dalí's religious feelings. An extraordinary number of Dalí's works dealt with religious subjects. As a result, we are faced with two conflicting ideas about Dalí's motivation in his life and work, his preoccupation and even paroxysm regarding death in all its might opposed by his encounter with God and religion. This book is the first time that these two conflicting ideas are dealt with in depth. My compliments to Bernard Durand for this excellent treatise regarding this very important aspect of Dalí, his life, and his work.

As with all great forces, the publications listed in the pages of this book are only a small part of the vast universe that Dalí staged. However, I have hopefully achieved a solid and compact collection of what has been written and published, and trust that the compilation of these books is a contribution to a better understanding of the life and work of Salvador Dalí.

THE ENVIRONMENT OF DALÍ

In the Dalínian world, I have met a multitude of important figures from all walks of life who have established businesses based on the work and figure of Dalí. Among them was a small group of very good people who felt real and sincere friendship for Dalí, not the least of whom was Gonzalo Serraclara, a lawyer and cousin of Dalí, who was involved in helping Dalí and Gala manage many of the daily routine affairs typical in any household.

After the death of Serraclara, I received a poignant letter from Eleanor Morse, written in Spanish, stating what an honest and serious person Dalí's cousin had been. In that letter, on behalf of her and Reynolds, she lamented the fact that Dalí had lost a good friend. A copy of the original letter (and its translation) written to me is reproduced here.

Salvador Dalí with his cousin Gonzalo Serraclara.

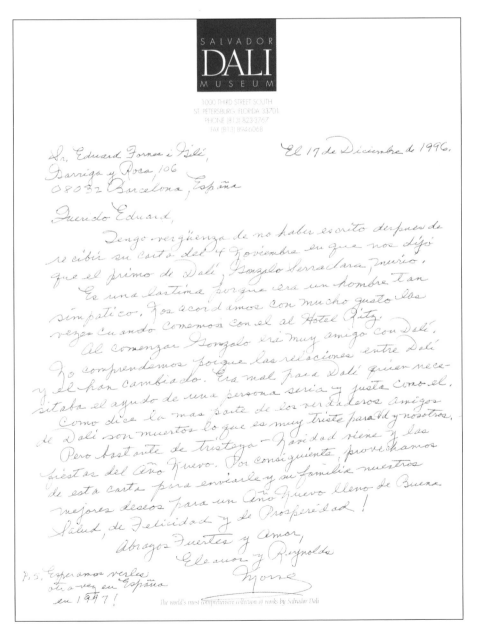

Eleanor Morse's hand-written letter in Spanish above (English translation on right).

Dear Eduard,

I am ashamed of myself for not writing back after receiving your letter of November 4. You said Dalí's cousin, Gonzalo Serraclara, has died.

It is sad because he was a very nice man. We remember with pleasure the times we ate at the Ritz Hotel.

At the beginning Gonzalo was a close friend of Dalí. We don't understand why the relationship between him and Dalí had changed. It was a bad situation for Dalí who needed the help of a serious and fair person like him.

It is very sad for all of us that most of Dalí's true friends are dead.

But enough of sadness. Christmas and New Year's festivities are coming, therefore we take advantage of this letter to send you and your family our best wishes for a new year filled with good health, happiness and prosperity!

Hugs and love.
Eleanor and Reynolds Morse

P. S. Hope to see you again in Spain in 1997!

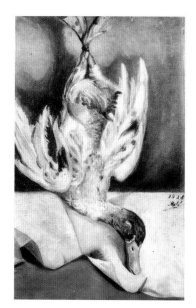

The Duck, 1918
oil on canvas, 53 x 34 cm.

Dalí with his faithful friend Artur Caminada.

Emilio Puignau and Salvador Dalí in
Cadaqués.

Montserrat Dalí, Dalí's cousin, was a woman with a great sense of humor. She cherished many childhood memories of the summers that she and Dalí spent in Cadaqués. I was fortunate, over the years, to have been able to spend a significant amount of quality time with her. Among my many visits with her were numerous trips to Cadaqués, Figueres, and to her favorite secret little restaurant in Paris on La Place des Victoires. At that time, it served the best wine of Sauterne. It was also a great pleasure to have accompanied her to the Dalí Museum in Saint Petersburg, Florida. I have many happy memories of my times with her during which I learned to appreciate her subtle humor. As an example, in her apartment in Barcelona overlooking the sea which was a daily joy for her to view, she expressed a wish to sell a 1918 oil painting by Dalí entitled *The Duck*. I was quite interested in the painting and asked for the price of *The Duck*. Curiously, she never gave me an answer. However, some days later, she rang me to ask if I had been to the 'Boqueria,' a very famous market in Barcelona. When I asked why, she answered: "To ask the price of the duck." Already knowing her dry sense of humor, I began a search for a buyer for this rare and special early Dalí painting, knowing that the price would come later. It finally was purchased by a Catalan industrialist.

Dalí's cousins, Montserrat and Gonzalo, were in my view the two people who had the greatest affection, love and respect for Dalí. Another person who had a real and sincere friendship with Dali was Artur Caminada, a faithful, loyal and honest man who was introduced to Dalí by his confidant Emilio Puignau, a builder. Artur Caminada was always the faithful butler, driver, gardener looking after the household, the personnel, etc. He had such love and esteem for Dalí that many of us, close to Dalí at the end, believed that Dalí and Gala would look after him in their Last Will and Testament. We were dumb-founded to learn they had left him nothing. I and others are truly convinced that it was not what Dalí wanted to do. I saw Artur Caminada cry while he was covering Dalí's face with a white linen veil at his funeral, carrying out Dalí's wish not to be photographed after he died. As it turns out, although he was still quite young, Artur Caminada was to die only a few years after Dalí's death.

Emilio Puignau, another of Dalí's close confidants, managed the financial affairs of Dalí and Gala for many years. Among his responsibilities were numerous renovations of Dalí's house at Port Lligat. He published a book about his personal experiences with Dalí, which through its simplicity and spontaneity showed his genuine and friendly relationship and respect for Dalí, free of selfish and self-serving motives and interests.

Ramon Guardiola, mayor of Figueres and initiator of the Theatre-Museum Dalí in Figueres, was very close to Dalí right up until his death. He visited him daily at Galatea Tower, adjacent to the Dalí museum, where Dalí spent the last years of his life. Guardiola wrote a detailed diary of his observations regarding what was happening in the life of Dalí. One day, Guardiola, already ill and in a wheelchair, called me and invited me to his home where he presented me with the gift of his intimate and personal diary. He said that he wished me to have it out of his love and respect for both Dalí and myself since he knew that by giving it to me it would be in the proper archives. Although I was able to see that he was in full possession of his mental faculties and perfectly understood his reasoning, before leaving his house I returned the diary to his wife who graciously thanked me.

Other good friends of Dalí were the father and son, Luis & Luis Durán. Dalí often dined at the famous restaurant they owned in Figueres. Their wine cellar holds many memories of the anecdotes and experiences of the numerous lunches and dinners that Dalí enjoyed with Gala, Amanda Lear, their secretaries, and other well-known figures from the celebrity world. I had the opportunity to dine with Dalí and many other people at that wonderful restaurant. I still remember one of my dinners there with Dalí, when before dinner was over he left us speechless by crying out: "My balls are full," and got up and left.

One of the rarely publicized facets of Dalí was his Roman Catholicism. Dalí was a Catholic, who only two days before he died, was visited by a priest. I met this priest, Father Narcís Costabella, priest of the church of Saint Pere de Figueres, through an introduction from Luis Durán at the time Dalí died. Father Costabella told me about this last visit with Dalí two days prior to his death. It was a moving story full of emotion. In a presentation held at the Ateneu Hall in Barcelona, of the last published book on Dalí, *Dalí y Dios, Un encuentro que no fue* (Dalí and God, a Missed Appointment) (2008), Father Costabella spoke about his last visit with Dalí. During the visit he showed Dalí an image of Christ crucified, which can be seen at the church of Figueres, and spoke of Dalí taking it close to him and kissing it. It was clear as he spoke that Father Costabella found this visit to be a particularly satisfying and moving part of his relationship with Dalí.

The topic that fascinates me most about Dalí was his remarkable, unique, intimate and personal relationship with God. Dalí painted more than 600 purely religiously-themed works. I cannot look at these works without having them evoke deep and mystical feelings. I can't help but think, when considering these magnificent paintings such as, *Christ of St. John of the Cross*

Ramon Guardiola, mayor of Figueres, was the initiator of the Dalí Theatre-Museum Dalí in Figueres.

Dedications to Luis Durán of Figueres by Salvador Dalí. In one of them, Dalí writes: "Para Luis Duran el Quijote de l'oca con peras. Dalí 1969."

Translation: To Luis Durán, the Quixote of Goose with Pears. ('Oca con Peras' is a popular Catalonian dish).

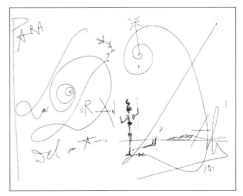

and the *Sacrament of the Last Supper,* that although they do not necessarily imply that Dalí was a believer during his life, can such a work of art be created if you do not believe in what you are painting? According to what Dalí wrote in the *Liturgical Arts* magazine in 1952: "The so-called abstract artists are primarily artists who do not believe in anything. And not believing in anything leads to NON-objective and NON-figurative painting. Those who do not believe in anything paint nothing or almost nothing." Then I ask myself, did Dalí want to express his relationship with God through his work and his writings? This is certainly the big question, the alpha and omega, the first and last about the life and work of the genius Dalí.

Up until this point I have only written in this book about those close to Dalí with whom I have had personal relationships. However there are others, some that I have met briefly or occasionally and others whom I never met, that I believe are worthy of comment in the roles they played in the life of Dalí.

For example, I never had the occasion to meet Amanda Lear personally, but this odd character in the life of Dalí is noteworthy of mention. According to her book *El Dalí d'Amanda* published in 1984, she first met Dalí in 1965. It is well known that Dalí was very fond of Amanda and that they were close friends for many years and Amanda spent many years at Dalí's side. For those interested in a deeper understanding of this relationship, it would be worthwhile to read the book.

A similar character was Nikita Kalashnikoff, who according to Puignau in his book *Vivencies con Dalí* (Living with Dalí) 1995, had a long and solid friendship with Dalí. Surprisingly, Nikita was accepted by Gala, and spent many summers with Dalí and Gala in Port Lligat, Paris or New York. Puignau says that after the death of Gala, Nikita visited Dalí often, and he welcomed her visits even when he was very ill, shut away and typically not wanting to see anyone.

Photographers Meli Casals and Marc Lacroix

Another good friend of Dalí, also from Figueres, was the photographer Meli Casals, whom the artist called '*Meli Color*' for having been the first one to take a color photograph of him. Another important friend and photographer was Marc Lacroix, who was commissioned by Gala in 1970 to take a series of photographs of her in the castle of Púbol. Dalí's relationship with Lacroix was intense and productive. Both Lacroix and Dalí were exploring flat painting in a manner that would cause it to appear three dimensional. These would come to be known as Dalí's stereoscopic paintings. Among the stereoscopic paintings that Dalí created were: *Dalí from the back painting Gala from the back eternalized by six virtual corneas provisionally reflected in six mirrors; Gala foot; The maids-in-waiting; Dalí's*

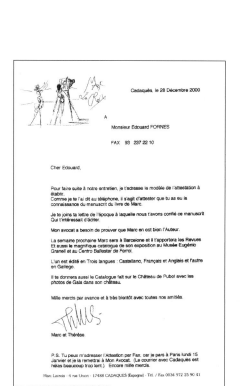

Marc Lacroix's letter sent to Eduard Fornés requesting a meeting in Barcelona.

hand drawing back the golden fleece in the form of a cloud to show Gala the dawn, completely nude, very, very far away behind the sun; Dalí lifting the skin of the Mediterranean Sea to show Gala the birth of Venus; The Chair; Gala's Christ; and *The Sleeping Smoker.* Some of these were painted by Dalí from photographs taken by Lacroix. Lacroix would photograph two distant objects to provide the eyes of the viewer with two different perspectives of the same object with a minor deviation just as both eyes naturally receive in binocular vision. By superimposing the two images, the painting is seen in 3-D.

I was fortunate to have had a very good relationship with Lacroix and his wife, Theresa. They were to introduce me to Gala's daughter, Cécile Eluard Boaretto, at Lacroix's home *Le Castillan* (Biot), on the French Riviera. Cécile herself had a house in Aut de Cagnes. Years later, Lacroix and I incorporated a stereoscopic tower with the photographs of Lacroix at the exhibition of *Dalí and His Books: Dalí, the Writer and Dalí, the Illustrator.*

Cover of the book: *The Rotting of Dalí and Lorca,* (1995) by professor Rafael Santos Torroella.

According to Lacroix in the book he published shortly before his death, entitled *The Privilege of Intimacy*, Dalí was always unpredictable. "Dalí," said Lacroix "liked to appear... and in a whirl disappear as fast as he had appeared." In 1973, he asked me to apply the principles of stereoscopy focusing on relief. "We will stage Dalí and Gala at the workshop in Port Lligat and then he will transform these photographs into 3-D paintings, which can now be seen in the mirrors, let's call them Magic, at his museum in Figueres."

The Writers and Art Critics Luís Romero and Rafael Santos Torroella

The Dalí scholar, Luis Romero, wrote the book *The Whole Dalí in a Face* (1974) and *PsicoDÁLIco DALÍ* (1991), which in my view is the most complete, convincing and best illustrated biography on Salvador Dalí. Luis owned a house in Cadaqués. During summer afternoons, while Dalí was painting at his house in Port Lligat, he would often receive visits from Luis. Luis was well known in Cadaqués as good friend to those who had the good fortune to meet him and share time with Dalí and him together. He was also the author of many articles on Dalí. It was a privilege for me to publish some of them; *The Hallucinogenic Toreador* and *PsicoDÁLIco DALÍ.*

From left to right - Dr. Giuseppe Albaretto (speaking), Dr. A. Reynolds Morse, the art critic Rafael Santos Torroella and Jean Estrade at the home of the Albaretto Family in Turin, Italy.

Any list of the important writers on Dalí and Surrealism must also include Rafael Santos Torroella. Rafael is not only an author but an expert on the works of Lorca and the Surrealist group. Among his important works are *Honey is Sweeter Than Blood* (1984), and his editing of books published by the Students' Residence in Madrid, *Dalí Resident,*

Round table in Cadaqués; from left to right: the journalist Josep Playá Masset, the publisher Eduard Fornés, the writer Luis Romero, the Minister of the City Hall of Cadaqués, the art critic Corredor Matheos and the artist painter Joan-Josep Tharrats.

Salvador Dalí and Luís Romero.

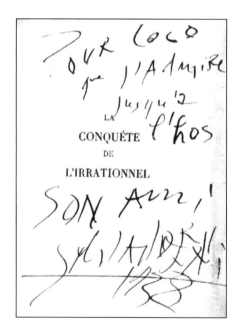

La conquête de l'irrationnel, dedicated to Coco Chanel in 1938.

The Morse couple with the Albaretto Family in Turin.

Dalí Period in Madrid, (1992), *Los putrefactos de Dalí y Lorca* (The Rotting of Dalí and Lorca) (1995). Other articles and presentations include those published in the magazine *Poesía* (Poetry) such as *Dalí Writes to Federico García Lorca* (1989), and his speech at the Sant Jordi's Royal Academy of Fine Arts in Barcelona, where he talked about Salvador Dalí and the Autumn Room, (1985). There are also texts in catalogs and articles in the newspapers *La Vanguardia* and *Diario 16.*

In 1986, with Editorial Mediterrània, I was fortunate to publish both in Catalan and Spanish, Rafael Santos Torroella's, *Salvador Dalí corresponsal de J.V. Foix, 1932-1936,* (1986). This is the book I mentioned earlier when I commented on the Gold Medal that the Catalan government finally bestowed on Dalí.

The Couple—A. Reynolds and Eleanor Morse

On March 7, 1992, in an emotional speech given by Eleanor Morse commemorating the 10th anniversary of the opening of the Dalí Museum of St. Petersburg, Florida, she told us how Reynolds and she met at a concert of the Cleveland Orchestra in October 1991. In her speech she stated: "The program was the music of Showboat adapted and arranged for the first time for the symphonic orchestra. I took my seat. The seat to my right was empty. Suddenly, a handsome, young man came and sat next to me. When we heard the song 'Why do I love you,' Cupid must have thrown his arrows because it was love at first sight." The following March, they married. Fifty years later when they celebrated the 10th anniversary of the museum, they also celebrated their golden wedding anniversary.

Prior to the wedding, they visited a retrospective exhibit on the works of Dalí at the Cleveland Museum of Art. They immediately fell in love with the Surrealist painter. In 1943 they bought their first painting and met Dalí, and soon after his wife, Gala. As their friendship developed and grew stronger, so did their collection, and in 1982 they opened the Dalí Museum in St. Petersburg, Florida.

On March 24, 1990, the 8th Anniversary Celebration of the museum took place. A group of people from Barcelona travelled to St. Petersburg, Florida to attend the ceremony and the dinner. H.E. Joseph Zappala, ambassador of the United States of America to the Kingdom of Spain, and the honorable Don Julian Santamaria, ambassador of the Kingdom of Spain to the United States of America, were present. Also among us was the Catalan sculptor Raimon Casals, who made a magnificent bust of Dalí in bronze which we presented to the Dalí Foundation of St. Petersburg so it could be exhibited at the entrance of the museum.

The program began with introductions of honored guests, toasts and other formalities. Our group from Spain was pleased to be a part of the program. I was honored to personally present a commemorative plaque to the Morses. Casals himself presented the bronze bust of Salvador Dalí to the museum. The program ended with speeches by both ambassadors, followed by dinner and dancing until midnight.

Eleanor Morse and Eduard Fornés at the Dalí Museum in St. Petersburg.

I have many fond memories of the visits of the Morses to Barcelona, and amongst my treasures are many dedicated books and correspondence from them. The Dalínian world owes a very great deal to the significant contributions made by the Morses to the life of the Dalís. It was a sad day when I contacted them and had to be the bearer of the sad news of Dalí's death. They thanked me and let me know that, as a result of waking them that morning and letting them know that Dalí had passed away, they were able to quickly make the necessary travel arrangements to be present at the funeral of their dear friend. They thanked me formally, once again, in the following issue of the museum's magazine for members (see page 88).

(1) The publisher of Salvador Dalí, Lady Arianne Lancel
(2) The author Eduard Fornés
(3) The painter Mr. Joan Abelló, friend of Salvador Dalí
(4) Mrs. Carme Farré curator of exhibitions
(5) Mrs. Eleanor Morse
(6) The cousin Salvador Dalí, Lady Montserrat Dalí
(7) The writer Mr. Luis Romero, friend of Salvador Dalí
(8) Dr. Reynolds Morse
(9) The lawyer Mr. Bernard Durand, author *Dalí and God a Missed Appointment?*
(10) Professor Mr. Joaquim Molas, scholar of the works of Dalí.

NEWSLETTER

SALVADOR DALI MUSEUM NEWSLETTER   SPRING 1989   VOL. 7 NO. 1

Salvador Dali, May 11, 1904 - January 23, 1989

Salvador Dali died in a hospital in Figueres, Spain, on January 23, 1989, at the age of 84. To honor the artist whose brilliance fills the Museum which bears his name, we dedicate this Newsletter. Inside, you will find statements from people around the world mourning the loss of this magnificent genius. Some, like Mr. and Mrs. Morse, knew him well and grieve for the loss of their friend. Others knew him only through his work. Each voice reflects a different reaction to the many facets of Salvador Dali.

Photo by Meli

Salvador Felipe Jacinto Dali i Domenech was born at 8:45 in the morning of May 11, 1904, in the small agricultural town of Figueres, Spain. Here, in the foothills of the Pyrenees, only sixteen miles from the French border in the region of Catalonia, he spent his boyhood. The family also had a summer home in the coastal fishing village of Cadaques, where his parents built his first studio. As an adult, he made his home with Gala in nearby Port Lligat. Many of his paintings reflect his love of this area of Spain.

The young Dali attended the San Fernando Academy of Fine Arts in Madrid. Early recognition of Dali's talent came with his first one-man show, held in Barcelona in 1925. He became internationally known when three of his paintings, including The Basket of Bread (now in the Museum's collection), were shown in the third annual Carnegie International Exhibition in Pittsburgh in 1928.

The following year, in 1929, Dali went to Paris and opened his first one-man show there. Later that year, he met Gala Eluard, who was visiting Cada-

ques with her husband, poet Paul Eluard. She was to become Dali's lover, muse, business manager and chief inspiration.

In 1930, Dali returned to Paris and joined the Paris Surrealists Group, led by author Andre Breton. He became a leader of the Surrealist movement and his painting Persistence of Memory (1931), is still one of the best-known surrealist works. However, as war approached, the apolitical Dali clashed with the Surrealists and he was expelled during a "trial" in 1934. Although he did exhibit works in International Surrealist Exhibitions throughout the decade, by 1940 he was ready to move into a new "classic" era.

Dali and Gala escaped from Europe during World War II, spending 1940-48 in the United States. These were very important years for the artist. The Museum of Modern Art in New York gave Dali his first major retrospective exhibit in 1941. This was followed in 1942 by the publication of Dali's autobiography, The Secret Life of Salvador Dali. As Dali moved away

from Surrealism and into his Classic period, he began his series of Masterworks - eighteen large canvases, many concerning scientific, historical or religious themes. Among the best known of these works are Hallucinogenic Toreador, The Discovery of America by Christopher Columbus (both from the Museum's collection), and The Last Supper (National Gallery, Washington, D.C.).

Dali's health began to fail following the death of his wife, Gala, in 1982. It deteriorated further after he was burned in a fire in his home in Pubol in 1984. Two years later, a pacemaker was implanted. Much of the past six years were spent in seclusion, first in Pubol and later in his apartments at the Torre Galatea, adjacent to the Teatro-Museo-Dali in Figueres, Spain.

Dali's most avid and scholarly collectors were A. Reynolds and Eleanor R. Morse. With the purchase of Daddy Longlegs of the Evening ... Hope! in 1942, Mr. and Mrs. Morse began a lifelong relationship with Dali and Gala that included vacations together, lectures and discussions, and numerous exhibitions. The Morse collection, which grew to be the largest private collection of Dali's works in the world, is unrivaled in scope and diversity. Originally displayed in a wing of their office building near Cleveland, Ohio, the collection was donated for the benefit of the people of Florida in 1980. The Salvador Dali Museum in St. Petersburg, Florida, opened on March 7, 1982, thereby giving the collection a permanent home and offering the public a unique opportunity to learn about the Catalan artist and his work.

Salvador Dalí Museum Newsletter announcing Dalí's death.

Salvador Dali's Funeral in Spain
- By Eleanor R. Morse

Port Lligat *cont. from page 2*

king as well as the distinguished governor of Catalonia on several occasions. But for the rest of us, there was no longer any place in his narrowing circle.

In trying to piece together an image of the world's greatest publicist turned total recluse, memories of the preceding happier years keep surfacing. More and more vignettes from people who knew Dali well, such as Amanda Lear and Ultraviolet are now appearing. None of them, however, look beyond 1979. Even in my own journal, the painful episodes and transitions of this sad decade are difficult to keep in perspective. Certainly the media has not distinguished itself in presenting the true poignancy of the last decade.

The real key is in the series of oils that Dali painted between 1979 and 1984. These show a new genius and a totally different personality as Dali's protective legends disintegrated on the one hand, and as his once-slick minutiae evolved into the pointillism of Seurat, and precursors such as Meissionier, Detaille and Fortuny --the ultimate realism of the totally abstract.

The sad vacuity of the lonely decade just ended only reinforces my regret for having so often looked without seeing. The Catalan painter said there is no such thing as a lazy genius. He also taught me that there should be no such thing as a dullard art collector. If I miss anything of the decades from 1943 on to 1979, it is the stern master's jolting admonition: "Morse you eez one e-stupid man. You is no know nozzing!" How right he was! The saddest thing of all about the sad decade has been the loss of all the "art lessons" Eleanor and I were privileged to have received in earlier years from both the artist and his wife.

Today, Dali and his art can teach us more about the future course of painting and creativity than any modern "art experts" are willing to concede. Our mission is -- and should remain -- to promulgate Dali's main thesis: The Art of Tomorrow will consist ONLY of art with intellectual content. Realism and the image must triumph over the abstract, or art will die!

Monday morning, January 23, 1989, we were awakened at 5 a.m. by a telephone call. It was our friend, Eduard Fornes, with sad news. Salvador Dali had just died in Figueres. It came as a great shock to us even though we had been expecting it for quite awhile.

The funeral was to take place on Wednesday because according to Spanish law, the burial must be within 72 hours. This caused a frenzy of hurriedly packing to catch a flight from Tampa in the early afternoon.

We arrived on Tuesday after a hectic trip just in time to see Dali in his casket in an alcove of his Teatro-Museo. There were lines of people waiting. Fortunately, we were given a short private session. We bid farewell to our dear friend, our eyes brimming with tears. Dali's expression was calm and serene as if he had found peace at last.

The funeral on the following day was at 4:30 p.m. in the Church of St. Peter where Dali had been baptized 84 years before. It was just across the square from the Teatro-Museo, and much too small for the hundreds who had come from all over the world for the last rites of the celebrated artist. Actually, the media took most of the space, even hanging from the rafters. But, of course, Dali would have liked this!

The service itself was very simple and austere, not at all Dalinian. Catalan was used throughout, but certain parts were repeated in several languages. Among those present were Jordi Pujol, Governor of Catalonia; Maria Lorca, Mayor of Figueres; Mayor of Cadaques and other dignitaries, including members of the Board of Trustees of the Gala-Salvador Dali Foundation with the "troika", Robert Descharnes, Antonio Pichot and Miguel Domenech and our dear friend, Meliton Casals (Meli). Dali's sister, Ana Maria, did not attend but watched the service on TV. (She told us this the next day when we visited her in Cadaques.)

Quite a few cousins were present, such as our friend Felipe Domenech and his wife. Arturo Caminada, faithful servant of Gala and Dali for fifty

years, looked very stricken. The Albarettos from Italy and Captain Moore, Dali's ex-secretary, were there, but notable by his absence was Dali's other manager, Enrique Sabater.

Most eminent among the friends attending were the French artist, Yves Tremois, with his collegue, Louis Pauwels, Director of Figaro Magazine and author of The Passions According to Dali. They were resplendent in their gorgeous uniforms of the Académie Francaise and added the only color to an otherwise drab ceremony, completely lacking in the pomp and circumstance so dear to Dali and really not elaborate enough for such an internationally celebrated artist. (Note: Dali became a member of the Academie Francaise on May 9, 1979 with a sensational speech entitled "Velazquez, Gala and the Golden Fleece".)

After the church ceremony, the casket, with the Museum guards as pallbearers, was taken to the Museum under the Geodesic Dome of Pinero. There was not enough space here either for the crowds from the church. We were among those who managed to squeeze in before the doors were closed. The actual burial was extremely brief, consisting only of lowering the coffin into the tomb in the floor. It seems that at the last moment Dali wished to be buried under the Cupola in the museum instead of beside Gala at the Chateau in Pubol. May he rest in eternal peace!

We have read quantities of obituaries in which the critics have not been kind to Dali. They have all judged him by his antics and not by his art We believe that our faith in Dali's genius will be justified by time, and that history will class him among the Titans.

As Marcel Proust said: "Besides the time that it takes an individual to penetrate a slightly profound work (of art) is only the shortening and like a symbol of the years and sometimes of the centuries that pass before the public can admire a really new masterpiece." (Vol. 3-In the Shade of Young Girls in Bloom-"Remembrance of Things Past" by Marcel Proust.)

Article in Salvador Dalí Museum Newsletter by Eleanor Morse.

Pierre Argillet

Pierre Argillet was a long-standing and important publisher of books illustrated by Dalí. He first met Dalí in 1934 and throughout the years maintained a close friendship with him. At the suggestion of Dalí, he was to purchase what Dalí told him was a 'proper surrealistic palace,' the castle Vaux-le-Penil.

Pierre Argillet in his castle of Vaux-le-Penil.

Located near the Seine and Fontainebleau, Castle Vaux-le-Penil had 78 rooms, some decorated by Dalí himself, along with a basement where an authentic castle jail had been. This peculiar palace became a kind of embryo of Argillet's own Surrealist museum, not the least of which was the room with a life-size figure of Dalí next to a piano containing a tap from which water could actually flow.

Dalí made several drawings of angels that Argillet would frame and keep as part of his collection. The drawings were studies used to make the lavish Dalínian angels that were to decorate the balconies of the castle façade in its transformation into the Musee du Surrealisme (Museum of Surrealism). From 1978, Argillet lived practically alone in the castle. He dressed impeccably, carried a walking stick embossed in silver and wore his hair in a ponytail like a courtier. He received many collectors and people from the Dalínian world seeking access to his rich files, while he recounted his many invaluable memories of the Surrealist world. Argillet always welcomed people with great kindness and friendliness, and offered good French champagne. He considered himself 'the last Surrealist.' From one of my visits, I still have a vivid memory of a group of horsemen dressed in medieval costume trotting through the rooms of the castle, and from another, a birthday celebration with a parade of Harley-Davidsons revving their engines while driving up and down the stairs and in and out of the rooms of the castle. Argillet was simply unique and brilliant.

Salvador Dalí with Pierre Argillet, 1962. Dalí gives approval for the "bon a tirer (ok to print)" for illustrations of the book *Les Rois Mages*.

During the numerous visits that Gala and Dalí made to the Castle Vaux-le-Penil, Argillet made a practice of filming Dalí as often as possible while Dalí was unaware. However, whenever Dalí would realize he was being filmed the Dalí show started, with Dalí giving free rein to the real and exaggerated true character that he invented. In the DVDs that Argillet was kind enough to offer me, one can see Gala busily looking for four leaf clovers in the gardens or Dalí pursuing her with a hose, trying to soak her, or the painter kicking a football, or dancing the Charleston – Dalí in his pure state.

Salvador Dalí signing illustrations edited by Pierre Argillet.

Portrait de Ronsard (Portrait of Ronsard),
Pierre de Ronsard, *LES AMOURS DE CASANDRE*,
Argillet Paris 1968
An image from the suite of 10 dry points.

Les Petits chevaux (The Little horses),
Mao-Tse-Tung, *POEMES*,
Argillet Paris 1967
An image from the suite of eight copper engravings.

Tête de veau (Calf's Head),
Johann Wolfgang Goethe, *FAUST*, Graphik
Europa Anstalt – Argillet Paris 1969
An image from the suite of 21 dry points.

Portrait de Marguerite (Portrait of Marguerite),
Johann Wolfgang Goethe, *FAUST*,
Graphik Europa Anstalt – Argillet Paris 1969
An image from the suite of 21 dry points.

Les Aigrettes (The Plumes),
Leopold von Sacher – Masoch, *VENUS AUX FOURRURES*,
Argillet Paris, 1969
An image from the suite of 20 copper engravings.

Femme à la guitare (woman with guitar),
Guillaume Apollinaire, *POEMES SECRETS*,
Argillet Paris, 1967
An image from the suite of 18 copper engravings.

The following is a list of books with original engravings by Dalí which Argillet published: *Les Rois Mages* (1960), *La Mythologie*, 16 gravures sur cuivre (1963-1965), *Poèmes*, Mao Tse Tung (1966), *La Tauromaquia* (1966), *Poèmes secrets* by Guillaume Apollinaire (1967), *Les amours de Casandre*, Pierre de Ronsard (1968), *Faust*, J. Wolfgang Goethe (1969), *La Venus des Fourrures*, Sacher-Masoch (1970), *La Serie de Hyppies* (1971), and the even numbered published later edition of *Les Chants de Maldoror*, Lautréamont (1974). Albert Skira had published the odd numbers in the first edition in 1934.

During a student demonstration in France in May of 1968, an excited delegation of students from the Sorbonne University showed up at Dalí's suite at the Hotel Meurice on the Rue de Rivoli, demanding that Dalí contribute a painting in support of their student cultural revolution. With his usual shrewdness and 'savoir faire', Dalí told them that his secretary was not there and asked them to return the next day, with the promise that he would prepare his contribution to the student movement. After the committee of students had left the hotel, Dalí immediately called Argillet. He asked him to come and see him at the hotel as soon as possible. That afternoon Dalí wrote the manifesto entitled *Ma revolution culturelle* (My Cultural Revolution). So on the night of May 18, 1968, Argillet printed 20,000 copies of the 16-page booklet, in small format. In this booklet, Dalí, after proclaiming himself Catholic, Apostolic and Roman, also proclaimed his strong opposition to the bourgeois culture, offering as his special contribution to the cultural revolution, his "paranoiac-critical method, particularly adapted, as it seems to me, to nature, happily irrational in the ongoing developments." The next day, euphoric, the student committee of the Sorbonne, left the Hotel Meurice with brochures that were distributed among their companions... but without a painting. Dalí had managed to avoid giving them anything more.

I had the opportunity to attend several dinners at the castle of Vaux-le-Penil. I once even stayed overnight in one of the damp and cold rooms of this ramshackle, medieval, surreal monstrosity. During one of these meetings, Argillet gathered together more than 20 ambassadors who resided in Paris. On arrival, we were welcomed by beautiful ladies dressed in the style of the Versailles court period, who announced the guests individually while the music played - really impressive! Moreover, the night revolved around a real feast in the style of Louis XV. I shared a table with one of the most distinguished Spanish ambassadors that I have ever known, Mr. Juan Durán-Loriga. Argillet was absolutely elated to be the host of this Dalí-type extravaganza. Before leaving my memories of this unique man, Argillet, I would like to mention his enormous indignation when we attended Dalí's funeral in Figueres. He could not understand how they could carry out such a

The manifesto *Ma Révolution Culturelle*. May 1968.

Salvador Dalí with Christina, the daughter of Pierre Argillet, at the castle of Vaux-le-Penil.

Eduard Fornés at Vaux-le-Penil, with Pierre Argillet.

traditional and "putrefied" ceremony. He was deeply offended, and when he had enough of it, he approached me and said: "Dalí would have never wanted anything like this comedy. We will arrange the real funeral in Paris in Vaux-le-Penil."

And so it was: the funeral was held at the castle on June 24, 1989, the feast of St. John. About 50 people came up from Barcelona to Paris, including myself, Dalí's cousin Montserrat, and the painter Joan Abelló, a friend of Dalí's who was to die in December 2008, the sculptor Raimon Casals, and a number of collectors, scholars and friends.

Photos above and below: the historic funeral wake that the publisher Pierre Argillet, organized in the gardens of the Castle Vaux-le-Penil, on June 24, 1989.

The funeral began with a special meal that lasted until midnight. Several television channels attended the event, including TV3, the Catalan Television. A variety of spectacles, performances and shows took place in the vast gardens of the castle Vaux-le-Penil: ballet; music bands; a parade of Rolls Royces; a parade of funeral carriages with mourners crying; a tremendous and fascinating parade of people with their heads adorned with huge deer antlers; a real hunt held with hundreds of dogs; and many performances on the stage - one of which was a dance of a 'Dalí' making a painting. We also enjoyed a catwalk of some models in dresses made of paper. One of the guests, a descendent of a noble family, the grandson of the Duke of Orleans, was dressed in full regalia and arrived in a horse-drawn carriage. There was also a papier maché elephant with long ostrich legs, which rose with a hot air balloon. Argillet himself walked around the gardens with one of these balloons to end the funeral-party with a kind of big monument that represented the castle of Púbol which he set on fire. This fire represented the fire that Dalí had suffered at his home in Púbol. All this was followed by a series of spectacular fireworks. At the end of the funeral, a huge buffet was served to more than 500 people, with each person getting lobster and French champagne among many other delicacies. Argillet, radiant and euphoric, said: "This was the funeral Dalí deserved."

Joseph Forêt

I had opportunities to visit Joseph Forêt in his office-workshop at the *Cartier de la Opera* in Paris. However, it is interesting to note that one of the most significant and lively conversations about our dear deceased friend Dalí I ever witnessed was between Montserrat Dalí, Argillet, Forêt and myself at the funeral-party in memory of Dalí, even amid the lavish celebration!

Forêt was an affable and observant man who had a great admiration for the genius of Dalí. He published the only editions of Dalí where Dalí worked directly on stone to create lithographs. Dalí worked on stone for the illustrations of his *Don Quixote* (1957). The stones were limestone or in Spanish 'esquit calcareo' (calcareous shale about 135 million years old) of very high quality and approximately 10 to 12 centimeters thick.

Dalí had them taken to Port Lligat. It was the first time that Dalí made lithographs and his restless spirit led him to experiment by using different ways to create images on them. One of the images was made by firing an old arquebus (an early muzzle-loaded firearm used in the 15th to 17th centuries). He loaded the arquebus with stones and ink before firing it at the limestone amazingly creating two enormous rhinoceros horns. In his illustration of *Don Quixote – Standing* drawn in a whirl of circular lines, one can appreciate a parade of soldiers of the court in uniform drawn on a band going from arm to arm across his chest. His approach was both amazingly creative and incredibly intricate.

In 1958, Forêt published *The Apocalypse* which at that time was, in my view as a publisher of books, clearly the most lavish and costly book ever published. There is only one example of this book (78-cm. by 86-cm. with a total net weight of 218 kilograms), and it was valued at $1 million in 1961! The cover by Dalí was embossed in bronze, and adorned with gold and precious stones. The text of the manuscript written by seven contemporary authors, was printed on parchment and contained commentaries about the Apocalypse related to our time. The scholars Jean Cocteau, Jean Rostand, Daniel Rops and Jean Guitton, the Romanian philosopher E.M. Cioran, the French novelist Jean Giono and the German writer Ernst Junger wrote, in their own hand, their personal thoughts, which were illustrated by seven painters from different countries, Salvador Dalí, Bernard Buffet, the Argentinean Leonor Fini, the Japanese Foujita, Mathieu, Pierre Yves Tremois and the Russian Ossip Zadkine.

Joseph Forêt presenting the great *L'Apocalipsis.*

Telegram from Joseph Forêt to the Albaretto family for the presentation of the *L'Apocalipsis* to his Holiness, John the XXIII, February 24, 1959.

Joseph Forêt's grand book of *L'Apocalipsis.*

Salvador Dalí editing one of the proofs of *Pages choisies de Don Quichotte de la Manche* with Joseph Forêt, 1957.

Pages choisies de Don Quichotte de la Manche, 1957.

93

Jean Estrade

Jean Estrade was the artistic director and creative force behind the publishing house, Les Heures Claires, located at 19 Rue Bonaparte, Paris. The company was founded in 1945 by Jean Estrade and his partner, Jean Riviere, and was one of the first publishing houses to achieve broad international recognition. Along with being responsible for the selection of the company's projects, Mr. Estrade was the editor and technical director for each project undertaken by the publishing house. The company continues to this day, with offices at 79 Boulevard Picpus in Paris under its current Director, Mr. Daniel David.

Invitation for dinner at the Elysee Palace by France's President, Valéry Giscard d'Estaing

Initially, the company focused on discovering and presenting new, young talent to the artistic world. In that effort Mr. Estrade formed a relationship with the master printer, Raymond Jacquet, which would change the course not only of Les Heures Claires, but of the bibliophile art world itself. Through the collaboration of Estrade's visionary concepts and Jacquet's innovative breakthroughs in the art of engraving, Les Heures Claires brought into existence some of the world's finest and most magnificent modern illustrated books. Estrade continued the advancement of Les Heures Claires by purchasing the highly respected publishing house of Piazza in Paris, and bringing into his company over the years respected and experienced professionals such as Robert Blairon, as a partner and director and; Antoine Branducci, as an honorary administrator and Director of Commerce; and Mr. Jean Tarico as technical expert.

Postcard to Jean Estrade from Dali dated the 26th October 1959.

In July 1959 the publisher Joseph Forêt contacted Jean Estrade to discuss the possibility of Les Heures Claires being the publisher of *The Divine Comedy*. Forêt explained that the 100 watercolors Salvador Dalí created for the Librereia dello Stato (the Italian State Library) for *The Divine Comedy* would not lead to publication because of a politically controversial decision by the Italian government wherein it would not support a non-Italian artist illustrating Dante's esteemed *Divine Comedy*. As a result, the 100 magnificent watercolors created by Dalí for *The Divine Comedy* did not have a publisher. As a result of that meeting, Forêt and Estrade came to an agreement for the publication of *The Divine Comedy*.

Even though Forêt had recently worked with Salvador Dalí on the publication of *The Apocalypse,* Forêt thought it best if Estrade himself discuss the publication with Dali directly. Forêt arranged a meeting between Jean Estrade and Salvador Dalí at the home of Salvador Dalí in Cadaquès. As a result of the meeting, an agreement was reached in which Editions d'Art Les Heures Claires became the publisher of *The Divine Comedy* and acquired the copyrights to the 100 watercolors. Thus commenced the creation of the six illustrated volumes of *The Divine Comedy* which included the 100 magnificent wood engravings based on the master's watercolors.

Jean Estrade was to enjoy a long professional and personal relationship with Dalí beginning in 1959 when Dalí was 54. This relationship lasted for more than two decades and resulted in the 100 wood engravings and magnificent illustrated book which was to become *The Divine Comedy* and 67 other graphic editions. Dalí was deeply involved in *The Divine Comedy* project and his numerous and often difficult demands were well suited to Estrade and Les Heures Claires. Even though an additional four years were needed in the collaboration between Dalí and Estrade for the creation of the 100 engravings, Dalí was pleased that this now thirteen year project came to such a magnificent end in the Dalí master pieces which were to illustrate Dante Alighieri's masterpiece epic poem.

With Jean Estrade as its editor and artistic director, Les Heures Claires would conceive, edit and publish illustrated books by important artists including: Henry LeMarié, Maurice Gonon, R.W. Thomas, Leonor Fini and a collaborative project entitled *Peintres mes amis,* which included illustrations by Dufy, Miró and Picasso.

In 1968, Les Heures Claires opened the Les Heures Claires art gallery at 19 Rue Bonaparte. Between 1971 and 1978, Mr. Estrade edited 67 different editions of lithographs and intaglios by Dalí that were printed by Les Heures Claires, Paris for Dr. Giuseppe Albaretto, who formed the company Les Heures Claires, Italy, as publisher (pages 261-277).

In October 1972, Jean Estrade and Robert Blairon were received by his holiness, Paul VI at the Vatican in Rome in recognition of the Les Heures Claires publication presenting "Imitation of Jesus Christ."

In 1977 Jean Estrade and his associate Robert Blairon were received for dinner at the Elysee Palace by France's President, Valéry Giscard d'Estaing, where Les Heures Claires was recognized as an important contributor to the cultural enhancement of the Republic of France and to the international world of art and culture.

Jean Estrade died on September 1, 2005.

Jean Estrade and Robert Blairon offering the "Imitation of Jesus Christ" to his holiness, Paul VI

*A ROME, LA SAINTETÉ PAUL VI
APPRÉCIE L'ŒUVRE QUI VOUS EST PRÉSENTÉE AUJOURD'HUI*

L'ŒUVRE

L'Imitation de Jésus-Christ est un classique de la littérature spirituelle qui a d'ailleurs trouvé auprès des laïques et même dans le public non chrétien, le plus étonnant accueil.
Sa lecture donne une impression de grande sagesse.
C'est l'ouvrage le plus reproduit après la Bible et c'est de l'avis de Fontenelle : « le plus beau livre sorti de la main de l'homme ».
C'était aussi l'œuvre préférée de Jean XXIII qui en était l'illustration vivante.

Translation:

ROME, POPE PAUL VI
APPRECIATES WORK PRESENTED TO YOU TODAY

THE WORK

The Imitation of Christ is a classic of spiritual literature which has also found among secular and even in non-Christian audiences, the most amazing welcome.

Reading it gives an impression of great wisdom.

It is the most reproduced work after the Bible and it is the opinion of Fontenelle: "the most beautiful book out of the hand of man."

It was also the favorite work of John XXIII who was a living illustration.

Dalí with Giuseppe (Beppe) and Mara Albaretto.

Dalí with Cristiana Albaretto.

Dalí with the ocelot.

Letter from Captain Moore to Mara Albaretto in 1998.

Giuseppe Albaretto

Giuseppe Albaretto, his wife Mara and their daughter Cristiana, lived in what could be described as a city palace in Turin. Giuseppe was a dentist, who for most of his life did not practice dentistry, but instead focused his time on art and almost exclusively the art of Salvador Dalí. Mara was a physician and the heiress of the well known Berio Olive Oil family. Giuseppe and Mara met Dalí at a bull fight in Spain in the 1950s and a close friendship developed between Dalí, the Albarettos, and their daughter Cristiana. This friendship was to last more than 30 years.

The most important collectors of paintings on canvas by Salvador Dalí were Dr. A. Reynolds Morse and his wife Eleanor. The most important collectors of paintings on paper by Dalí were Dr. Giuseppe Albaretto and his wife, Dr. Mara Albaretto. There were no other persons or institutions, including museums, dealers or collectors, that remotely approached these two couples in both the quality and number of the paintings they collected directly from Dalí. There was one substantial difference. The Albarettos were also important publishers of Dalí whereas the Morses did not get involved in any significant way in the publishing of Dalí's works. The Albarettos, along with their daughter Cristiana, would visit Dalí and Gala often. They spent significant time together in Cadaqués and would also often meet in Paris and New York, where Mara and Gala Dalí would go shopping together or simply just go out walking and sightseeing.

Dalí was Cristiana's godfather, and among the gifts he gave her, he would regularly create drawings as special gifts. For her confirmation, and for every Christmas and Easter, Dalí would send her a drawing as a gift. The Albaretto family accumulated a significant collection of original works by Dalí; oil paintings, watercolors and drawings as well as hundreds of photographs, contracts signed by Dalí, other documents and over 200 original letters and telegrams. The Albaretto collection of Dalí artwork was without question the largest private collection in Europe.

Importantly, the Albaretto collection has the very unique characteristic of having many of the drawings, projects and studies that Dalí created from 1960 to 1970 as preliminary sketches for major graphic works.

Their numerous memories of experiences and their anecdotes could easily fill the pages of a book. The hours they spent together in Port Lligat, whether at the swimming pool or the beach or on the boat, are only a portion. For instance, one afternoon, they brought Dalí a live ocelot so he could have his photo taken with it, but once that was done, Dalí had no further use for the feline. Cristiana wanted to keep it, but her parents would not hear of it as it could be dangerous. Eventually, the ocelot was kept by Captain Peter Moore, one of Dalí's secretaries. [1]

1). On the top floor of the home in Turin, Cristiana still keeps an ocelot which is an offspring of that very ocelot which was the gift of her parents to Dalí.

The nearly 30-year relationship between Dalí and the Albarettos is a rich subject for a book in and of itself. Contained here is a very small sampling of some of those meetings. There were countless meetings between Giuseppe, Mara, Dalí and Gala at the Meurice Hotel in Paris. Among the most notable of those meetings were those where the Albarettos were accompanied by Angelo Rizzoli, when they presented the many color proofs for the lithographs of the *Sacred Bible* to Dalí for his corrections and eventual approval. There were also countless lunches and dinners together in their homes and in the restaurants they loved in Cadaqués, Figueres, New York and Paris. They would often dine together in Paris at La Tour d'Arget or Maxim's, or with Alfonso de Borbón at the Hotel Meurice. Cristiana has many memories and anecdotes of the people she met when they were in the company of Dalí. Cristiana tells a funny story about an incident that took place during a lunch with her parents, Dalí, Gala and Don Alfonso de Borbón, which gives some insights about both her father and the French mentality regarding wines. Beppe, as they all called Giuseppe Albaretto, asked for strawberries with wine for dessert (a typical Italian dessert). But in Paris, and in an upscale restaurant at that, one cannot ask for wine, even if it is mixed with fruit for a dessert, unless the *sommelier* knows the qualities the bottle of wine should have and to what purpose. And so the waiter had to ask the *maître*, who in turn had to ask the *sommelier* who then had to study the wine menu in order to decide which wine would go well with strawberries. They eventually served the strawberries mixed together with a fine French wine.

Christ of the Vallés, oil on canvas acquired by the Albaretto family in 1962.

I could go on describing intimate experiences, although this might not be the most appropriate place since it serves no purpose other than to highlight the friendship the couples shared. As this friendship is already so well known, I only comment on it further to demonstrate the open and generous character of Dr. Giuseppe Albaretto. He was a true 'head of family' and from my own experience, I can unequivocally state his house was always open to any friend of Dalí.

Invitation from the Honor Committee to the reception and presentation of the Academic Sword to Salvador Dalí.

It is worthwhile to mention one very special painting by Dalí that was collected by Giuseppe, *The Christ of Vallès* (1962). Dalí completed this oil painting in the Saló del Tinell in Plaça del Rei in Barcelona for the sole purpose of submitting it as a donation for an auction with the proceeds going toward the damage caused by the floods in Spain in 1961, which had caused many deaths and much damage. At Dalí's urging, Giuseppe acquired this painting for what at the time was a small fortune, since his dear friend Dalí pled with Giuseppe that he buy it no matter the price. This was all done by Dalí so that the painting might not be sold at a lower price than a painting by Picasso which was also in the auction. Now, even years after the death of Beppe, at the time of the completion of this book, *The Christ of Vallès* is still presiding in the living room of his house in Turin.

Receipt from Andres Francois Petit, for the contribution of 1.000 francs from the Albaretto family to create Dalí's Academic Sword.

The Albarettos continued to show their love and appreciation for Dalí and Gala throughout the years. One poignant example took place, when Dalí was nominated in France to the Academy of Fine Arts in 1979. They honored Dalí by accepting his personal invitation to the ceremony and by purchasing and gifting the handmade gold embossed sword, designed by Dalí himself, which was presented to Dalí in commemoration of his entry into the Academy.

Dalí at the ceremony for the Académie des Beaux Arts conducted at the Hotel Meurice, Paris.

Woman with drawers, being given to the Albaretto's by Dalí at Dalí's studio in Port Lligat.

Dalí with the Albaretto family at Dalí's home in Port Lligat.

L'Académie des Beaux-Arts a l'honneur d'inviter

Monsieur Albaretto

à la réception qui suivra l'installation
de M. Salvador DALI

Le Mercredi 9 Mai 1979
(après la séance sous la Coupole)
Salle Comtesse de Caen, 27, quai de Conti

Cette carte, rigoureusement personnelle, *sera demandée à l'entrée*

L'Académie des Beaux-Arts a l'honneur d'inviter

Mademoiselle Albaretto

à la réception qui suivra l'installation
de M. Salvador DALI

Le Mercredi 9 Mai 1979
(après la séance sous la Coupole)
Salle Comtesse de Caen, 27, quai de Conti

Cette carte, rigoureusement personnelle, *sera demandée à l'entrée*

Personal invitations to Dr. Albaretto and Christiana Albaretto, to the reception that will follow the Academic inauguration, May 4, 1979.

The close and intimate relationship between Dalí and his dear friend and dealer Giuseppe (Beppe) Albaretto is also evident in the drawings illustrated here.

In the drawing at the right, you see Dalí referring to Beppe Albaretto as the "ideator supreme of the Bible".

In the drawing below, Dalí writes in both French and Italian about his friends and dealers the Albarettos. At the top of the drawing Dalí writes in French: "Pour les condotieri, mes grand amis les Albarettos" (For the leaders, my great friends, the Albaretto family). At the left of the drawing Dalí writes in Italian in a spiraling upward line: "Echelle de Jacob, La Monte' des Anges, Desoxiribonucleinique perfection ascentionelle avec les Albarettos" (Jacob's ladder, the ascent of the Desoxiribonuclenic Angels, the perfection of the ascent with the Albarettos). At the top of the right of the drawing is a crown and a Cross which was part of the blind stamp that was created by Dalí for Giuseppe Albaretto.

These drawings reference Dalí's closeness and respect for the Albarettos using the religious reference of the Bible and the Cross (Dalí was well aware of the strong faith of the Albarettos). We also see the religious reference by Dalí regarding the Albarettos and Dalí ascending together on Jacobs Ladder with angels guiding them to perfection.

A drawing by Dalí on the inside page of a *Sacra Biblia* dedicated "To Beppe Albaretto ideator supreme of the Bible".

A drawing by Dalí dedicated to the Albarettos.

LES CHANTS DE MALDOROR

Count of Lautréamont

In 1934, in the Galerie des Quatre Chemins of Paris, Albert Skira presented 42 magnificent intaglios created by Dalí to illustrate *Les Chants de Maldoror* by the Count of Lautréamont (pseudonym of the French-Uruguayan romantic poet Isidore Lucien Ducasse, 1846-1870). Between 1932 and 1934 Dalí, by his own hand, created 44 intaglios. Thirty-two are full-page and 12 are vignettes that illustrate the text.

Only 50 "Deluxe" edition examples of the book were created. These were hand-signed by Dalí and numbered on the page adjacent to the title page. The Deluxe edition contained 207 pages of text with typography by the Phillipe Gonin presses, along with 12 text pages combined with the vignettes created by Dalí to accompany the text. In the "Deluxe" edition only, the twelve vignettes were also included as individual intaglios without text (see pages 107 - 121). The "Deluxe" examples of the book also contained one or more images, printed on one plate (see page 121), that were not used in the First "Popular" Book Edition or the Second "Popular" Book Edition (referred to as "planche refuse").

Additionally incorporated into the first, "Deluxe" book edition, were detailed remarques appearing beneath and occasionally above the 30 full size Dalí intaglio illustrations. These 30 plates were eventually cut-down which removed the remarques. The "Deluxe" editions of the book incorporated the complete set of intaglios from both the large and reduced plates, along with the 12 intaglio vignettes, and the complete text.

Drawing by Dalí that illustrates a portion of the text of *Les Chants de Maldoror.*

During the printing of the second "Popular" book edition, less than half of the edition was printed, and these were annotated with odd numbers only. It is likely that Dalí's and Skira's limited financial resources were the reason it was done this way. The tirages for the three editions are as follows:

First Deluxe edition:
1934; Skira, Paris/Graphik Europa Anstalt Lacouriere
29.8 x 18.4 (book), 22 x 16.5 (sheet)
Print technique: engravings on celluloid, with graphite rubbed into the lines. Heliogravure and drypoint etching were used to make the copper intaglio plates. 44 intaglios produced by Dalí as illustrations for the book.

"Deluxe" edition consists of:
50 books including 72 unbound intaglios (consisting of 30 full-page intaglios with remarques, 30 reduced plate intaglios without remarques (one plate with two intaglio illustrations was not incorporated into the later editions), 12 vignette intaglio illustrations printed without text, and the complete text by Count of Lautréamont.

"Deluxe" editions were printed on Arches paper, numbered 1-40 and hand-signed by Dalí on the adjacent tirage page. In addition, 10 Roman numbered hors commerce examples, reserved for the artist and collaborators were printed.

The "Deluxe" books were printed in 1934, and the prints were issued unbound in a clamshell case.

First "Popular" Book Edition:
1934; Skira/Graphik Europa Anstalt Lacouriere
32.5 x 25 (book)
Book consists of 30 intaglios, without remarques (from the cut down plates), and the complete text by Count of Lautréamont, printed on Arches wove paper.

First "Popular" edition consists of:
160 Arabic numbered examples, numbered 41-200 (the "Deluxe" edition was numbered 1-40).

Only 80 unevenly numbered copies of the book were printed by Skira (According to Field "signed by Dalí in Paris" however there is no reference to the date, place or eye witnesses to the signing. We also found no modern references to hand signed examples in auction records).

Second "Popular" Book Edition:
1974; Pierre Argillet/printed by Leblanc
32.8 x 25 (book)
38 intaglios, consisting of the 30 intaglio illustrations created by Dalí in 1934 along with 8 new intaglio remarques (cul-de-lampes) created by Dalí c. 1970, which substituted the original remarques that were cropped off the plates after the deluxe edition of 1934.

Second "Popular" Book Edition consists of:
100 books with text (according to Lopsinger - evenly numbered, however, only some of the examples were printed by Argillet)

100 suites on hand-made paper, evenly numbered, each intaglio was also hand-signed by Dalí.

The illustrations on pages 107 to 121 are in the same order as in the first Deluxe Edition suite of engravings.

Les Chants de Maldoror, which praised murder, sadomasochism, violence, blasphemy, obscenity, putrefaction and dehumanization, was rescued from oblivion by the Surrealists as it fit so nicely into the framework of their thinking. It was to become one of the precursor texts of the movement. In 1974, 40 years after the publishing of the first edition containing the odd numbers, Argillet published the second part of the edition containing the even numbers. Argillet must be praised for completing this project, thus preserving and reinforcing its importance to the Surrealist movement.

It is noteworthy that in 1931, it was Picasso who suggested to Skira that Dalí should be the artist to illustrate this fundamental and transcendental writing that is clearly an important reference point for the Surrealists. *Maldoror* embodies adolescent rebellion and the victory of imagination over reality: his hatred towards reality dramatically separates him from his contemporaries, and as a result he suffers. These etchings by Dalí, which illustrate *Les Chants de Maldoror*, represent one of Dalí's most significant series of illustrations and hence they bring forward many of the major issues that were reflected in his paintings. They present some of the famous myths that the artist will develop in his later works. These works reflect the most surreal Dalí, cannibalism, love, autophagy (self-digestion), death, *The Soft Watches*, *The Angelus* of Millet, *The Spectrum of Sex-Appeal*, *The Spectrum of Vermeer of Delft*... Not by chance, the grotesque, the fright and the ridicule in *Les Chants* remind us of the work of another pictorial precedent of Surrealism, El Bosco. And not by chance, either, was Lautréamont an inspiration to writers such as Louis Aragon or André Breton, as well as artists like René Magritte, Amadeo Modigliani, Man Ray as well as Dalí.

One of the themes (in 4 of the engravings) is *The Angelus* of Millet, the painting by Jean François Millet (1859) that can be seen at the Musée d'Orsay in Paris. It is interesting to highlight that, curiously, a copy of this masterpiece was hung in the hallway of the school of the Hermanos de la Doctrina Cristiana of Figueres, where Dalí attended his first years of education. In *The Secret Life of Salvador Dalí* (Chapter V), Dalí writes: "After *The Angelus*, and at almost the same instant that the window went black at night, the hallway that led into the classroom lit up and then through the door windows I could observe the oil paintings that decorated the hall covering the wall completely. From where I was, I could only clearly see two things: one was a fox head coming out of a cave, carrying a dead duck hanging from its mouth, and the other was a copy of *The Angelus* by Millet."

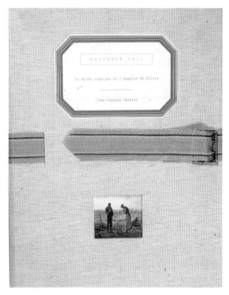

Cover of the first edition of *The Tragic Myth of the Angelus of Millet*, 1963.

In a footnote Dalí writes: "The painting that resulted in having such a profound impression on my childhood had completely disappeared from my imagination for years. But in 1929, suddenly, when I looked at a reproduction of *The Angelus* it took me back to the original anxiety and emotional disorder that it had caused me as a young man. Shortly after that I decided to do a systematic analysis of a series of 'events' that began to occur around the image and brought out in me my obsessive character; and after using this image of *The Angelus* in various forms, such as objects, paintings, poems, etc., I finally wrote an essay of paranoid interpretation entitled '*The Tragic Myth of The Angelus of Millet*,' a book which will be published soon and which I consider one of the fundamental documents of Dalí's philosophy."

Unfortunately the original manuscript, *The Tragic Myth of the Angelus of Millet,* was lost when Dalí and Gala hurriedly left the town of Arcachon just a few hours before its Nazi occupation. Twenty-three years later, the original was unexpectedly recovered and published in 1963 without any modifications to the original text in any way.

In the preface to the French edition, Dalí explains that someone told him that Millet had painted a coffin in which the dead child of the peasant couple, piously praying, lay between them. But a friend of Millet sent him a letter stating that the painting produced 'some kind of rejection' because of the powerful and excessive melodramatic effects it provoked. Millet was probably convinced, and as a result shrouded the dead child with a layer of soil so that the couple seems to be holding a wake over nothing, rather than the coffin that was previously at their feet.

Dalí understood then why he felt so much anguish and uneasiness when he looked at those lonely figures joined by such a strong missing element. If this story was true, traces or marks of the modified picture painted by Millet should exist. Following a request by Dalí, the laboratory of the Louvre Museum x-rayed *The Angelus* and discovered, in actual fact, a painted-over geometric shape strikingly similar to a coffin at the mother's feet.

Dalí's drawing *Angelus,* 1959.

This myth of Dalí was displayed in various oil paintings and interpreted in many different ways. It is precisely in the terrible illustrations of *Les Chants de Maldoror* that Dalí expresses by way of his 'paranoiac-critical method' that a set of elements from the subconscious help us to interpret his most difficult and complex works of art. To analyze these elements, we can turn to Dalí himself, who wrote the foreword to the catalog of the exhibition at the Galerie des Quatre Chemins. In his foreword, Dalí makes the argument that in this well-known painting of *The Angelus,* the famous comparison written by Lautréamont in *Les Chants de Maldoror*: "as beautiful as a chance meeting on a dissection table of a sewing machine and an umbrella" is justified. This, according to Dalí, constitutes one of the most distinctive features of Surrealist irrationalism: "the combination of disjointed, dislocated and even contradictory realities."

The dissection table is for Dalí, the ploughed fertile land driven into by the pitchfork of the peasant. The table represents the complex and ambiguous relationship between man and woman, so typical of Surrealists. Also the pitchfork is a Surrealist tool used to play with the objects, the umbrella represents the male figure and the sewing machine the female figure; according to Dalí, it is a "...feminine symbol known by all – because her work is identified with the superfine perforation of the Holy shroud." Starting from this Surrealist analysis, Dalí proposes in his foreword in the catalog that: "It is possible for one not only to read about but become absorbed in the deep meaning of the images of the 42 works."

Illustrations:

FO 1a. Here we see Gala naked carrying in her hand a lamb chop with a spoon and a fork. In the text quoted in the foreword of Dalí, the painter compares the worked land with meat. During these same years, Dalí painted the oil painting *Gala with two lamb chops balanced on her shoulders* (1933). So as not to practice cannibalism and devour Gala, Dalí placed the chop on her shoulder.

FO 2a. Dalí's first illustration for the text, here he depicts a male figure, decomposing, caught between life and death. He sits atop an incongruous object, perhaps a desk or dresser, which is foreign to the setting. The figure looks off into a deeply receding landscape, Dalí's recurring theme of the set upon which his Surrealist theatre evolves. The figure appears to contemplate his journey and provides a visual equivalent of the literary narrative which is about to begin.

FO 3a. We can see Gala's head, with the fork going through the lamb chop – the pitchfork of the peasant digging the land. In the background, the plains of the Empordà, and in the foreground a figure holding the hand of a child. This image, which projects an elongated shadow, is often repeated in the illustrations by Dalí. In the outline of the cloud we have the allusion to *The Angelus* of Millet.

Illustration FO 1b from the reduced plate.

Illustration FO 2b as it appears with text.

Illustration FO 3b from the reduced plate.

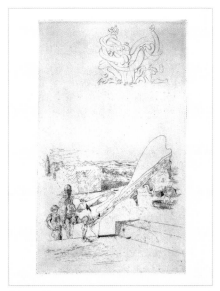

FO 4a. The grand piano turned into a skull is another of the elements that Dalí often uses to show the relationship in the Oedipus complex which relates to the myth of William Tell. In the same manner as in the previous illustration, the cypress refers to the Mediterranean landscape.

FO 5a. These illustrations develop with vividness and passion themes that Dalí will repeat throughout his work; the soft structures like the camembert cheese, and the hard ones like the bones and deformations are a clear reference to death.

FO 6a. A manifestation of disorder and confusion, and a mixture of hard and soft structures. At the bottom of the image in the plain, there is a soft watch, while at the top there are the mountains of the Empordà.

Illustration FO 4b from the reduced plate.

Illustration FO 5b from the reduced plate.

Illustration FO 6b from the reduced plate.

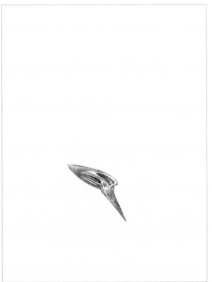

FO 7a. Dalí employs a recurring theme in his work, the human skull. In it resides symbols of life, death, time and decay. Here he elongates it and transforms its material into a soft malleable form, further intensifying the associations he arouses and its suggestive mystery as a visual device.

FO 8a. Two human limbs, one appearing dead and masculine, and the other, female and living, move toward each other, attached to a plush chair and surrounded by organic shapes. A violent tone is introduced through the piercing of the chair by the masculine arm and a long plank.

FO 9a. The figure of bones is transformed into the two figures of *The Angelus*.

Illustration FO 7b as it appears with text.

Illustration FO 8b as it appears with text.

Illustration FO 9b from the reduced plate.

FO 10a. The crutches are incorporated, which are repeated in all the soft structures to support them, and at the bottom, the skull is crushed by a stone.

FO 11a. The figure of *The Spectre of Sex Appeal* was used in an oil painting dated 1934. The figure is supported by crutches and in front of it there is the figure of the child, Dalí dressed as a sailor with a hoop.

FO 12a. Standing figure with its back to us and raising flowers. The bones that appear give the impression of a decomposing body. Dalí has this often used figure of a female standing in many of his drawings.

Illustration FO 10b from the reduced plate.

Illustration FO 11b from reduced plate.

Illustration FO 12b from the reduced plate.

FO 13a. In this illustration of great violence and mutual destruction are the two figures of *The Angelus*. We see the elements of the crutch, with the spoon on the floor and over the highest figure a raw chop with the fork through it. The two figures are pierced by a kind of javelin while they are decomposing.

FO 14a. The crutch appears again, the soft clock and the figure of Dalí as a child with a bone-shaped phallus and the hoop. Sitting on the beach with her back to us, is the figure of Lucia, the wet nurse Dalí had as a child.

FO 15a. It's the dissection table, on which the lamb chops with the fork are both on top of the spoon. The soft watch appears and places us in the space-time that reminds us of the destruction of the physical, and of death.

Illustration FO 13b from the reduced plate.

Illustration FO 14b from the reduced plate.

Illustration FO 15b from the reduced plate.

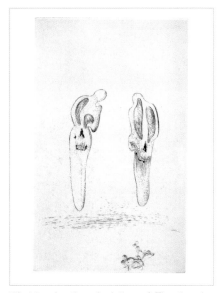

FO 16a. Another depiction of *The Angelus* appears before the final depiction in illustration 40. Here the two figures maintain the identity of *The Angelus* man and woman, but have transformed into elongated human skulls, hovering above ground. The emptiness of the background adds to the haunting and otherworldly quality of the image.

FO 17a. The cavalier dismounts and stands next to his steed, in conversation with a now female rider. Dalí continues to allude to the masters through his use of classical drawing devices, such as the sphere, cone and cylinder throughout. The image however, moves away from Surrealism and into a narrative depiction.

FO 18a. One of the most mysterious and obtuse illustrations for the entire text, we see an elongated, oval shape lying on the ground. It suggests allusions to a halo, or perhaps the sun, and it radiates an unknown energy depicted through Dalí's rhythmic, short linear punctuations (a crown of thorns?), which hover and pulsate above the form.

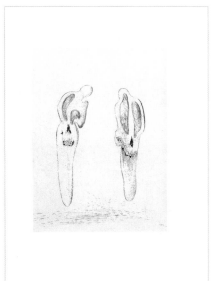

Illustration FO 16b from the reduced plate.

Illustration FO 17b as it appears with text.

Illustration FO 18b as it appears with text.

FO 19a. This illustration includes the following Dalínean elements, the plains of the Empordà with a figure projecting its elongated shadow, a soft deformed monster leaning on a crutch above which a soft watch rests, devouring a child, and the sewing machine, which Dalí uses to represent women, sewing a skull.

FO 20a. Once again, *The Angelus*. As explained in the foreword to the exhibition of the illustrations of *Les Chants de Maldoror,* which took place in the Galerie des Quatre Chemins, the peasant's bone-shaped phallus is erect and is supported by a crutch while, at the same time, holding a hat that covers it. The two figures are on the vast plain of the Empordà, on which father and son project their shadows while strolling.

FO 21a. The peasant from *The Angelus* has his hat hanging from his phallus. The stylization of the figures and their simplification maintain an attitude of prayer.

Illustration FO 19b from the reduced plate.

Illustration FO 20b from the reduced plate.

Illustration FO 21b from the reduced plate.

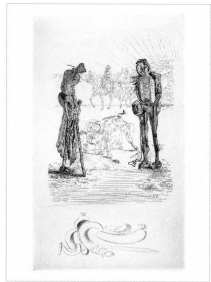

FO 22a. This is a new representation of the two figures of *The Angelus*. The upper body of the peasant is, on this occasion, the sack of potatoes that leans on a crutch. The two figures wear the wooden shoes of Millet's painting. Dalí also incorporates the wheelbarrow, which is the upper body of the male peasant, on which there is the chop. The central figures are from another painting by Millet, *Los segadores*, (The Gleaners), who are picking up the fork and the spoon. The silhouette of the cloud is transformed here into Napoleon on horseback.

FO 23a. A lovely composition of nondescript, soft and malleable forms coexist in a balanced arrangement. The illusion of movement is conveyed through the tilting of the forms and the shading within and behind them.

FO 24a. The same idea is developed as in the previous illustration, but more complex in form and composition, and Dalí introduces recognizable elements, a dresser, a bottle, swimming figures. These elements serve to enhance the Surrealist quality of the image. Their irrational relationships to the soft forms are open to interpretation and dreamlike.

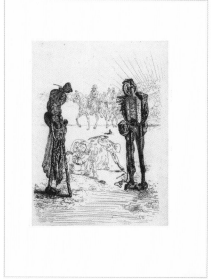

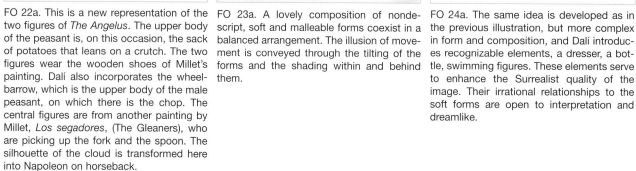

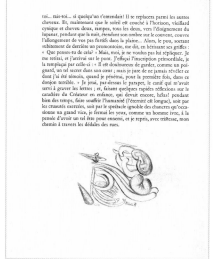

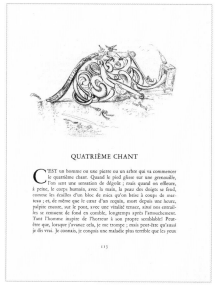

Illustration FO 22b from the reduced plate.

Illustration FO 23b it appears with text.

Illustration FO 24b as it appears with text.

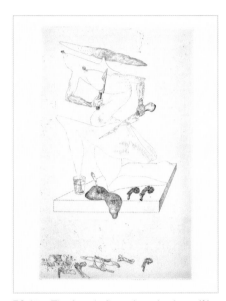

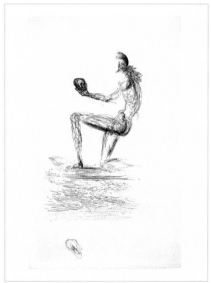

FO 25a. The female figure harming herself by cutting her breast and buttock with two knives. Above the same dissection table are two raw chops. The left leg ends with a bone inside a glass containing liquid and a fork piercing a body that is in putrefaction.

FO 26a. On the vast plain of the land of Dalí, the Empordà, the two figures of father and son, expectantly observe the shadow projected by the two soft entwining volumes as if embracing each other. This is another theme that Dalí tirelessly repeats in his works.

FO 27a. "To be or not to be." The figure is kneeling while looking and talking to the skull held in its hand.

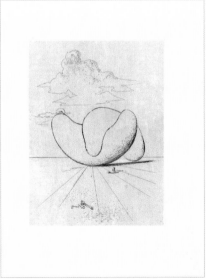

Illustration 25b from the reduced plate.

Illustration FO 26b from the reduced plate.

Illustration FO 27b from reduced plate.

FO 28a. The Surrealist object had the value of an amulet. Dalí created some objects on which he outlined several theories. The shoe, entitled *Surrealist Object* (1932) that functions symbolically, or the aphrodisiac telephone, *Lobster Telephone* (1936). In this illustration, Dalí incorporated a diversity of object-amulets: the shoe, the inkwell, the chop, and the soft watch, everything on a trunk of a tree from which a shirt hangs and a hand, a foot and a thigh emanate.

FO 29a. Dalí incorporates his trompe l'oeil (trick the eye) technique by placing simple objects together to form an illusion of a face. This images is further developed and expanded upon in illustrations 30, 32, and 43.

FO 30a. A second variation of the preceding image, Dalí places the image into the foreground of the deep Emporda space. The image is again developed in illustrations 32 and 43.

Illustration FO 28b from the reduced plate.

Illustration FO 29b from the reduced plate.

Illustration FO 30b as it appears with text.

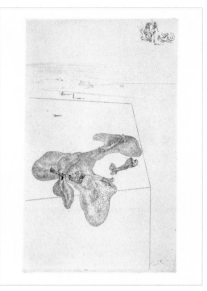

FO 31a. A dismembered foot, suggestive of a Greek or Roman statue appears. An extra toe lies beside it. The allusion suggests a food item, perhaps meat or vegetable, sliced and ready for consumption.

FO 32a. Further developing the image that appears in illustration 29, We see a clearly delineated and developed face, balanced between two cubes. It becomes clear now that the roses have become cheeks, inverted spoons have become eyes, the bone-nose has taken a prominent position and the chin has become rendered by an orange pinned through the two chops (lips).

FO 33a. The rocks of Cadaqués in the background. The figure on the beach with its elongated shadow and on the dissection tables some substances in putrefaction perforated by the chops.

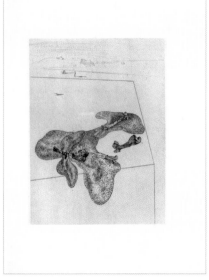

Illustration FO 31b as it appears with text.

Illustration FO 32b from reduced plate.

Illustration FO 33b from the reduced plate.

FO 34a. As if it were a monument, a structure of bones welcomes a rider mounted on soft elements.

FO 35a. The rocks of the landscape of Cap de Creus in Port Lligat were one of the places that inspired Dalí to paint so many of his complex forms. The Rolls Royce that goes toward infinity dragging the rocks is a foreign element in the midst of all the illustrations of *Les Chants de Maldoror.* At no time must we forget the provocative characteristic of feeling and being surreal that Dalí bestows upon himself.

FO 36a. Returning to the surreal, Dalí portrays a partially human creation, composed of legs and a breast, apparently wrestling with itself and a disembodied hand, fighting to possess an enigmatic shape nestled in a cloth.

Illustration FO 34b from the reduced plate.

Illustration FO 35b from the reduced plate.

Illustration FO 36b as it appears with text.

FO 37a. Here, the deep Catalan plain provides a context for Dalí's arrangement of soft elongated forms. They intertwine and appear to move rhythmically as if in a choreographed arrangement. Smaller, amorphous, bean-like shapes accompany the two dominant figures as they pursue their unknown and imagined purpose.

FO 38a. Two new elements are incorporated, in addition to the spoon, the chop and the wrist-watch. In the struggle between the two figures, one is strangling the other with a soft cello and a metal plate on the calf at their feet.

FO 39a. The deformation of the bodies is extreme. Amputations, crutches, more chops, bones, and a male corpse performing cannibalism on the floor.

Illustration FO 37b as it appears with text.

Illustration FO 38b from the reduced plate.

Illustration FO 39b from reduced plate.

FO 40a. The two figures of *The Angelus* are embracing. At their feet, the jaw of a donkey with excrement on its teeth. The vast plain without a horizon gives it a disturbing and distressing aspect.

FO 41a. We see a scene of cannibalism in which the figure on the right is decomposing the other figure with the fork and the knife. They are both supported by crutches with chops next to the substance in decomposition.

FO 42a. Dalí's brilliant draftsmanship is revealed in this small and meticulous drawing of the cavalier, one of his recurring themes. The swirling lines and delineation of form through light and shadow suggest an allusion to the old-masters.

Illustration FO 40b from the reduced plate.

Illustration FO 41b from the reduced plate.

Illustration FO 42b as it appears with text.

FO 43a. Here, Dalí simplifies the apparition through minimal contour lines, suggesting, perhaps a stone sculpture through a more classical drawing approach. He removes the light source found in illustration 29, and the extensive detail in illustration 32, and only briefly suggests a shadow above the spoon to articulate the solidity of the top form of the bone-nose.

FO 44a. Dalí's elongation of form, in this case a skull, alludes to his frequent art historical references, and the mannerist approach. Like the mannerist painters, he imbues the subject with an emotional charge and pushes it toward abstraction. This plate was not used in the published book.

Illustration FO 43b from the reduced plate.

THE DIVINE COMEDY

Italy vs. Dalí

In 1950 to celebrate the 700ᵗʰ anniversary of the birth of Dante, the Italian government commissioned Salvador Dalí to illustrate one of the most important works of Italian literature, Dante's *Divine Comedy*. In November 1949, Pope Pius XII granted Dalí a private audience and lo and behold! His Holiness consented, and to everyone's surprise also agreed to Dalí's request that Dalí paint the Immaculate Conception. The painting he finally created was to become his masterpiece, *The Madonna of Port Lligat*. By many, this was considered not only an amazing gesture by a Pope, but an audacious act considering that Dalí outrageously proclaimed himself "a Surrealist void of all moral values" during what many considered a 'blasphemous' stay in Paris in 1929 with the Surrealist group presided over by Ándre Breton. The Italian government, jealous of the pontifical audience, did not want to be left behind, and the Libreria dello Stato Italiano signed a contract with Dalí for him to illustrate a work of one of the greatest symbols of the country, Dante Alighieri. It was already incredible that the *Madonna of Port Lligat,* appearing with a transparent abdomen with the baby Jesus having a framed hole in his body containing some floating bread, was allowed in Roman Catholic Italian society at that time. But to allow Dalí to be the one to illustrate *The Divine Comedy* was a completely different matter – according to some in government, a crime against the state. The dispute reached the Italian Parliament, and rather than face a lawsuit from a left-wing member, the government decided to terminate the contract of Libreria dello Stato with Dalí, and the exhibition of the watercolors of *The Divine Comedy,* which should have taken place in Rome, was cancelled.

Dalí, however, was enthralled with the work of Dante and was also already deeply immersed in the project. As a result, he decided to offer the project to the French publisher, Joseph Forêt, editor of important illustrated books. In 1959, Mr. Forêt's company, Editions d'art Les Heures Claires, the well-known publisher of limited edition books illustrated with fine art, agreed to undertake the project and proceeded to purchase the watercolors and all of the copyrights for the publication of *The Divine Comedy*.

Between 1951 and 1960, Dalí painted 100 watercolors in preparation for the publication of *The Divine Comedy*. These watercolors explored the many myths and elements of this magnificent work of literature by the great Dante Alighieri. The illustrations of *The Divine Comedy* are considered by many to be the most creative total body of work ever by Dalí. In my opinion, there is no doubt. They represent the long journey that Dante took in 1300. It was on a Good Friday that he is lost in a dark woods and attacked by three beasts, a panther, a lion and a she-wolf. His platonic love Beatrice sends him Virgil to protect and guide him through the beyond – Hell, Purgatory and Paradise which Dante was to name *The Divine Comedy*.

Dante envisages Hell in nine circles, with steps descending to the very depths of the earth. On this journey into Hell, they find the damned in a series of terraced levels where they are punished according to how bad and perverse their sins are. They all suffer terrible torments in scenes of terror, violence and the presence of monstrous creatures. And worst of all, that is where they must remain for all eternity. It is in the watercolors illustrating *The Divine Comedy* that the genius of Dalí is so overwhelmingly evident. For Dalí, it was instinctual for his creativity and talent to be completely unrestricted through his surreal imagination. No where is it more evident than in the visual power of these watercolors by Dalí, offering levels into Dante's *Divine Comedy* that could never before be reached by words alone.

Purgatory is presented to Dante and Virgil as an imposing mountain. They arrive at the mountain after following a secret pathway from the deepest abyss of Hell. The mountain is surrounded by seven circles in the shape of a cornice, where the souls are being purged of their sins in order to reach the nine circles of Paradise.

To complete their journey and arrive at Paradise, Virgil cedes his place as a guide to Beatrice. Beatrice, accompanied by the angels as their mediators, then takes Dante, her old lover on earth, to the presence of God himself.

Throughout all of the journey, one can see that Dalí, through these 100 watercolors, possessed an astounding capacity to penetrate the essence of the Italian author.

Dante was a man with a great presence in 13th and 14th century Italy. He went from holding the highest positions in the society of medieval Florence, to being branded a stateless outlaw, and was even threatened with being burned at the stake. He was a rebel, a talented man of the Renaissance, a great lover of beauty and a literary genius of his time. All of this comes through in Dante's depiction of Beatrice. The objective of the writer is the personification of Beatrice as the maximum expression of beauty. This writing of Dante, where the premature death of Beatrice takes her to the beyond, a place where she finds eternal happiness, fits so well with Dalí and his Surrealist views, particularly when combined with his underlying fascination with Roman Catholicism.

The life of Dante Alighieri

Dante lived in a time and era of great turmoil and social confusion which fueled power struggles, feuds and wars. Dante, who came from a noble family, enlisted to fight the feared Ghibellines in 1289. However, he became involved in a faction which was defeated, bringing him ill-fated consequences and tremendous drawbacks. He became contracted in a marriage with Gemma Donati. The couple had two sons and two daughters, and named one of them

Beatrice. In 1300, Dante at 35 years old began to write about the times in which he lived, which for many was like Hell itself. In the years that followed, he wrote, refined and completed the famous 14,000 verses which compose the great three-part poem of *The Divine Comedy*.

In 1300, the tense social situation in Florence had worsened to such an extent that Pope Boniface VIII had to intervene. The struggles to gain control of the rich principality of Tuscany reached levels of strife and warfare which were to coin the definition for a situation to be called *Dantesque.* Because of his efforts to protect the poet Cavalcanti, Dante was discredited and fell into disgrace and on the night of November 1, 1301, when Charles de Valois entered Florence, Dante along with his two sons were sentenced to death.

To avoid the death sentence, he fled from Florence and went into exile for 20 years. He was never to return to his native city. For the remainder of his life he lived in Verona, first as a guest of the Scaligere family, and afterwards, under the protecting wing of Guido Novello, lord of Ravenna.

During his exile, Dante never gave up hope of returning to Florence. However, while in exile, his reputation continued to grow throughout Tuscany to greater and greater levels as a poet, an astrologer and an accomplished scientist. In 1312, the new emperor of Luxemburg, Henry VII, in his conquest of northern Italy, offered Dante the hope of returning to Florence, but the emperor was to die without fulfilling this promise.

It was after this, that Dante lived the saddest moments of his life while under the wing of Novello who would send him on diplomatic missions to handle business. During his travels, he turned into a kind of solitary globe-trotter, going from city to city. He managed to only just survive, like a ship without sails or a captain adrift "taken by the dry wind that suffers the pain of poverty." At the age of 56, Dante caught a fever and died on September 14, 1321 while visiting Venice.

It was not only well known, but apparent, that Dalí was deeply touched by the ordeals suffered by Dante, ordeals which were so authentically 'Dantesque.' In many respects Dalí felt himself to be Dante. As his interpreter, he felt obliged to follow the verses of *The Divine Comedy,* and through his watercolors not only explain but reconcile the writing of Dante. By attempting to pictorially take the viewer through Dante's series of incredibly complex situations, he set himself a difficult task, one almost impossible to achieve. However, being Dalí, it was impossible for him to refrain from applying his own interpretations - free and new. His fantasy flew and gave free rein to his own symbols and ghosts, so that on many occasions, he unforgivably (to some) went off the track of the images as Dante described them in the text. However, in many of the watercolors Dalí was able to create powerful scenes, quite parallel to the fabulous poem, which were also powerfully striking as purely Dalí paintings in themselves.

From Paper to Wood

On May 19, 1960, an exhibition of the 100 watercolors that illustrate the 14,000 verses of Dante Alighieri's *The Divine Comedy* was presented, with Dalí in attendance, by Josef Forêt and Les Heures Claires at the Museum Galiera in Paris. Dalí created 34 watercolors illustrating Inferno, 33 illustrating Purgatory and 33 illustrating Paradise.

In 1959, Jean Estrade, the artistic director of Les Heures Claires of Paris, commissioned Raymond Jacquet to be the engraver of the blocks which were used to create the 100 wood engravings of *The Divine Comedy*. Raymond Jacquet, working in collaboration with and under the supervision of Dalí himself for a period of four years (1959-1963), engraved the blocks that were used in the printing of the engravings. Although referred to as wood engravings, rather than working on wood, Jacquet worked on resin blocks which were harder and were able to retain a more consistent quality when printed. In viewing what are known as the decompositions - the single color proofs - of the wood engravings, one can see more than 30 colors for just one of the completed engravings. The decompositions are rare in the ouevre of *The Divine Comedy* since relatively very few were ever printed. Decompositions of specific images have been included in some of the complete sets of *The Divine Comedy*.

Raymond Jacquet utilized the technique of engraving the same block to print different colors. By engraving again on the same block, it could never be used again to print the previous color. As a result, *The Divine Comedy* could never be reprinted from the blocks as the blocks were permanently changed during the process. In total, he would end up engraving the resin blocks for printing more than 3,500 times, an arduous job which took four years with Dalí's collaboration and supervision. The ability of the blocks to print the engravings was eradicated at the time of printing by engraving again and again on the same block after the colors were printed. In hindsight, it can be seen how clever and important this decision of engraving the same blocks repeatedly in order to print different colors was, since as a result, un-authorized examples or forgeries of the wood engravings can never successfully be made.

The project was carried out under the supervision of Jean Estrade working closely together with Salvador Dalí, who himself approved each of the wood engravings with a "bon à tirer" (good to pull) proof. Both Estrade and Jacquet interacted closely with Dalí, who spent a great deal of time in Paris during these four years. The artist approved and worked on the drawings for each of the engravings and personally approved, through continuous modification, each of the colors used.

Work of the engravings on resin.

The process for the execution of these 3,500 resin blocks meant complete dedication on the part of the engraver. Jacquet's technical and artistic talent achieved a quality that has rarely been equaled, and as a result of this project, arguably never surpassed.

The technique of woodcutting is one of the oldest known forms of printmaking. Great artists, including Dürer, Gauguin, Munch, Dubuffet, de Staël and others, have used this ancestral medium to create art. These artists selected this medium in order to obtain a richness of expression and depth. As a result, using the technique of woodcut, these past masters have created many masterpieces which have stood the test of time. A special type of treated wood is needed in order to produce wood engravings of artistic quality. Until the use of resin blocks was developed, as in the case of *The Divine Comedy*, the best surface for this process was boxwood.

The engraver must first draw on a piece of paper using a carbon or lithographic pencil to be able to transfer the drawing onto the wood, or in this case the resin, which in itself is no easy task. He must be able to create a type of perfect negative from the original. Because the printed image and block are in reverse, Jacquet worked with a mirror in front of him to see the final result of the print.

From this point, one begins by making a clean incision into the block with a burin, leaving the areas to be inked for printing standing in relief. It is important to painstakingly check the thickness of the lines with partial ink and colors in order to understand the effect that the thickness of the line produces in each of the engravings. For color engravings this process must be repeated for each color, in order to see the result produced as each of the colors is added. Considering the fine drawing and utilization of color which at the same time is intense, yet subtle and often graduated in Dalí's art works, the complexity and difficulty not only increases but multiplies dramatically. This is why the ongoing presence, active participation and collaboration of Dalí was so important for the end result.

The printing of the images was done under the supervision of Jacquet and Estrade, using the process fundamentally known as typographic printing, derived from the Greek 'typos' meaning blow and 'graphos' meaning writing. In the typographic method, the result varies in accordance with the relief press itself which can cause the color tones to be more or less intense, and the process will dictate the sequence in which the colors are overlaid and their level of darkness. As the individual sheets were passed through the press many times, in some cases the paper required an additional sheet of backing as a further support, adding yet another level of craftsmanship to the project. In the creation of wood engravings, each detail is important! I have permitted myself this small and humble digression for the simple fact that I am by profession an editor, and a confirmed lover of art books.

Salvador Dalí (left) with Marc Ways (far right).

Marc Ways (left) with Salvador Dalí.

A wood engraving from *The Divine Comedy* with an original drawing by Dalí.

I believe that this masterpiece, *The Divine Comedy* of Salvador Dalí with its superb 100 engravings, would never have been achieved without the unconditional support of Les Heures Claires or the genius of the engraver and printer who dared to carry out such an exceptional work, working alongside the extraordinary genius Salvador Dalí. *The Divine Comedy* of Salvador Dalí is unique in the world and in the history of modern art, and can comfortably and properly be referred to as 'spectacular.'

The artistic value and craftsmanship of Raymond Jacquet and his assistants, Jean Taricco and Paul Bassin, must also be recognized as extremely important elements and exceptional achievements even if considered by themselves.

The time commitment, difficulty, incredible quality and the magnitude of the scope of the work itself came at a tremendously high cost. Dalí himself was quite pleased with the completed project, which achieved the highest level of quality and could be brought, at least initially, to a large number of collectors at an affordable price.

The justification page of Les Heures Claires explains why this French edition of *The Divine Comedy* by Dante required 56 months of patient and continuous work. It had started in April 1959 and the edition was not completed until November 23, 1963.

The Divine Comedy was released in French and Italian editions, and what is referred to as the so-called German edition was compiled from the original French edition.

The French edition of *The Divine Comedy*:

The justification page for the Forêt edition of *The Divine Comedy* states that the edition created by Les Heures Claires for Joseph Forêt, bibliophile and art editor, consists of thirty-three (33) sets. There are twenty-one (21) sets on Japon paper numbered from I to XXI on the frontispiece, enriched by the addition of original watercolors that Dalí painted as studies for the images. Twelve (12) sets were printed on Rives paper, with two (2) reserved for the artist, and ten (10) personalized with the name of the collector. Set I included nine (9) original watercolors, three (3) inked plates, a suite on silk of the copper plate engravings, a suite on Rives of the copper plate engravings, a suite on silk of the woodcut engravings, and a suite of decompositions of one illustration by Dalí. Sets II and III each included six (6) original watercolors, one (1) inked plate, a suite on silk of the copper plate engravings, a suite on silk of the woodcut engravings, and a suite of decompositions of one illustration. Sets IV to VIII, each included three (3) original watercolors, one (1) inked plate, a suite on silk of the copper plate engravings, a suite on silk of the woodcut engravings, and a suite of decompositions of one illustration. The remaining sets, numbered from IX to XXI, each included one (1) original watercolor by Dalí, a suite on silk of the copper plate engravings, a suite on silk of the woodcut engravings, and a suite of decompositions of one illustration. All these volumes were hand-signed by Dalí on the frontispiece. Inferno was signed in red crayon, Purgatory in violet and Paradise in blue.

The edition for *The Divine Comedy* published and distributed by Les Heures Claires consisted of four thousand seven hundred sixty five (4,765) sets on Velin de Rives paper which were accompanied by text and the images. Each individual set was comprised of six volumes, two each for Inferno, Purgatory and Paradise, numbered in Arabic on the frontispiece.

Fifteen (15) sets, numbered from one to 15, to which a copper plate engraving was added, a suite of all 100 images as copperplate engravings printed in black and white, a second suite of the 100 wood engravings, and a decomposition of the colors of one image (It is noteworthy that one can view the printing of each individual block and their progressive overlays and see the wonderful blending of colors that Dalí utilized to achieve the final result of each image).

One hundred fifty (150) sets, numbered from 16 to 165, with a suite of all one hundred (100) images as copperplate engravings printed in black and white, a second suite of the one hundred (100) wood engravings, and a suite of decompositions of the colors of one image.

Three hundred fifty (350) sets, numbered from 166 to 515 which contains a second suite of the one hundred (100) wood engravings, and a suite of decompositions of the colors of one image.

Three hundred fifty (350) sets, numbered from 516 to 865, which have a suite of decompositions of the colors of one image.

Three thousand nine hundred (3,900) sets, numbered from 866 to 4,765, which have the text with the images.

Nine hundred fifty (950) suites released without text, grouped into three boxed sets with each engraving in its own mat-sleeve: a red box dedicated to Inferno, a violet dedicated to Purgatory and a blue dedicated to Paradise. Each of the one hundred (100) engravings in the nine hundred fifty (950) suites contained block signatures which are illustrated on pages 185 -197.

The Italian edition of *The Divine Comedy*:
There was also an Italian edition of *The Divine Comedy* published by Les Heures Claires for Arti e Scienzie, Salani, Verona with all the images on Rives paper which was printed at the same time. The justification page for the Italian edition states:

Four (4) sets, "Ad Personam (personalized)," including a second suite of the one hundred (100) wood engravings, a decomposition of one image, and a suite of all one hundred (100) images as copperplate engravings printed in black and white. The text was printed by Officina Boldoni Verona on handmade Japanese "Kaji Torinoko" paper.

Fifteen (15) sets, "(personalized) Ad Personam," including a second suite of the one hundred (100) wood engravings, a decomposition of one image, a suite of all one hundred (100) images as copperplate engravings printed in black and white and an original watercolor by Dali. The text was printed by Officina Boldoni Verona on handmade Japanese Kaji Torinoko paper.

Twenty-five (25) sets, annotated on the cover page with an alphabet letter, including a second suite of the one hundred (100) wood engravings, a decomposition of one image, and a suite of all one hundred (100) images as copperplate engravings printed in black and white. The text was printed by Officina Boldoni Verona on handmade Japanese Kaji Torinoko paper.

One hundred (100) sets, numbered in Roman on the frontispiece page, including a second suite of the one hundred (100) wood engravings. The text was printed by Valdonega de Verona on handmade Brotherhood Magnani Pescia paper.

Two thousand nine hundred (2,900) sets with the text and one hundred (100) wood engravings, numbered in Arabic on the frontispiece. The text was printed by Valdonega de Verona on handmade Brotherhood Magnani Pescia paper.

Each engraving released in this edition is stamped on the back with the number corresponding to "tavola" (chant or verse) of Inferno, Purgatory and Paradise.

The German edition of *The Divine Comedy:*
In 1974, Dr. Jawdat Naffouj purchased complete sets of the Les Heures Claires French edition of *The Divine Comedy* from Les Heures Claires, Paris for distribution through his gallery in Germany. Each engraving contained a signature in the block and each volume contained some text sheets in German with English translations. These engravings were released, each in its own mat-sleeve, in three color box volumes. Although a justification page stated that there were 1,000 total in the so called 'German Edition,' to the best of our knowledge the full number of sets were never compiled or released.

Mr. Antoine Branducci, honorary administrator of Les Heures Claires, was responsible for arranging exhibitions of Joseph Forêt's *The Apocalypse* as well as Dalí's watercolors of *The Divine Comedy*. He was also responsible for the sales of the edition of the six volumes of *The Divine Comedy* containing 100 wood engravings.

With the exception of Inferno 1, which contained a block signature, the initial publication of *The Divine Comedy* did not include signatures in the block on the other 99 images of *The Divine Comedy*. The signatures in the block which appear on many of the examples were added, with the approval and control of Dalí, after many of the sets and individual examples had already been sold. As a result some complete series of *The Divine Comedy* will include examples of the wood engravings some of which contain block signatures and some of which do not.

There are fifty-nine (59) different block signatures of Dalí on the images of the wood engravings of *The Divine Comedy*. Ninety three (93) of *The Divine Comedy* wood engravings contain a single different block signature on each of the block signed examples. However the same block signature often appears on more than one different image. For example signature type DC BS 43 appears on eight (8) different images of *The Divine Comedy:* IN 31, PU 3, PU 10, PU 13, PA 10, PA 11, PA 19 and PA 27.

Seven (7) images of *The Divine Comedy* wood engravings have two different block signatures for the same image. On pages 185 - 197 illustrated for the first time in any publication are the block signatures which are on each image of *The Divine Comedy* wood engravings.

JUSTIFICATION DU TIRAGE

15 SUITES OF THE 100 WOOD ENGRAVINGS ON PURE RAG VELLUM RIVES PAPER together with an inked copper plate, a suite of 100 engravings from copper plates, an additional suite of the 100 wood engravings in color on pure rag vellum rives paper, and a decomposition of the colors of one of the wood engravings.

Numbered 1 to 15

150 SUITES OF THE 100 WOOD ENGRAVINGS ON PURE RAG VELLUM RIVES PAPER together with a suite of 100 engravings from copper plates, an additional suite of the 100 wood engravings in color on pure rag vellum rives paper, and a decomposition of the colors of one of the wood engravings.

Numbered 16 to 165

350 SUITES OF THE 100 WOOD ENGRAVINGS ON PURE RAG VELLUM RIVES PAPER together with an additional suite of the 100 wood engravings in color on pure rag vellum rives paper, and a decomposition of the colors of one of the wood engravings.

Numbered 166 to 515

350 SUITES OF THE 100 WOOD ENGRAVINGS ON PURE RAG VELLUM RIVES PAPER together a decomposition of the colors of one of the wood engravings.
Numbered 516 to 865

3,900 SUITES OF THE 100 WOOD ENGRAVINGS ON PURE RAG VELLUM RIVES PAPER

Numbered 866 to 4,765

*Translated from French, a copy of the original document is in the documentation section herein.

JUSTIFICATION DU TIRAGE

4 SUITES OF THE 100 WOOD ENGRAVINGS ON PURE RAG VELLUM RIVES PAPER with text pages on Japanese Kaji Torinoko paper printed by hand by Bodoni printers of Verona, Italy together with an additional suite of the 100 wood engravings in color on pure rag vellum rives paper, a suite of 100 engravings from copper plates, and a decomposition of the colors of one of the wood engravings.

15 SUITES OF THE 100 WOOD ENGRAVINGS ON PURE RAG VELLUM RIVES PAPER with text pages on Japanese Kaji Torinoko paper printed by hand by Bodoni printers of Verona, Italy together with an additional suite of the 100 wood engravings in color on pure rag vellum rives paper, a suite of 100 engravings from copper plates, a decomposition of the colors of one of the wood engravings and an original watercolor by Salvador Dali.

25 SUITES OF THE 100 WOOD ENGRAVINGS ON PURE RAG VELLUM RIVES PAPER, marked with the letters from A to Z, with text pages on Japanese Kaji Torinoko paper printed by hand by Bodoni printers of Verona, Italy together with an additional suite of the 100 wood engravings in color on pure rag vellum rives paper, a suite of 100 engravings from copper plates, and a decomposition of the colors of one of the wood engravings.

100 SUITES OF THE 100 WOOD ENGRAVINGS ON PURE RAG VELLUM RIVES PAPER, marked with the Roman numbers from I to C, with text pages printed by Valdonega Printers of Verona, Italy on hand made paper produced by the Magnani Brothers of Pescia, Italy together with an additional suite of the 100 wood engravings in color on pure rag vellum rives paper.

2,900 SUITES OF THE 100 WOOD ENGRAVINGS ON PURE RAG VELLUM RIVES PAPER, with text pages printed by Valdonega Printers of Verona, Italy on hand made paper produced by the Magnani Brothers of Pescia, Italy numbered from 1 to 2,900.

*Translated from Italian, a copy of the original document is in the documentation section herein.

Illustrations:

AUTHENTIC HAND SIGNATURES: A selection of works from the archives of Les Heures Claires Paris where the signing by Dalí was witnessed by the editor of *The Divine Comedy* Jean Estrade, and Jean Estrade signed the back of the works. The works and the signatures of Dalí on the forso and Jean Estrade in the verso are included on pages 139, 141, 144, 147, 150, 158, 166, 169, 171, 173, 175, 177, 180, 181 and 183. In addition, there are authentic Dalí hand signatures on works from *The Divine Comedy* and authentic Dalí hand signatures on certificates for *The Divine Comedy* on pages 289 - 299 where the hand signatures of Dalí were confirmed as authentic by graphologist and documents examiner Alfredo Ghio.

FRONTISPIECE: Below is an example of a frontispiece of *The Divine Comedy* signed by Dalí in 1965 which is in the archives of Les Heures Claires, Paris.

Inferno - The Nine Circles Of Hell

Detail of hand signature of Dalí.

Departure on the Grand Voyage   (FO 45) IN 1

I looked on high and saw its shoulders clad already with the planet's beams whose light leadeth men straight, through all paths good or bad.

Detail of hand signature of Editor Jean Estrade on verso, witnessing Dalí signing the work.

Verso of IN 1

Virgil Comforts Dante　　　　　　　　(FO 46) IN 2

I was among those biding in suspense, when hailed me a dame,
so blessed and so fair, I begged her to command my obedience.

Sharon and the Passage of Acheron　　　(FO 47) IN 3

And lo, to us-ward on shipboard drew near one, white with hoary
locks, exceeding old, exclaiming, 'Woe to you, spirits sinister!

Legs　　　　　　　　　　　　　　　　(FO 48) IN 4

but all the while were passing through the wood, the wood, I
mean, of spirits crowded thick.

Minos   (FO 49) IN 5

There presides Minos, grisly sight to face, snarling; inspects the faults as they come in, dooms and, by how he girds him, allots their place.

Detail of hand signature of Dalí.

Verso of IN 5

Detail of hand signature of Editor Jean Estrade on verso, witnessing Dalí signing the work.

From left to right: Dali, Jean Estrade and Joseph Forêt, at the exhibition of the Dalí watercolors illustrating *The Divine Comedy*, presenting wood engraving proofs to the artist; Museum Galiera, Paris; May, 19, 1960.

Dali with Jean Estrade at the exhibition of the Dalí watercolors illustrating *The Divine Comedy*, presenting wood engraving proofs to the artist; Museum Galiera, Paris; May, 19, 1960.

Cerberus   (FO 50) IN 6

Cerberus, fell beast, whose like was never found, with three gullets in dog-like fashion howls over the people lying there half-drown'd.

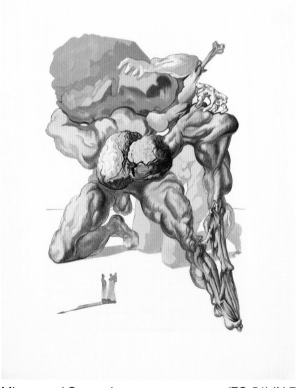

Misers and Squanderers   (FO 51) IN 7

Here saw I crowds, more dense than elsewhere, throng this side and that, who, with loud howls, by sway and heave of chest were rolling weights along.

Choleric People   (FO 52) IN 8

For, fighting, not with hands alone they came to blows, but with the head and breast and feet: with teeth, too, did piece-meal each other maim.

Erinnyes   (FO 53) IN 9

He ceased. Each with her nails was clawing her breast; self-smitten with their palms, they screamed so shrill, that I, for dread, close to the poet press'd.

Heretics   (FO 54) IN 10

When I at his tomb's foot was standing now, he eyed me awhile: then, almost with disdain, he asked me: 'Of what lineage are thou?'

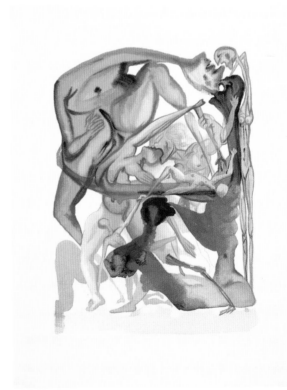

At the Edge of the Seventh Bolge   (FO 55) IN 11

hence in the second circle, thither bann'd, nest hypocrites, and flatterers, whoso takes to witchcraft, forging, theft and simony, procurers, barrators and suchlike jakes.

Detail of hand signature of Dalí.

Minotaur   (FO 56) IN 12

*'Haply thou deemst that the duke of Athens, by whom done
to death wast thou in the upper world, draws near' my sage,
turn'd tow'rds him, cried*

Detail of hand signature of Editor Jean Estrade on verso,
witnessing Dalí signing the work.

Verso of IN 12

The Forest of Those who Committed Suicide (FO 57) IN 13

Each of us, once the human shape, here takes a stock's:

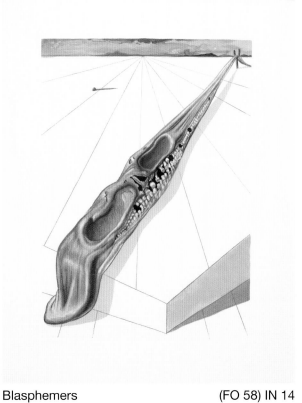

Blasphemers   (FO 58) IN 14

*The latter far outnumbered, it was plain, those who were lying
in the torment, though these had their tongues more loosened
by the pain.*

The Borders of Phlegethon   (FO 59) IN 15

*Each hand in counterdance with tortured hand, this side and
that, sought ever without rest to fend off the fresh burning ere it
should land.*

The Climb of Geryon   (FO 60) IN 16

so down from a sheer precipice we found that tinted water falling
with a din, such that the ear had soon thereby been stunn'd.

Usurers   (FO 61) IN 17

Lo, the fierce monster with the pointed tail, who crosses
mountains, storms the strongest fort, lo, that which makes the
whole world stink of hell !'

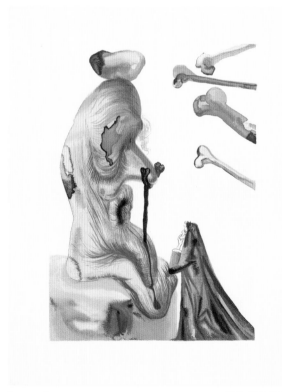

Imposter   (FO 62) IN 18

It goes its way, still slowly swimming on, wheels, sinks, but I aware
of this nowise save by the head-wind from beneath me blown.

Simoniacs   (FO 63) IN 19

*Horned demons stood, where the rock, glooming, rose, this side
and that, huge whips in hand, prepared to flog them from behind
with cruel blows.*

Detail of hand signature of Dalí.

Verso of IN 19

Detail of hand signature of Editor Jean Estrade on verso,
witnessing Dalí signing the work.

Soothsayers and Sorcerers   (FO 64) IN 20

*'they've sunk me down to this, the flatteries of which
my tongue could never have enow.'*

The Black Devil   (FO 65) IN 21

*Protruding from the mouth of each were seen a sinner's feet and
legs so much as came up to the calf: the rest remained within.*

Jean Estrade, of Editions d'Art Les Heures Claires editions, publisher of *The Divine Comedy.*

The Dishonest (FO 66) IN 22

See the vile hags who forsook huswifry, shuttle and distaff for divining, fain to charm with herbs and with and effigy.

The Torment of Hypocrites (FO 67) IN 23

and I beheld a black devil come running behind us up the rock.

Robbers (FO 68) IN 24

And, as at the edge of water in a ditch frogs set themselves, with just the snout outside, their feet and bulk else hidd'n ; on either beach so did the sinners squat:

Detail of hand signature of Dalí.

Centaur   (FO 69) IN 25

*They had their hands, which were behind them, tied with
serpents: through their loins these thrust the tail*

Detail of hand signature of Editor Jean Estrade on verso,
witnessing Dalí signing the work.

Verso of IN 25

Joseph Forêt, Salvador Dalí and the engraver, Raymond Jacquet, examining the results of an engraving of *The Divine Comedy*.

Inhabitants of Prado   (FO 70) IN 26

I saw a Centaur full of fury race, and 'Where's the ribald, where?' I heard him yell.

The Logician Devil   (FO 71) IN 27

"May be thou didst not think that I was a logician!"

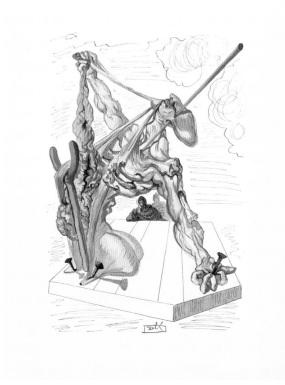

Bertrand de Horn   (FO 72) IN 28

*Dangling between his legs the entrails hung: the pluck
appeared, and the foul sack thereunder, which turns whate'er is
swallowed into dung.*

Falsifiers   (FO 73) IN 29

*It held in its hand by the hair and to and fro'me let the
dissevered head swing lantern-wise;*

Men Who Devour Themselves   (FO 74) IN 30

*Come to Capocchio, one so fanged him nigh the neck-joint that
he made his belly grind on the hard rock-floor as he dragged
him by.*

Complete five activities to finish a challenge. There are four challenges. Activities may be repeated.

Activities

1. Attend or watch a virtual Library event
2. Book that's part of a series
3. Book with pictures
4. Try a Library online resource/app
5. Fairytale, myth, or legend
6. Book about a culture, race, or ideology that is different from your own
7. Classic you've never read
8. Read or write a poem
9. Nonfiction book
10. Re-read a favorite book
11. Featuring a library or bookstore
12. Write a handwritten letter
13. Graphic novel or comic book
14. Newspaper or magazine
15. Book about food
16. Audiobook
17. Biography or memoir
18. 'How-to' book/article
19. Make a picture inspired by a book
20. Free Choice!

Library

Summer
Reading
June 8 – August 15

https://stmalib.beanstack.org
or Download the
Beanstack App!

Imagine Your Story 2020

Collect a free glow-in-the-dark
t-shirt when you complete your
first challenge!

**Each challenge will earn you
one ticket to be entered into
our end of summer drawings.
Also be entered to win our
mid-summer Amazon giftcard
drawing!**

Giants   (FO 75) IN 31

a moment this, when I would fain have gone by another road.

Traitors Against Their Country   (FO 76) IN 32

Whereat I seized him by the neck upon the nape and said: 'Thou shalt declare thy name or of the locks on this be left with none.'

Dalí signing *Divine Comedy* wood engravings for Mara Albaretto (right).

Traitors Against Their Hosts   (FO 77) IN 33

I wept not, so within I'd turned to stone:

The Ghost Spoken of   (FO 78) IN 34

*The imperial monarch of the realm of woe
stood forth at midbreast from the ice;*

Purgatory

The Fallen Angel   (FO 79) PU 1

*and of that second realm my song will treat, which is the human
spirit's purifier and to ascend to heaven makes it fit.*

The Grim Boatman's Boat   (FO 80) PU 2

*Like one whose bliss by his look seemed ratified, on the poop
stood the heavenly mariner; and more than a hundred spirits sat
inside.*

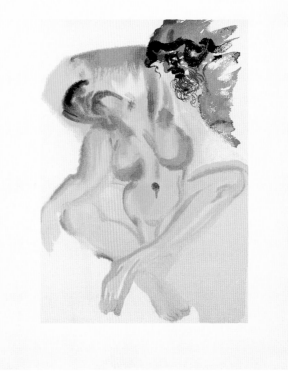

Indolents   (FO 81) PU 3

*for that which heeds it is one faculty, another that which holds
the soul entire: bound as it were is this, and that is free.*

The Negligent   (FO 82) PU 4

and persons had sunk down there in the shade behind the rock,
like those whose indolence is by their posture shown.

Reproaches of Virgil   (FO 83) PU 5

'Why strays thy mind in such perplexity' the master said, 'that
thou art dawdling so? The things here whispered, what are they
to thee? Follow thou me, and let them talk

Deaths by Violence   (FO 84) PU 6

We all, of old, were slain by violence, and went on sinning
up to our last hour,

Princes of the Flowered Valley   (FO 85) PU 7

Drawing his finger along the ground, the good Sordello said:
'Look, e'en beyond this line, the Sun gone, pass nor thou nor
any could.

Guardian Angels of the Valley   (FO 86) PU 8

And I saw, issuing from on high, descend two angels with
two swords of flame,

The Dream   (FO 87) PU 9

in dream meseemed I saw, as I looked up, an eagle in the sky, with
plumes of gold, with wings wide open, and prepared to stoop;

Detail of hand signature of Dalí.

The Face of Virgil (FO 88) PU 10

and in her gesture were these words she said, 'Ecce ancilla
Dei', as clearly impressed
as is in wax the shape a seal hath made.

Detail of hand signature of Editor Jean Estrade on verso,
witnessing Dalí signing the work.

Verso of PU 10

The Proud   (FO 89) PU 11

My forbears' feats set my proud blood on fire:

The Beauty of the Sculpture   (FO 90) PU 12

Ah, vain Arachne, thee I saw distraught, already turned half spider, in the shreds of that which thou to thine own ill had'st wrought!

The Second Level   (FO 91) PU 13

Upon the stairway's summit now we stood where for the second time is cut away the mount which, as one climbs, turns bad to good:

A Spirit Interrogating Dante   (FO 92) PU 14

'O folk assured of seeing the light supreme,' turning to them I thus began, 'the sum of all your prayers and their abiding theme,

Envy   (FO 93) PU 15   In the Stream of Anger   (FO 94) PU 16

The blessed angel, whom we had reached by now, with a glad voice said: 'Here's the entrance; nor is this stair half as steep as the other two.'

Gloom as of Hell and night, night that allow'd no planet's gleam, under a straitened sky, night to the utmost darkened by dense cloud, over my sight ne'er spread a canopy so thick, of frieze so rasping to the sense, as did that smoke we there were covered by,

Jean Estrade and Giuseppe Albaretto at the offices of Les Heures Claires at 23 Rue Bonaparte, Paris.

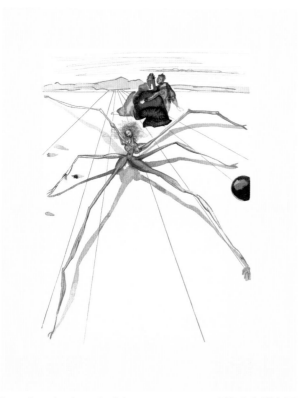

Leaving the Level of Anger   (FO 95) PU 17

O imagination, oft with power endow'd so to transport us that we heed it not, though round us blare a thousand trumpets loud,

The 4th Level: Accidia   (FO 96) PU 18

And as of old by night a fury and rout along Ismenus and Asopus hied, if but the Thebans aid from Bacchus sought,

Dante's Dream   (FO 97) PU 19

'I'm,' she sang, 'I'm the sweet-voiced Siren skilled to enchant mariners in mid-ocean, so with pleasing magic is my utterance filled.

Greed and Lavishness   (FO 98) PU 20

'Adhaesit pavimenta,' 'anima mea,'

The Source   (FO 99) PU 21

Truly we often see things which provide false matter for misdoubting, just because their real causes deep within them hide.

Lavishness   (FO 100) PU 22

The primal age, which was as fair as gold, with hunger made the acorn delicate, and every brook with thirst a nectar hold.

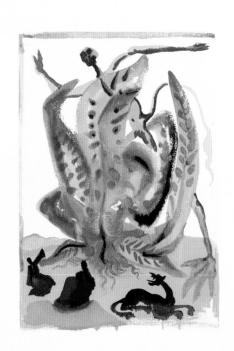

Gluttony   (FO 101) PU 23

Who, unless told the cause thereof, would guess that the mere smell of fruit and of a spring had thus wrought, by engendering greediness?

The Tree of Chastisement   (FO 102) PU 24

'Pass farther on, without drawing near, and go higher up; there stands the stock whereof Eve chose to eat, and thence did this, its scion, grow.'

Rising to the 7th Level: Lustful   (FO 103) PU 25

I saw in the midst of it souls walking;

HOTEL MEURICE
228, Rue de Rivoli
75001 PARIS

Je Soussigné Mâitre Salvador Dali

certifie par la presente d'avoir signé par ma main au Docteur Giuseppe Albaretto de Turin, un lot de trois series de 100 illustrations de la "DIVINE COMEDIE" Réalisées en gravure sur bois.

Fait à Paris le 24 Novembre 1974

Mâitre SALVADOR DALI

HOTEL MEURICE
228, Rue de Rivoli
75001 PARIS

I the undersigned Master Salvador Dalí

hereby certify to have hand-signed for Doctor Giuseppe Albaretto of Turin, a group of three series of 100 illustrations of "The Divine Comedy" produced in wood engraving.

Done in Paris, November 24, 1974

Master Salvador Dalí

/signed/

Dalí certificate of authentic hand signatures for three *Divine Comedy* suites signed for Giuseppe Albaretto.

English Translation.

Meeting of the Two Groups of Lechers   (FO 104) PU 26

*Then, like to cranes which flying some might be to the Riphaeans,
some tow'rd the sandy waste, these from the frost, those from the
sun to flee; the one band going, the other coming,*

The Last Oratories of Virgil   (FO 105) PU 27

thee o'er thyself I therefore crown and mitre.'

The Divine Forest   (FO 106) PU 28

*Here, in his innocence, man's root was set; here spring is, aye,
and fruits in plenitude; the nectar this, that they all celebrate.'*

Meeting of Dante and Beatrice   (FO 107) PU 29

I recognize the signs of the ancient flame!'

Announcement of the Grand Event (FO 108) PU 30

*Into my heart such self-conviction drove its barb,
that I fell conquered:*

Dante's Confession (FO 109) PU 31

*Thus threading the tall forest, empty still — her fault who in the
snake had credit shown — we timed our steps to the angels'
canticle.*

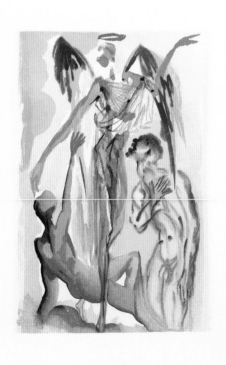

Earthly Paradise (FO 110) PU 32

I, all in doubt, said: 'Where is Beatrice?'

Dante Purified (FO 111) PU 33

and ready now for mounting to the stars.

Paradise

Detail of hand signature of Dalí.

Dante   **(FO 112) PA 1**

Within the heaven his brightest beams caress was I, and things beheld which none returning to earth hath power or knowledge to express;

Detail of hand signature of Editor Jean Estrade on verso, witnessing Dalí signing the work.

Verso of PA 1

The Angel (FO 113) PA 2

The holy spheres, with virtue and motion fired, like hammer guided by the workman's skill, by their blest movers needs must be inspired;

The First Heaven (FO 114) PA 3

Whence I to her: 'Your faces, thus array'd, glow with I know not what of heavenly sheen, making one's former notions of you fade:

Beatrice (FO 115) PA 4

Beatrice did as Daniel did, when he Nebuchadnezzar from an anger freed which drove him to unrighteous cruelty.

The New Aspect of Beatrice (FO 116) PA 5

I saw my lady there so radiate joy, as within that shining heaven she passed, that the bright planet grew thence brighter yet.

| The Sky of Mercury (FO 117) PA 6 | Dante's Men Doubt (FO 118) PA 7 |

The Sky of Mercury (FO 117) PA 6

And when the Holy Church lay gored and rent by the fierce Lombard's tusk, beneath its wings Charlemain, in triumph, to her rescue went.

Dante's Men Doubt (FO 118) PA 7

A doubt within me 'Say it,' whispered, 'say, oh, say it to my lady! Be it confess'd to her whose gentle dews my thirst allay.'

LA MAISON D'ÉDITIONS D'ART
«LES HEURES CLAIRES»

a réalisé une édition de la DIVINE COMÉDIE de DANTE illustrée par le MAÎTRE SALVADOR DALI, en dix exemplaires numération romaine de I à X, en trois tomes, sans texte, avec toutes les illustrations encadrées dans un elegant carton noir frisé en or.

Chaque illustration est signée avec signature en entier par le Maître, en encre de chine sépia.

Le MAÎTRE SALVADOR DALI s'engage à ne plus signer aucune autre illustration de la DIVINE COMÉDIE en encre de chine sépia avec signature en entier.

PARIS 1964

Maître
Salvador Dali

Les Heures Claires
Directeur General et Fondateur
Robert Blairon

The Art Publishing House
Les Heures Claires

has produced an edition of Dante's *Divine Comedy*, illustrated by Master Salvador Dalí in ten suites, numbered in Roman numerals from I to X, in three volumes, without text, with all illustrations matted in elegant black mat-board bordered in gold.

Each illustration is signed with the full signature by the master in sepia india ink.

Master Salvador Dalí commits to no longer sign any other illustration of the *Divine Comedy* in sepia ink with a full signature.

Paris 1964

Master
Salvador Dali

Les Heures Claires
General director and Founder
Robert Blairon

Certificate of Authenticity for one of 10 sets of *the Divine Comedy* signed in sepia ink by Dalí.

English Translation.

Detail of hand signature of Dalí.

The Grandest Beauty of Beatrice (FO 119) PA 8

That in it now was I the proof was clear because, tho' all unconscious that we rose, I saw my lady's face had grown more fair.

Detail of hand signature of Editor Jean Estrade on verso, witnessing Dalí signing the work.

Verso of PA 8

The Heaven of Venus   (FO 120) PA 9

To those that knew if Folco was my name;

The Angel of the Sun   (FO 121) PA 10

song that in those sweet pipes the loveliest lay of earthly muse
or siren doth excel as much as primary light the reflex ray.

Antoine Branducci - First art dealer for *The Divine Comedy.*

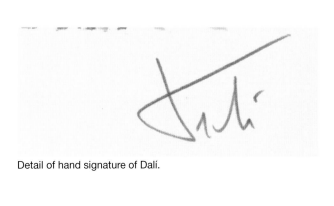

Detail of hand signature of Dalí.

The Opposition   (FO 122) PA 11

E'en as, both limned alike and parallel, two bows are drawn o'er
softly clouded skies, should Juno's hest her handy-maid impel,

Detail of hand signature of Editor Jean Estrade on verso, witnessing Dalí signing the work.

Verso of PA 11

Uproar of the Glorious Corps   (FO 123) PA 12

Thus the Earth Was Created   (FO 124) PA 13

*Thus moulded once to form that paragon
of living creatures was "the dust of the ground";*

for beaconing so upon that cross was Christ,

Certificate of Jean Estrade, Les Heures Claires, for a hand-signed
Divine Comedy suite.

English Translation.

Ghost of Christ (FO 125) PA 14

even so on earth do atoms in the air, aslant and level, slow and rapid, none like-sized, remaining never as they were, move though the ray of light we notice run at times athwart the shade

Detail of hand signature of Dalí.

Detail of hand signature of Editor Jean Estrade on verso, witnessing Dalí signing the work.

Verso of PA 14

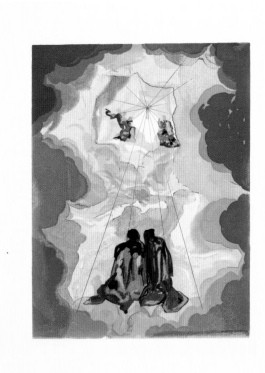

Dante's Ecstasy (FO 126) PA 15

darting adown that cross to its foot there came a star, of those that cluster bright thereon.

Ghost of Ancestors (FO 127) PA 16

with these words: 'From the say when "Hail" was said.

The Divine Presence (FO 128) PA 17

From thence, e'en there stealeth on the ears sweet harmony from organ, comes to me a vision of thy life in future years.

The Splendor of Beatrice (FO 129) PA 18

*That blessed mirror now enjoyed alone his word within himself,
and I too fed, tempering the sweet with bitter, on my own.*

Detail of hand signature of Editor Jean Estrade on verso,
witnessing Dalí signing the work.

Verso of PA 18

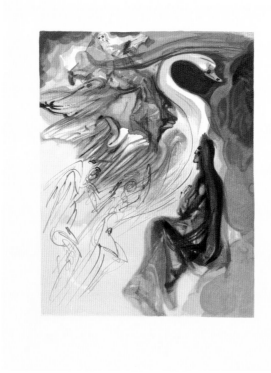

Language of the Birds   (FO 130) PA 19

Confronting me appeared with wings outspread the fair image which,
revelling in their sweet fruition, the souls thus interwoven made.

Certificate of Jean Estrade and Daniel David, Les Heures Claires,
for a hand-signed *Divine Comedy* suite.

ATTESTATION

We the undersigned, Jean Estrade and Daniel David, respectively
Founding President and Director of "Editions d'Art Les Heures
Claires" attest to the sale:
To GPL Promotions/PASS 220 Madison Avenue New York USA
The following piece:

1 collection no. 4648 of the *Divine Comedy* by Dante and illustrated
by Salvador Dalí, comprised of 6 volumes of sheets, including the
text and 100 illustrations.

The 100 illustrations bear the original signature of Salvador Dalí lower
right and are counter signed on back by Jean Estrade.

This collection edited by "Les Editions d'Art Les Heures Claires" was
bought back from one of our clients.

Done in Paris January 7, 2005

                                         Daniel DAVID

                                         Director
/signed/

Jean ESTRADE

President and one of the founders
of Les Heures Claires, Paris

English Translation.

Detail of hand signature of Dalí.

The Sixth Heaven of Jupiter   (FO 131) PA 20

When he who floods the whole, wide world with light so far beneath our hemisphere is gone, that day on every side melts into night, the sky, lit up before by him alone, suddenly yet again begins to shine with many lights, which but reflect the one:

Detail of hand signature of Editor Jean Estrade on verso, witnessing Dalí signing the work.

Verso of PA 20

The Mystical Ladder   (FO 132) PA 21

*coloured like gold, translucent, glittering, I saw a stairway
reaching up so high, that to my sight it was past following.*

The Angel of the Seventh Heaven   (FO 133) PA 22

*But by that most enlightened soul in heaven, that Seraph who on
God most pins his glance, to thy demand no answer could be given;*

The Triumph of Christ and the Virgin (FO 134) PA 23

*The rose which bore the incarnate Word is there: there are the
lilies whose sweet odour gave men strength along the narrow
way to fare.'*

The Joy of the Blessed   (FO 135) PA 24

*Thus on the circling music was impress'd its seal, and 'Mary'
was the name that rung through heaven, by all the other lights
confess'd.*

Saint John and Hope   (FO 136) PA 25

and those joyful spirits straightway made themselves spheres
on fixéd poles, thereby flashing, revolved, with a comet's fiery ray.

Meeting of the Forces of Luxury   (FO 137) PA 26

'Look, look: behold the baron who on earth draws pilgrims to Galicia'
— thus, elate, my lady made me know that spirit's worth.

Daniel David, director of Les Heures Claires, Paris.

Detail of hand signature of Dalí.

Gloria Patri   (FO 138) PA 27

And thou, son, who to Earth must be restor'd by reason of thy mortal burden, hide nought that I hide not; tell it, word for word.'

Detail of hand signature of Editor Jean Estrade on verso, witnessing Dalí signing the work.

Verso of PA 27

Detail of hand signature of Dalí.

The Creation of Angels   (FO 140) PA 29

but now, as poet, I must needs give o'er pursuit that
every artist knows is vain,
when, having done his best, he can no more.

Detail of hand signature of Editor Jean Estrade on verso, witnessing Dalí signing the work.

Verso of PA 29

The March Towards God   (FO 139) PA 28

*thus by enlightening grace and by their own desert their vision
was uplifted so, that will in them is full and steadfast grown.*

At the Empyrean   (FO 141) PA 30

*with act and voice of guide whose task is done, resumed:
'We've left the largest body, and move now in the heaven
composed of light alone:*

The Archangel Gabriel   (FO 142) PA 31

*angels on the wing saw I in thousands round it dance and play,
each one in glory and function differing.*

Prayer Of Saint Bernard   (FO 144) PA 33

*pray thee instantly — oh, spurn not my desire — by means
of thy own prayers to chase away all clouds of his mortality,*

Detail of hand signature of Dalí.

Preparation of the Last Prayer   (FO 143) PA 32

since he it is who did the palm convey to Mary, when the Son of God most high vouchsafed to assume the burden of our clay.

Detail of hand signature of Editor Jean Estrade on verso, witnessing Dalí signing the work.

Verso of PA 32

Wood Block Signatures

The images of *The Divine Comedy*, containing block signatures, have 59 different block signatures for block signed *Divine Comedy* wood engravings.

Each of the 59 block signatures is described by the block signature numbers DC BS 1 through DC BS 59. They are shown as they appear on the wood engraving with the description of each wood engraving appearing on the right. For example, DC BS 1 on the left indicates *Divine Comedy* block signature type 1 and DC IN 15 indicates *The Divine Comedy* Inferno 15.

The list below illustrates the type of block signature found on each image of *The Divine Comedy* wood engravings:

Inferno 1	DC BS 42	Purgatory 1	DC BS 12	Paradise 1	DC BS 45
Inferno 2	DC BS 7	Purgatory 2	DC BS 32	Paradise 2	DC BS 38
Inferno 3	DC BS 23	Purgatory 3	DC BS 43	Paradise 3	DC BS 33
Inferno 4	DC BS 28	Purgatory 4	DC BS 6	Paradise 4	DC BS 17
Inferno 5	DC BS 30	Purgatory 5	DC BS 46	Paradise 5	DC BS 38
Inferno 6	DC BS 15	Purgatory 6	DC BS 29	Paradise 6	DC BS 41
Inferno 7	DC BS 49	Purgatory 7	DC BS 44	Paradise 7	DC BS 45
Inferno 8	DC BS 31, DC BS 41	Purgatory 8	DC BS 18	Paradise 8	DC BS 47
Inferno 9	DC BS 7	Purgatory 9	DC BS 59	Paradise 9	DC BS 20
Inferno 10	DC BS 36	Purgatory 10	DC BS 43	Paradise 10	DC BS 43
Inferno 11	DC BS 26	Purgatory 11	DC BS 46	Paradise 11	DC BS 43
Inferno 12	DC BS 41, DC BS 55	Purgatory 12	DC BS 4	Paradise 12	DC BS 39
Inferno 13	DC BS 41, DC BS 56	Purgatory 13	DC BS 43	Paradise 13	DC BS 9
Inferno 14	DC BS 4	Purgatory 14	DC BS 7	Paradise 14	DC BS 10
Inferno 15	DC BS 14	Purgatory 15	DC BS 48	Paradise 15	DC BS 1
Inferno 16	DC BS 35	Purgatory 16	DC BS 5	Paradise 16	DC BS 6
Inferno 17	DC BS 22	Purgatory 17	DC BS 11	Paradise 17	DC BS 6
Inferno 18	DC BS 1	Purgatory 18	DC BS 48	Paradise 18	DC BS 37
Inferno 19	DC BS 24, DC BS 41	Purgatory 19	DC BS 3	Paradise 19	DC BS 43
Inferno 20	DC BS 19	Purgatory 20	DC BS 20	Paradise 20	DC BS 22
Inferno 21	DC BS 44	Purgatory 21	DC BS 23	Paradise 21	DC BS 8
Inferno 22	DC BS 47	Purgatory 22	DC BS 2	Paradise 22	DC BS 53
Inferno 23	DC BS 9	Purgatory 23	DC BS 16	Paradise 23	DC BS 38
Inferno 24	DC BS 54	Purgatory 24	DC BS 23	Paradise 24	DC BS 37
Inferno 25	DC BS 13	Purgatory 25	DC BS 52	Paradise 25	DC BS 23
Inferno 26	DC BS 5	Purgatory 26	DC BS 39	Paradise 26	DC BS 57
Inferno 27	DC BS 51	Purgatory 27	DC BS 9	Paradise 27	DC BS 1, DC BS 43
Inferno 28	DC BS 38	Purgatory 28	DC BS 49	Paradise 28	DC BS 21
Inferno 29	DC BS 50	Purgatory 29	DC BS 48	Paradise 29	DC BS 3
Inferno 30	DC BS 27	Purgatory 30	DC BS 8	Paradise 30	DC BS 2
Inferno 31	DC BS 41, DC BS 43	Purgatory 31	DC BS 1	Paradise 31	DC BS 34
Inferno 32	DC BS 7, DC BS 41	Purgatory 32	DC BS 9	Paradise 32	DC BS 1
Inferno 33	DC BS 25	Purgatory 33	DC BS 22	Paradise 33	DC BS 40
Inferno 34	DC BS 58				

The 59 Signatures in the Block which are on Divine Comedy Wood Engravings

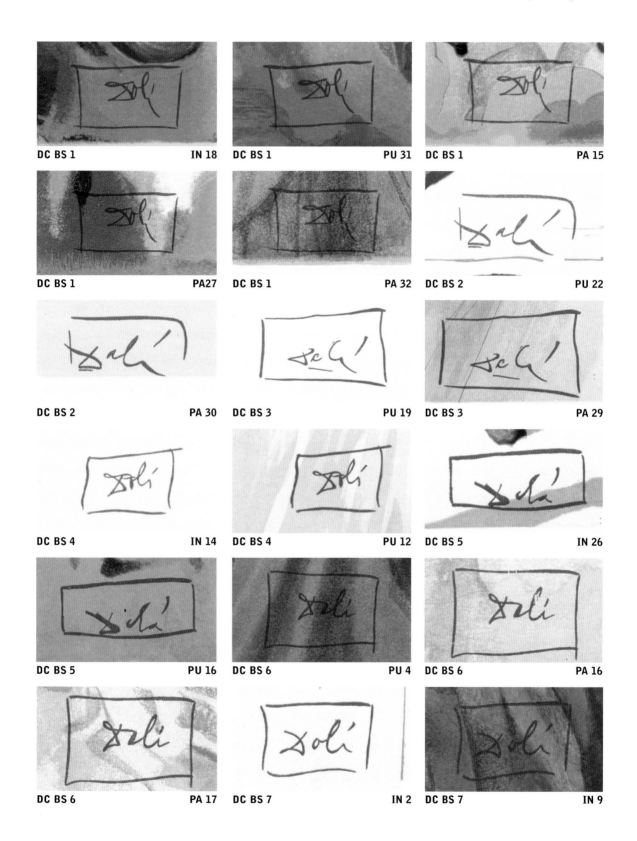

DC BS 1 IN 18	DC BS 1 PU 31	DC BS 1 PA 15
DC BS 1 PA27	DC BS 1 PA 32	DC BS 2 PU 22
DC BS 2 PA 30	DC BS 3 PU 19	DC BS 3 PA 29
DC BS 4 IN 14	DC BS 4 PU 12	DC BS 5 IN 26
DC BS 5 PU 16	DC BS 6 PU 4	DC BS 6 PA 16
DC BS 6 PA 17	DC BS 7 IN 2	DC BS 7 IN 9

The 59 Signatures in the Block which are on Divine Comedy Wood Engravings

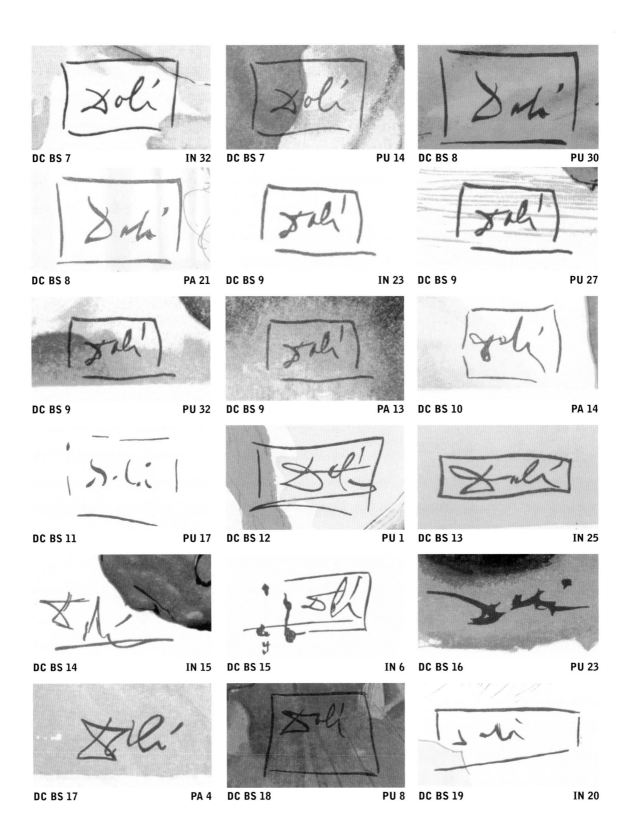

DC BS 7 IN 32	DC BS 7 PU 14	DC BS 8 PU 30
DC BS 8 PA 21	DC BS 9 IN 23	DC BS 9 PU 27
DC BS 9 PU 32	DC BS 9 PA 13	DC BS 10 PA 14
DC BS 11 PU 17	DC BS 12 PU 1	DC BS 13 IN 25
DC BS 14 IN 15	DC BS 15 IN 6	DC BS 16 PU 23
DC BS 17 PA 4	DC BS 18 PU 8	DC BS 19 IN 20

The 59 Signatures in the Block which are on Divine Comedy Wood Engravings

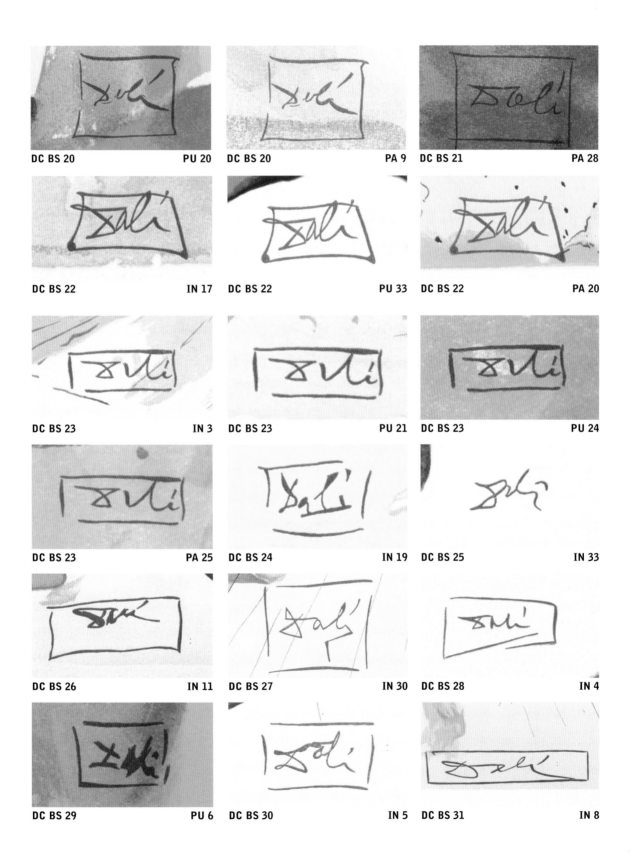

DC BS 20	PU 20	DC BS 20	PA 9	DC BS 21	PA 28
DC BS 22	IN 17	DC BS 22	PU 33	DC BS 22	PA 20
DC BS 23	IN 3	DC BS 23	PU 21	DC BS 23	PU 24
DC BS 23	PA 25	DC BS 24	IN 19	DC BS 25	IN 33
DC BS 26	IN 11	DC BS 27	IN 30	DC BS 28	IN 4
DC BS 29	PU 6	DC BS 30	IN 5	DC BS 31	IN 8

The 59 Signatures in the Block which are on Divine Comedy Wood Engravings

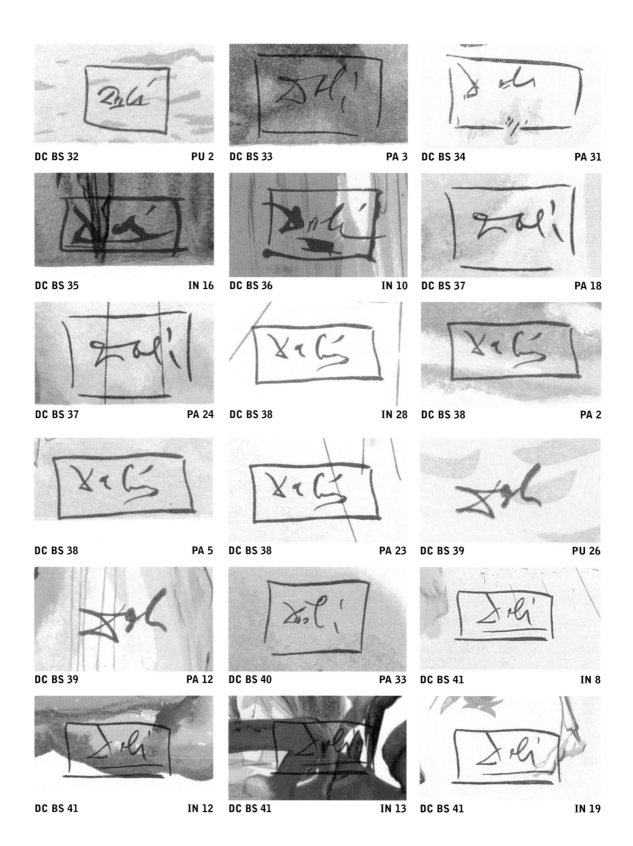

DC BS 32 PU 2	DC BS 33 PA 3	DC BS 34 PA 31
DC BS 35 IN 16	DC BS 36 IN 10	DC BS 37 PA 18
DC BS 37 PA 24	DC BS 38 IN 28	DC BS 38 PA 2
DC BS 38 PA 5	DC BS 38 PA 23	DC BS 39 PU 26
DC BS 39 PA 12	DC BS 40 PA 33	DC BS 41 IN 8
DC BS 41 IN 12	DC BS 41 IN 13	DC BS 41 IN 19

The 59 Signatures in the Block which are on Divine Comedy Wood Engravings

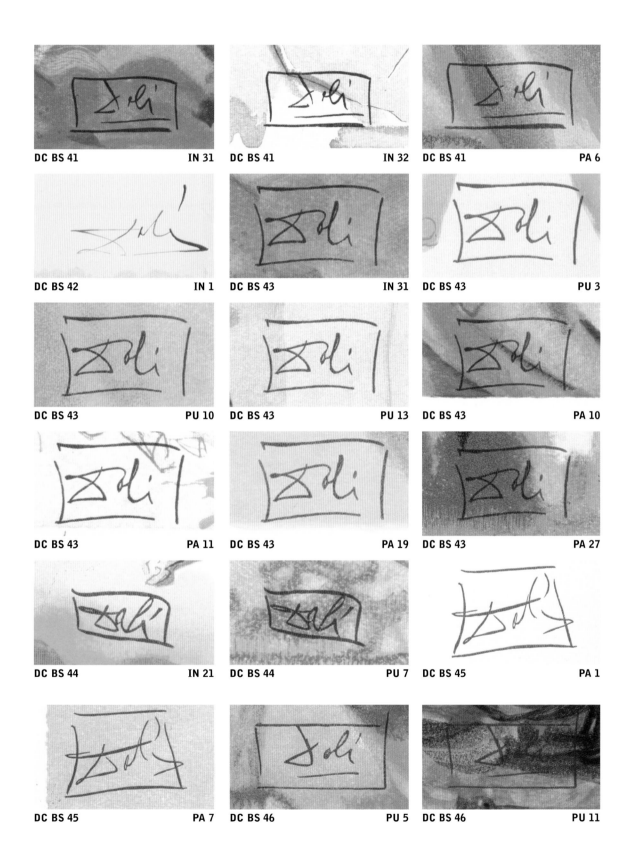

DC BS 41 IN 31	DC BS 41 IN 32	DC BS 41 PA 6
DC BS 42 IN 1	DC BS 43 IN 31	DC BS 43 PU 3
DC BS 43 PU 10	DC BS 43 PU 13	DC BS 43 PA 10
DC BS 43 PA 11	DC BS 43 PA 19	DC BS 43 PA 27
DC BS 44 IN 21	DC BS 44 PU 7	DC BS 45 PA 1
DC BS 45 PA 7	DC BS 46 PU 5	DC BS 46 PU 11

The 59 Signatures in the Block which are on Divine Comedy Wood Engravings

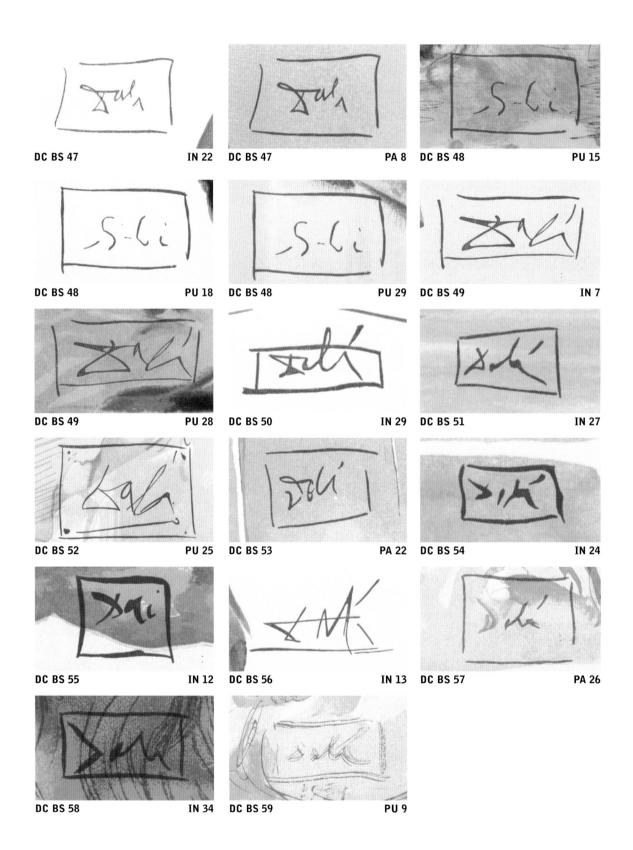

DC BS 47 IN 22	DC BS 47 PA 8	DC BS 48 PU 15
DC BS 48 PU 18	DC BS 48 PU 29	DC BS 49 IN 7
DC BS 49 PU 28	DC BS 50 IN 29	DC BS 51 IN 27
DC BS 52 PU 25	DC BS 53 PA 22	DC BS 54 IN 24
DC BS 55 IN 12	DC BS 56 IN 13	DC BS 57 PA 26
DC BS 58 IN 34	DC BS 59 PU 9	

Seven Divine Comedy Wood Engravings which have Two Different Block Signatures for the Same Image.

Inferno 8

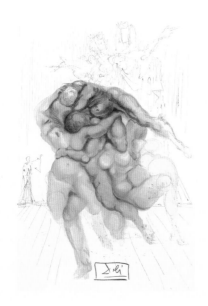

DC BS 41

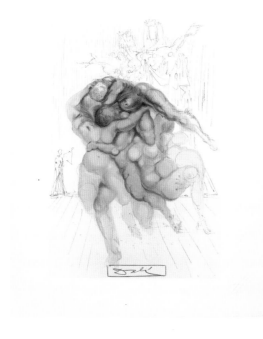

DC BS 31

**Seven Divine Comedy Wood Engravings which have
Two Different Block Signatures for the Same Image.**

Inferno 19

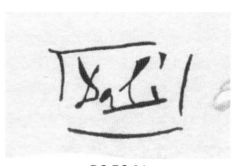

DC BS 24

DC BS 41

**Seven Divine Comedy Wood Engravings which have
Two Different Block Signatures for the Same Image.**

Paradise 27

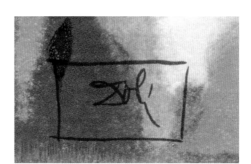

DC BS 1

DC BS 43

**Seven Divine Comedy Wood Engravings which have
Two Different Block Signatures for the Same Image.**

Inferno 32

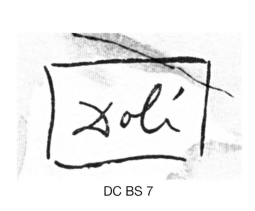

DC BS 7

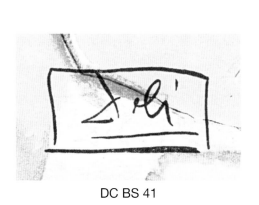

DC BS 41

**Seven Divine Comedy Wood Engravings which have
Two Different Block Signatures for the Same Image.**

Inferno 31

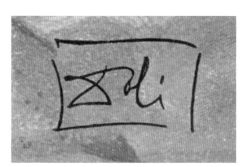

DC BS 43

DC BS 41

**Seven Divine Comedy Wood Engravings which have
Two Different Block Signatures for the Same Image.**

Inferno 12

DC BS 41

DC BS 56

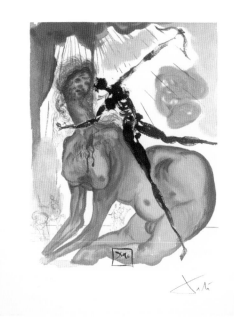

**Seven Divine Comedy Wood Engravings which have
Two Different Block Signatures for the Same Image.**

Inferno 13

DC BS 57

DC BS 41

Divine Comedy Wood Engravings with drawings by Salvador Dalí.

Inferno 1

Inferno 1

Inferno 1

Divine Comedy Wood Engravings with drawings by Salvador Dalí.

Inferno 33

Purgatory 1

Purgatory 2

**Divine Comedy Wood Engravings with
drawings by Salvador Dalí.**

Paradise 2

Paradise 3

Paradise 14

Divine Comedy Wood Engravings with drawings by Salvador Dalí.

Paradise 18

Paradise 18

Purgatory 9

Examples of Watercolors for The Divine Comedy

The signatures in the block which appear on the wood engravings of *The Divine Comedy* are not the signatures which appear on the mixed media paintings for *The Divine Comedy*. Following are three illustrated examples:

Purgatory 12

Wood engraving.

Watercolor painting, painted by Dalí for *The Divine Comedy.*

Signature type DC BS 4 appears on wood engravings for Purgatory 12 of *The Divine Comedy.*

Signature from the watercolor painting.

Watercolor painting, painted by Dalí for *The Divine Comedy.*

Wood engraving.

Signature from the watercolor painting.

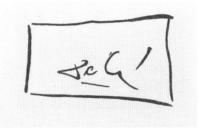

Signature type DC BS 3 appears on wood engravings for Purgatory 19 of *The Divine Comedy.*

Wood engraving.

Watercolor painting, painted by Dalí for *The Divine Comedy.*

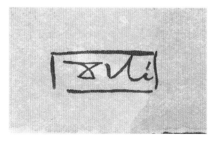

Signature type DC BS 23 appears on wood engravings for Purgatory 24 of *The Divine Comedy.*

Signature from the watercolor painting.

Authentic Signatures by Salvador Dalí on Divine Comedy Wood Engravings

The vast majority of *The Divine Comedy* wood engravings were initially not offered with individual examples of the engravings hand-signed by Dalí. However, at various times, Dalí signed by hand each example of complete sets of *The Divine Comedy* wood engravings. Dalí is known to have signed his name in more than 1,000 substantially different stylistic ways, and as a result, the definitive way to determine the authenticity of a Dalí hand signature on a *Divine Comedy* wood engraving is by a comparison to a known signature where there was a documented eye-witness to Dalí signing. This book contains more than 200 authentic Dalí signatures and adds to the body of knowledge of Dalí signatures as the third definitive such work. The other two are *Les 678 Tres Riches Signatures de Salvador Dalí* by Captain John Peter Moore which contains 678 different Dalí signatures, and *Dedicatories* by Eduard Fornés, published by Editorial Mediterrània, which contains more than 200 additional different Dalí signatures. Since Dalí's signature was as enigmatic as Dalí himself, no one will ever be able to definitively compile the number of different ways in which Dalí signed his name.

Jean Estrade, editor of *The Divine Comedy*, arranged for Dalí to hand-sign complete sets of *The Divine Comedy*. Although these works were not annotated on the forso, Mr. Estrade would often hand-sign the back of the wood engravings which he witnessed Dalí signing and retain them in the archives of Les Heures Claires, Paris. In this manner, Jean Estrade provided provenance as well as security for the authenticity of every *Divine Comedy* wood engraving signed by Salvador Dalí at his request. Documentation regarding the arrangements for Dalí to sign are contained in the Documentation section of this book on pages 317-327.

In the publication of this book, I contacted all parties that were reported to have had known collections of hand-signed *Divine Comedy* engravings, and requested their documentation for review and possible inclusion herein. I submitted all documentation which was presented to me to Daniel David, director of Les Heures Claires, the publisher and copyright holder of *The Divine Comedy,* whom I particularly wish to thank for his significant help both in making his archives available in an unlimited manner and for his independent evaluation.

The substantial documentation and independent confirmation of this documentation by Daniel David and Alfredo Ghio, expert graphologist and documents examiner, allows me to state that: *Divine Comedy* wood engravings with a written provenance from Giuseppe Albaretto, Jean Estrade and Marc Ways contain authentic Dalí signatures on wood engravings of *The Divine Comedy*.

I did not receive any documentation regarding signing by Dalí from the four sources listed below in the Field book. As a result I make no statement regarding the authenticity, or lack thereof, of these collections. The collections mentioned in the Field book are the following:

- Edition Orangerie numbered 150 sets in Arabic in 1964 which were hand-signed by Dalí in crayon and sets I to III numbered in Roman which were hand-signed by Dalí in crayon.

- Alex Rosenberg in 1970 purchased 70 sets from Jean Estrade which were signed by Dalí in black pencil, some numbered /100 and others marked E.A.

- Abe Lublin provided Collector's Guild with 150 sets which Dalí signed in color.

- Dalí signed 150 sets of *The Divine Comedy* wood engravings in New York City with colored pencil with the Inferno engravings signed in red, the Purgatory engravings in purple and the Paradise engravings in blue. The signing began in the window of the F.A.R. Gallery in New York City and concluded at the St. Regis Hotel in New York City.

Albert Field and Giuseppe Albaretto.

Annotation and Numbering - Divine Comedy

Dr. Giuseppe Albaretto also arranged for Dalí to hand-sign complete sets of *The Divine Comedy*. With agreement from Jean Estrade, Director of Les Heures Claires, Paris (copyright holder of *The Divine Comedy*), his successor, Daniel David, and Dr. Giuseppe Albaretto, owner of Les Heures Claires, Italy, (copyright holder of the *Sacred Bible*), examples of the wood engravings hand-signed by Dalí from the Albaretto Collection were annotated and numbered.

Twenty-five (25) sets were annotated 'g.a.' (for Giuseppe Albaretto) and numbered in Arabic, 1/25- 25/25. The sets were authenticated by Albert Field who reviewed documentation (including certificates signed by Dalí for Dr. Albaretto) relevant to each individual wood engraving for Field's Salvador Dalí Archives.

There are eight (8) hand-signed sets of *Divine Comedy* wood engravings from the Albaretto collection which are annotated 'g.a.' and numbered in Roman, I/VIII-VIII/VIII. Other hand-signed *Divine Comedy* sets and individual wood engravings from the Albaretto collection are annotated 'g.a.' and designated with sequential alphabetic letters. Albert Field also reviewed documentation and authenticated these sets.

A limited number of examples of hand-signed *Divine Comedy* wood-engravings from the Albaretto collection without annotations on the forso also exist.

Other examples of alphabetic annotations appearing on the graphic work of 20th-century masters include Marc Chagall's *In the Land of the Gods* lithograph proofs published by A.C. Mazo (1967, marked A to Y), and Joan Miró's *Homenatge a Joan Prats* lithograph proofs published by Galerie Maeght (1971, marked A to H).

Ten (10) *Divine Comedy* sets were signed in sepia ink by Dalí with his full signature, annotated in Roman numerals in ink on the verso of each wood engraving, and Roman numerals in pencil on the forso in the bottom left margin. Each engraving also contains the annotation 'g.a.' in front of the number. This signifies Giuseppe Albaretto's arrangement of the signing, verification by Dalí of the exclusivity of the signings, and the limited number of each work signed in this manner.

Annotation in pencil from the collection of Giuseppe Albaretto (g.a.), numbered in Arabic.

Annotation in pencil from the collection of Giuseppe Albaretto (g.a.), numbered in Roman.

Annotation in pencil from the collection of Giuseppe Albaretto (g.a.), with alphabetical letter.

Annotation in pencil from the collection of Giuseppe Albaretto (g.a.), with alphabetical letters.

LA MAISON D'ÉDITIONS D'ART
«LES HEURES CLAIRES»

a réalisé une édition de la DIVINE COMÉDIE de DANTE illustrée par le MAÎTRE SALVADOR DALI, en dix exemplaires numération romaine de I à X, en trois tomes, sans texte, avec toutes les illustrations encadrées dans un elegant carton noir frisé en or.

Chaque illustration est signée avec signature en entier par le Maître, en encre de chine sépia.

Le MAÎTRE SALVADOR DALI s'engage à ne plus signer aucune autre illustration de la DIVINE COMÉDIE en encre de chine sépia avec signature en entier.

PARIS 1964

Maître
Salvador Dali

Les Heures Claires
Directeur General et Fondateur
Robert Blairon

Certificate of Authenticity for one of 10 sets of *The Divine Comedy* signed in sepia ink by Dalí. See Documentation section for translation.

SACRED BIBLE

Sacred Bible

I knew Giuseppe Albaretto to be a dynamic, communicative and energetic man. He was an open and fervent believer and supporter, and regular partaker of the sacrament of communion of the Roman Catholic Church. As a close friend of Dalí, he was concerned that Dalí, also a Roman Catholic, had fallen from grace. Through their close relationship, Albaretto knew that Dalí had deep feelings regarding his faith. Later in this book, we discuss the fact that Dalí had a Catholic priest at his bed two days before his death.

It was Albaretto's hope that Dalí's immersion in the project of painting the Bible would bring Dalí closer to God and reinforce the faith which Albaretto believed Dalí possessed. Dalí accepted the project, and the result was the 105 watercolor paintings and the 105 lithographs which would become monumental works in the oeuvre of Dalí. I have included an illustration of a drawing Dalí did for his friend Giuseppe whom he called "Beppe." The drawing is a dedication from Dalí to Dr. Albaretto and contains the following writing in Dalí's own hand in French: "A Beppe Albaretto, ideateur supreme de la Bible."

At Rizzoli Book Store, 712 Fifth Avenue, New York, on January 17, 1968. Dalí unveils his 105 illustrations for the *Sacred Bible* published by Rizzoli in a massive five volume edition.

Dr. Giuseppe Albaretto and Joseph Forêt were to meet through their mutual friend, Salvador Dalí, during the time when Forêt was publishing his monumental illustrated book, *The Apocalypse*. Albaretto and Forêt developed a very close friendship. Forêt would often visit the Albarettos in Turin, and the Albarettos would often visit Forêt in Paris. Cristiana, then a child, also has many memories of these visits with her parents to Paris and to the offices of Les Heures Claires, where Robert Blairon, one of its directors and owners, had a boxer named Castor with whom she played while her parents talked about publishing projects.

It was Joseph Forêt who first presented the project of *The Divine Comedy* to Mr. Jean Rivière, Mr. Jean Estrade and Mr. Robert Blairon, the owners of Les Heures Claires.

Dalí was getting more and more enthusiastic about the Bible project, but believed that the publishing contract should be done with Les Heures Claires in view of the fact that they had already published *The Divine Comedy* with excellent results. In addition, they were experienced and prestigious editors, while his good friend Beppe was a collector but not an editor.

However, it was Jean Estrade himself who suggested to Giuseppe Albaretto that the publishing of the *Holy Bible* should be offered to the famous internationally renowned book publisher, Rizzoli. As a result, Dalí entered into the agreement for the project with Giuseppe. Cristiana still has Dalí's letter where Dalí agreed that Beppe would go ahead with the contract for the edition of the *Holy Bible*. Albaretto then entered into a contract

Dalí with the Albarettos showing a painting of the *Sacred Bible.*

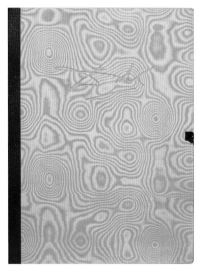

Portfolio cover for 6 loose sheets of the *Sacred Bible.*

Insert included in the portfolios of 6 loose sheets, as issued by Rizzoli.

with Rizzoli for publication. Whether it was Dalí's urging or Albaretto's desire to protect the interest of his dear friend Dalí, Albaretto retained the copyrights. When Rizzoli was contacted, Angelo Rizzoli was immediately interested in the project and visited the Albaretto family at their home in Turin requesting to see the first 10 watercolors that Dalí had painted to illustrate the *Holy Bible* and discuss the project. Albaretto agreed and the parties entered into serious discussions at the Albaretto home. At one point during the discussions, Rizzoli suggested that they should own all of the watercolors and the copyrights as well. Cristiana told us that her mother, Mara, discretely ignored the remarks and offered coffee and, thus, politely rebuffed the offer and turned the discussions to other points. A week later, Angelo Rizzoli called the Albaretto residence and said, "You have won. We will do the edition with equal shares and we will each keep half of the original watercolors, but you will retain the copyrights."

During 1963 and 1964, Dalí painted the 105 watercolors to illustrate the Old and New Testament. In the following months, the department of Grand Works Rizzoli commissioned the manufacture of a special paper with a watermark, and after that the printing trials started. Rizzoli Editorial worked until 1967 to publish the five-volume sets bound in leather with a total print run of 1,797 suites.

- Ninety nine (99) sets "ad personum (personalized for subscribers)" unnumbered in the colophon.

- One hundred ninety-nine (199) sets "magni luxus (deluxe)" numbered in the colophon

- Fourteen hundred ninety-nine (1,499) sets "luxus" numbered in the colophon

- Rizzoli only assembled a limited number of the complete bound sets in five volumes with text, and never completed the binding of all of the volumes described above. Subsequently, six different illustrations were released for sale as loose sheets in a portfolio without text. These sheets were from the original tirage as shown above and are identical in technique and printed on the same stock as those bound in the sets with text.

The Printing Quality and Printing Techniques of the Sacred Bible Edition.

The printing technique was a combination of silk screen (serigraph), and offset lithographic printing. For these prints, Rizzoli used the term "original mixed technique." However, the previous catalogs of Albert Field and Michler Lopsinger refer to them as lithographs and they are typically referred to as lithographs in various other catalogs. As a result, we follow this practice and describe these mixed media works as lithographs herein.

According to Rizzoli, the thick paper stock used for the *Holy Bible* lithographs was specially fabricated for the project (see the description from the insert in the loose sheet portfolios on page 334). Although slight variations exist, the stock is .26 inches thick and weighs 2.8 oz, including ink. It is 100 percent cotton, neutral ph and has a "vellum" finish applied.

With regard to the printing technique and quality, there is the following commentary in an insert included in the portfolios of six loose sheets as issued by Rizzoli:

"To reach such an exceptional result of which the six illustrations here presented are excellent examples, it was resorted to, after a series of tests and experiments, all possible modern and ancient techniques. On special cardstock specifically made to capture the multiple color impressions overlapping one another, the diverse techniques, the most refined and subtle, coexist: to restore intact in its magnificent richness, the textural sumptuousness of Salvador Dali's chromatic language he 'invented' under the inspiration of 'The Book of the Books'"

Frankfurt International Book Fair - photo of Dalí and the Albaretto family.

Dalí's way of thanking Albaretto for the excellent work carried out was shown at the Meurice Hotel when he handed him some of the watercolors from the sets he exhibited and asked him to tell the original apart from the print. Salvador Dalí, Giuseppe Albaretto and Angelo Rizzoli were clearly quite pleased about the quality obtained in the masterpiece they had published.

Albert Field in his Dalí print catalog commented on the printing quality as follows:

"Rizzoli / New York exhibited the original paintings and the prints side by side. The prints are so like the originals that the only sure way to distinguish one from the other was that the paint on the originals made the surface uneven. (69.3 Biblia Sacra; pg. 201 - *The official catalog of the graphic works of Salvador Dalí by Albert Field*)"

Presentation of the *Sacred Bible* at the Frankfurt International Book Fair with Chancellor Helmut Kohl.

Considering that it was the *Holy Bible* being published, Beppe Albaretto and Angelo Rizzoli sought and received the '*Nihil Obstat y el Imprimatur del Vaticano*', the Vatican's Seal of Approval, as acknowledgement of its acceptance by the Vatican. Albaretto's good standing and friendship with the Congregation of the Salesians was instrumental in having the Catholic Church accept and recognize the edition. Albaretto had a five volume set bound in white leather and sent to Pope Paul VI. Subsequently Dalí received a thank you letter from the Secretary of the State of the Vatican.

An example of the bound *Bible* was viewed by the Chancellor of Germany, Helmut Kohl, at the Frankfurt International Book Fair along with photos of the Albaretto family with Dalí.

Authentic Signatures by Salvador Dalí, Annotation and Numbering - Sacred Bible

Cristiana Albaretto, her husband Beniamino and certain documents provided the following information: the numbering along with the annotations 'E.A.' and sometimes also 'g.a.' on graphic works of the *Biblia Sacra* and *The Divine Comedy* were added with the authorization of the Albarettos to certify the origin of the works and to catalog and control them, allowing in this manner, protection for the buyers from prints appearing later in the market, or copies, and not works from the original editions.

The Albaretto family presently remains the exclusive owner of the rights of the *Sacred Bible* edition illustrated by Salvador Dalí. In a written agreement between the Albarettos and Ediciones Rizzoli of Milan house, Rizzoli published a single edition of the *Sacred Bible* in 5 volumes illustrated with lithographs of the 105 images based on the *Sacred Bible* watercolors purchased from Salvador Dalí by the Albarettos. The copyrights to the *Sacred Bible* which were allowed to be used in the creation of the *Sacred Bible* remained and still remain with the Albaretto Family. During the creation of the *Sacred Bible* in the 1960s, Dalí was in excellent health and in complete possession of his mental capacities, and was completely aware of and fully involved in this incredible publication by Rizzoli.

Mr. Roberto Mastella purchased complete sets of illustrations and individual unbound lithographs of the *Biblia Sacra* directly from Rizzoli. With the assistance of Giuseppe Albaretto, Robert Mastella along with his assistant, from time to time a Mr. Aprili, took these works from the *Sacra Biblia* to Salvador Dalí's home in Port Lligat (Cadaqués) and to Paris where Dalí signed complete series and individual lithographs by hand. The unbound individual lithographs which were hand-signed by Dalí were stamped on the verso with the number "5."

The works were annotated "g.a." in pencil or ink, followed by Roman numerals for the bound sets and Arabic numbers for the loose sheets. The denominator varies from illustration to illustration and reflects the quantity of hand-signed examples which are numbered in this manner.

Dalí with the Albaretto family in Cadaques.

Dalí with Giuseppe and Mara Albaretto at Dalí's house in Port Lligat.

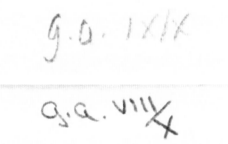

Examples of annotation with Roman numerals from the ten sets signed in sepia ink, originating from the collection of Giuseppe Albaretto (g.a.)

Annotation in pencil, numbered in Roman from bound volumes.

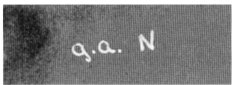

Annotation in pencil, numbered in Arabic from loose sheets and portfolios.

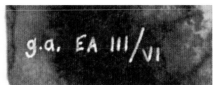

Annotation in white ink with alphabetic letter from loose sheets and portfolios.

Annotation in white ink Epreuve d'artiste (EA), numbered in Roman from bound volumes.

New York 1978

HÔTEL MEURICE
228, Rue de Rivoli
PARIS-1

Je certifie que toutes les illustrations

du livre " Sacra Biblia " illustré par moi

et edité par la Maison Rizzoli -Editore

Milano marqué avec cette chiffre **5**

ont été signées par ma main en crayon.

New York 78

Maître Salvador Dali.

Attestation of Dalí that he hand-signed the Mastella collection and that the collection has been stamped with the number "5" on the verso. Above is a copy of an authentication certificate that was signed by Mara Albaretto.

Annotation in pencil Epreuve d'artiste (EA), numbered in Arabic from loose sheets and portfolios.

Illustrations

The 105 lithographs of the *Sacred Bible* are illustrated on pages 219 - 251

Each of these illustrated works came from the archives of Giuseppe Albaretto and contain an authentic hand signature of Dalí.

In addition there are authentic Dalí hand signatures on works from the *Sacred Bible* on pages 303 - 308.

Saint Jerome
(FO 145) SB 1

In the Beginning God Created Heaven and Earth
(FO 146) SB 2

The Creation of Earthly and Sea Animals
(FO 147) SB 3

The Creation of Flying Things
(FO 148) SB 4

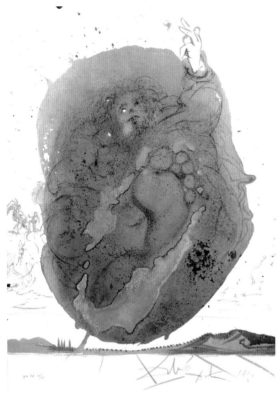

Let Us Make Man in our Image and Likeness
(FO 149) SB 5

Woman From the Side of Man
(FO 150) SB 6

Man and Woman in the Garden of Pleasure
(FO 151) SB 7

Original Sin
(FO 152) SB 8

Flood Waters Over the Earth
(FO 153) SB 9

Noah Who Planted the First Vineyard
(FO 154) SB 10

The Tower of Babel
(FO 155) SB 11

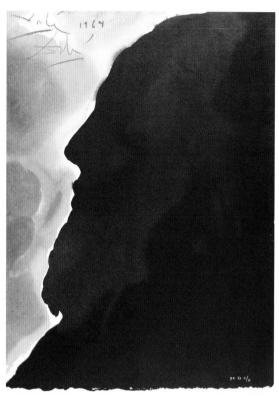

Abraham, the Father of Many Nations
(FO 156) SB 12

Lot's Wife, Turned Into a Statue of Salt
(FO 157) SB 13

Abraham, Abraham!
(FO 158) SB 14

Joseph and His Brothers in Egypt
(FO 159) SB 15

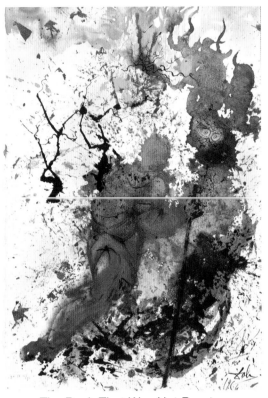

The Bush That Was Not Burnt
(FO 160) SB 16

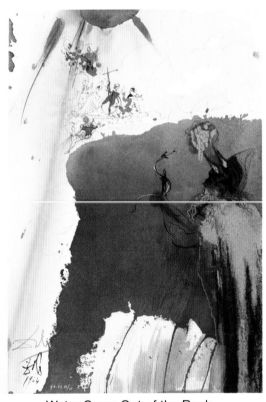

Water Come Out of the Rock
(FO 161) SB 17

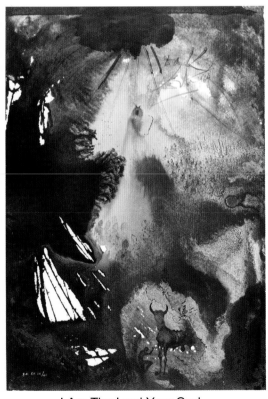

I Am The Lord Your God
(FO 162) SB 18

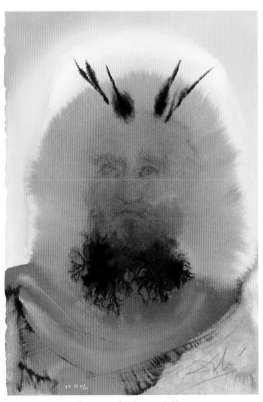

The Glory of Moses' Face
(FO 163) SB 19

Josuah, Brave in War
(FO 164) SB 20

Dalí presenting the Albarettos one of his watercolors of the *Sacred Bible*.

The Family Of Ruth, The Moabite
(FO 165) SB 21

David and the Philistine
(FO 166) SB 22

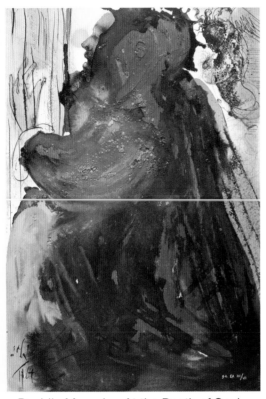

David's Mourning At the Death of Saul
(FO 167) SB 23

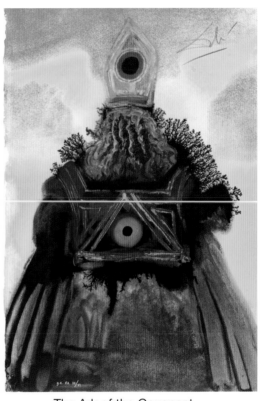

The Ark of the Covenant
(FO 168) SB 24

A Cherub Over the Threshold of the Lord
(FO 169) SB 25

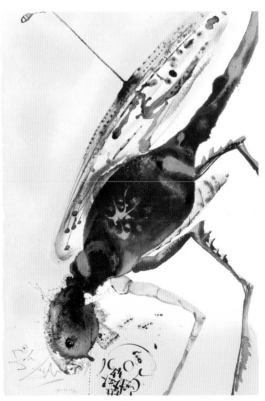

Locust and Grasshopper
(FO 170) SB 26

Elijah by Means of Whirlwind On a Chariot of Fire
(FO 171) SB 27

A Corpse in the Tomb of Elijah
(FO 172) SB 28

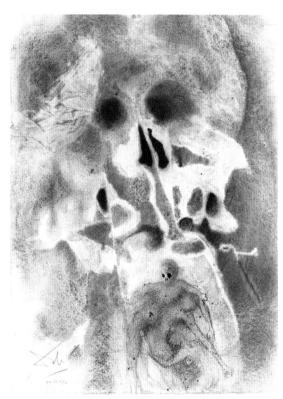

Josiah Buried in The Mausoleum of His Fathers
(FO 173) SB 29

Eduard Fornés and Giuseppe Albaretto in Torino.

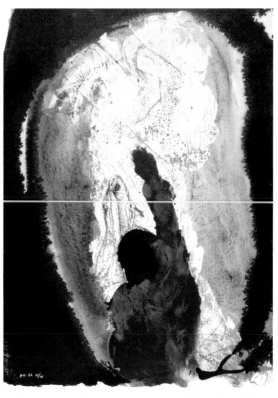

Jeremiah's Prophecy Against King Joachim
(FO 174) SB 30

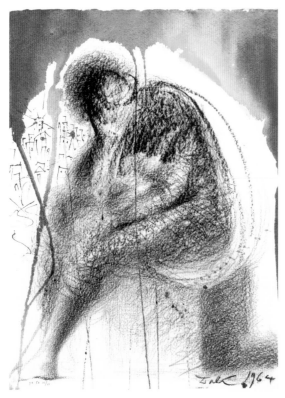

Lonely Sits the City That Was Full of People
(FO 175) SB 31

Nebuchadnezzar King Of Babylon
(FO 176) SB 32

Saint Raphael and Tobias
(FO 177) SB 33

Eleanor and Reynolds Morse with Giuseppe Albaretto.

May He Himself Join You in Marriage
(FO 178) SB 34

And Immediately Tobit Recovered His Sight
(FO 179) SB 35

The Liturgy Of Penance
(FO 180) SB 36

Judith Beheads Holoferness
(FO 181) SB 37

Ahasuerus Loved Esther Greatly
(FO 182) SB 38

Dalí with Giuseppe and Mara Albaretto.

Lament, Virgin, Girded with Sackcloth
(FO 183) SB 39

I Give Up My Body and Life for the Laws of Our Fathers
(FO 184) SB 40

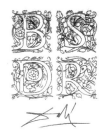

And Satan Also Was Present Among the Sons of God
(FO 185) SB 41

Certificate from a *Sacred Bible* volume.

Leviathan
(FO 186) SB 42

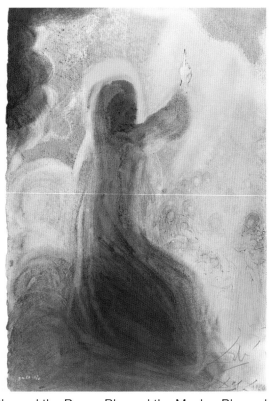

Blessed the Poor... Blessed the Meek... Blessed...
(FO 187) SB 43

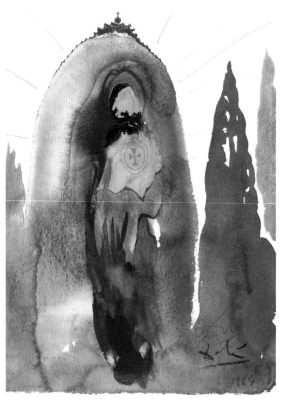

Who Will Go Up to The Mountain of the Lord
(FO 188) SB 44

You Will Sprinkle Me With Hyssop
And I Will Be Cleansed
(FO 189) SB 45

And After the Morsel, Satan Entered Into Him
(FO 190) SB 46

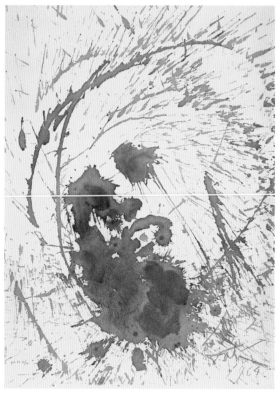

Behold the Man
(FO 191) SB 47

Away With Him, Away With Him, Crucify Him
(FO 192) SB 48

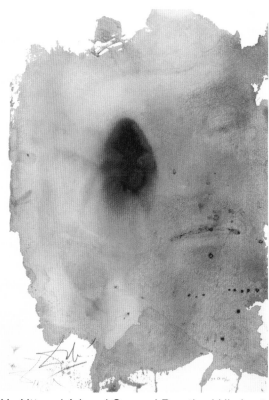

He Uttered A Loud Cry and Breathed His Last
(FO 193) SB 49

...And Took the Body of Jesus Away
(FO 194) SB 50

And They Bound the Body of Jesus in Linen Cloths with the Spices
(FO 195) SB 51

Jesus Walking on the Sea
(FO 196) SB 52

Blow the Trumpet in Zion
(FO 197) SB 53

Vanity of Vanities
(FO 198) SB 54

I Will Betroth You to Me Forever
(FO 199) SB 55

All the Nations in the Valley of Jehoshaphat
(FO 200) SB 56

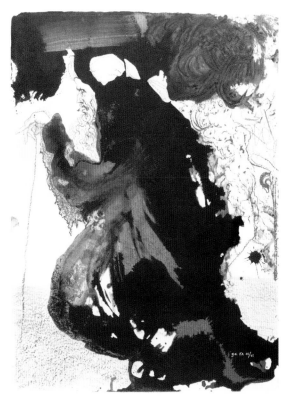

A Mason's Trowel in the Hand of the Lord
(FO 201) SB 57

Jonah in the Belly of the Fish
(FO 202) SB 58

The Foolish and the Wise Maidens
(FO 203) SB 59

The Money Changers Thrown Out of the Temple
(FO 204) SB 60

Give Me a Drink
(FO 205) SB 61

The Chosen Vineyard
(FO 206) SB 62

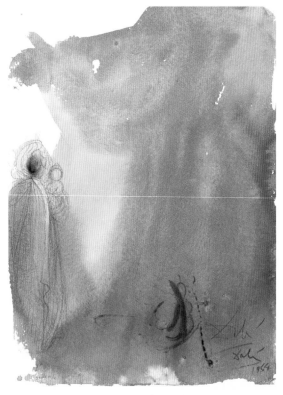

Behold, A Virgin Shall Conceive
(FO 207) SB 63

The Lion Eating Straw Like the Ox
(FO 208) SB 64

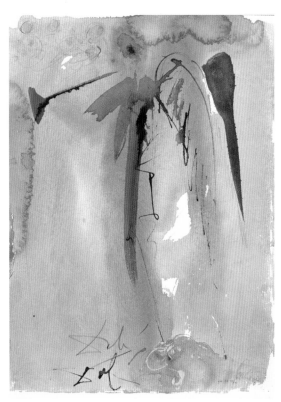

The Voice of One Crying Out
(FO 209) SB 65

Dalí with Giuseppe, Mara and Cristiana Albaretto.

They Will All Come from Saba
(FO 210) SB 66

Before You Came Out from the Womb I Sanctified You
(FO 211) SB 67

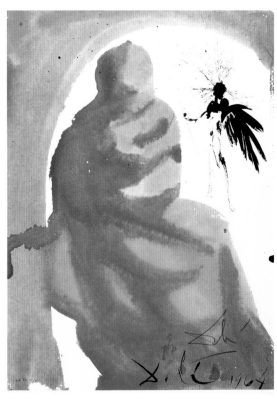

O Lord, You Have Deceived Me
(FO 212) SB 68

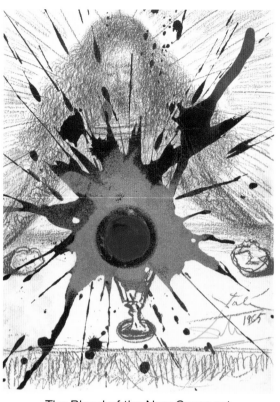

The Prodigal Son
(FO 213) SB 69

The Blood of the New Covenant
(FO 214) SB 70

Behold, One As The Son of Man
In the Clouds of Heaven
(FO 215) SB 71

An Idol By the Name of Baal
(FO 216) SB 72

The Angel Drove Out the Fiery Flame
(FO 217) SB 73

Mene, Tekel, Parsin
(FO 218) SB 74

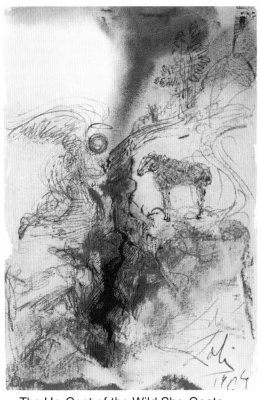

The He-Goat of the Wild She-Goats
On the Face of the Earth
(FO 219) SB 75

The Beauty Of Susanna
(FO 220) SB 76

Out of Egypt I Have Called My Son
(FO 221) SB 77

Is It Lawful to Pay Taxes to Caesar?
(FO 222) SB 78

The Spotless Offering
(FO 223) SB 79

He Himself Was Elijah
(FO 224) SB 80

The Annunciation To Mary
(FO 225) SB 81

The Birth of Jesus
(FO 226) SB 82

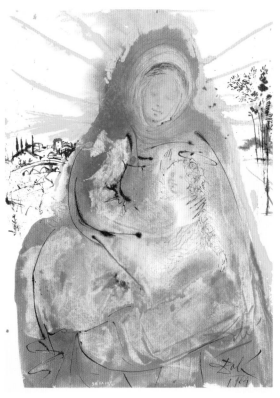

Mary Gathering Within Her Heart
(FO 227) SB 83

And You, Child, The Prophet of the Most High
(FO 228) SB 84

And He Was Baptized by John in the Jordan
(FO 229) SB 85

Jesus Is Tempted By Satan
(FO 230) SB 86

The Dance of Herodias' Daughter
(FO 231) SB 87

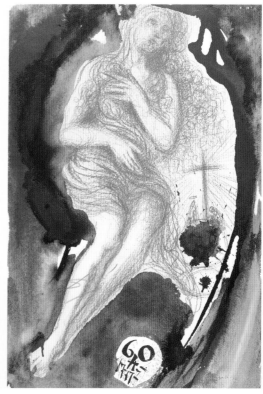

Many Sins Are Forgiven to the Sinful Woman
(FO 232) SB 88

The Transfiguration of Jesus
(FO 233) SB 89

You Are Peter
(FO 234) SB 90

Lazarus, Come Forth
(FO 235) SB 91

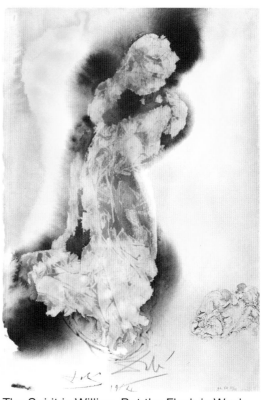

The Spirit is Willing, But the Flesh is Weak
(FO 236) SB 92

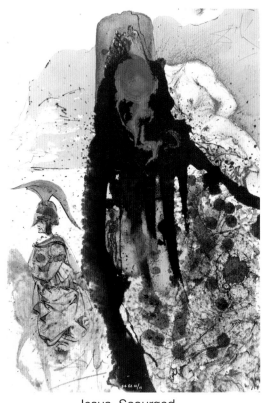

Jesus, Scourged
(FO 237) SB 93

He Went Out Carrying His Own Cross
(FO 238) SB 94

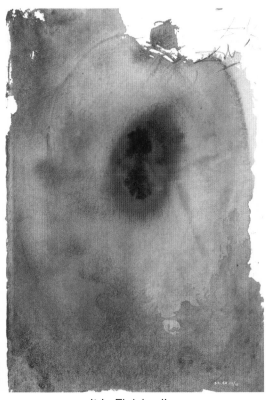

It Is Finished!
(FO 239) SB 95

Truly, This Was a Just Man
(FO 240) SB 96

The Taking Down From the Cross
(FO 241) SB 97

Dalí with Giuseppe and Mara Albaretto and secretary.

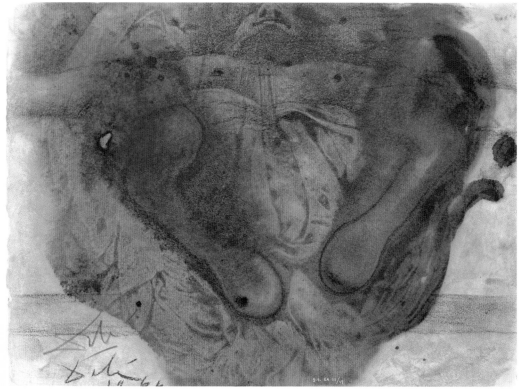

And They Placed Him In A Tomb
(FO 242) SB 98

On the Third Day He Rose From the Dead
(FO 243) SB 99

Don't Touch Me!
(FO 244) SB 100

And They Recognized Him In
The Breaking of the Bread
(FO 245) SB 101

There Appeared To Them Separated Tongues
(FO 246) SB 102

A Woman Clothed With the Sun
(FO 247) SB 103

A Great Battle in Heaven
(FO 248) SB 104

Come, Lord Jesus
(FO 249) SB 105

The Sacred Bible Lithographs
Plate Signatures

There are 96 different plate signatures (PS) on 96 different images of the *Sacred Bible* (SB). On pages 253 - 257, illustrated for the first time in any publication, are the plate signatures which are on each image of the *Sacred Bible* lithographs.

The plate signatures which appear on the mixed media lithographs of the *Sacred Bible* are reproductions of the hand signatures of Dalí which are on the mixed media paintings of the *Sacred Bible*.

However, nine of the 105 mixed media lithographs of the *Sacred Bible* were printed without plate signatures. They are:

The Glory of Moses' Face (SB 19),
The Ark of the Covenant (SB 24),
Josiah Buried in the Mausoleum of his Fathers (SB 29),
I Give Up My Body and Life for the Laws of Our Fathers (SB 40),
Jesus Walking on the Sea (SB 52),
I Will Betroth You to Me Forever (SB 55),
A Mason's Trowel in the Hand of the Lord (SB 57),
An Idol By the Name of Baal (SB 72),
Many Sins Are Forgiven to the Sinful Woman (SB 88).

The other 96 mixed media lithographs of the *Sacred Bible* contain plate signatures which are illustrated on pages 253 through 257.

Each of the 96 plate signatures is described by the plate signature numbers SB PS 1 through SB PS 96. They are shown as they appear on the lithographs with the plate signature description appearing on the left and the description of each lithograph appearing on the right. For example on page 251 the plate signature SB PS 96 appears on SB 105.

96 Signatures in the Plate on Sacred Bible Mixed Media Lithographs

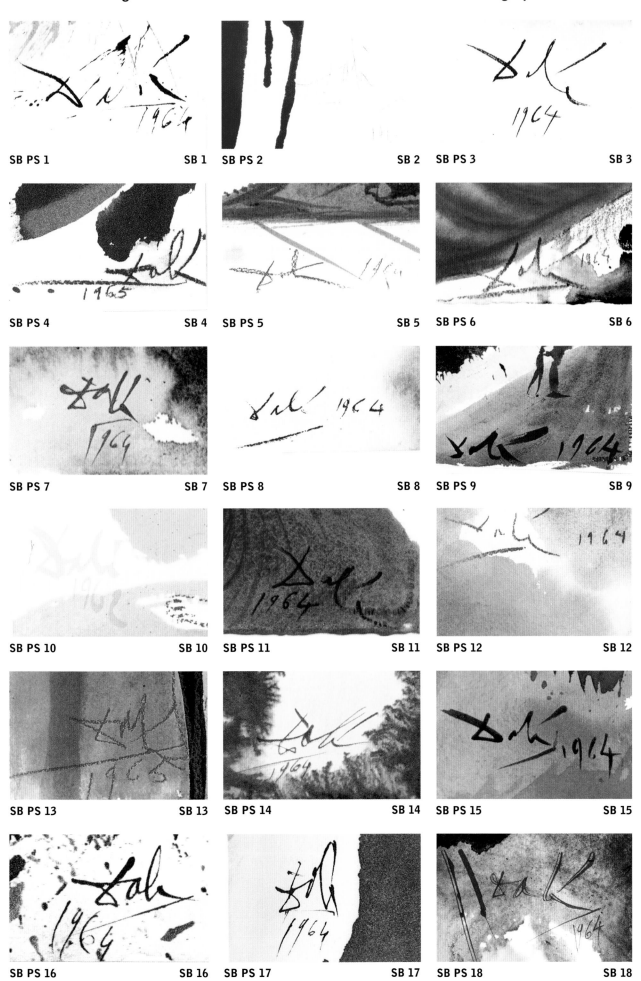

SB PS 1   SB 1   SB PS 2   SB 2   SB PS 3   SB 3

SB PS 4   SB 4   SB PS 5   SB 5   SB PS 6   SB 6

SB PS 7   SB 7   SB PS 8   SB 8   SB PS 9   SB 9

SB PS 10   SB 10   SB PS 11   SB 11   SB PS 12   SB 12

SB PS 13   SB 13   SB PS 14   SB 14   SB PS 15   SB 15

SB PS 16   SB 16   SB PS 17   SB 17   SB PS 18   SB 18

96 Signatures in the Plate on Sacred Bible Mixed Media Lithographs

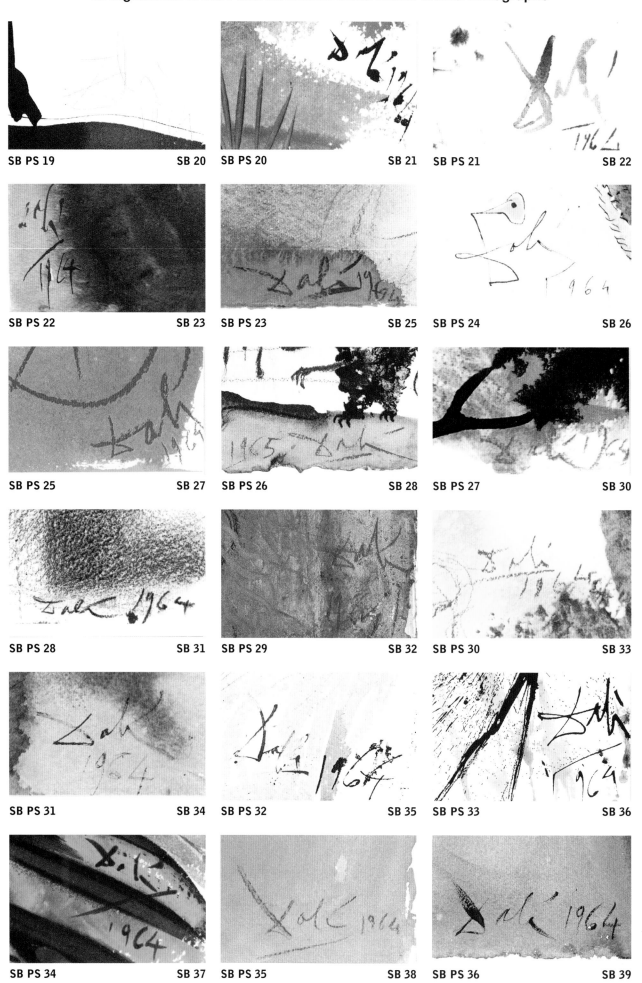

SB PS 19 — SB 20	
SB PS 20 — SB 21	
SB PS 21 — SB 22	
SB PS 22 — SB 23	
SB PS 23 — SB 25	
SB PS 24 — SB 26	
SB PS 25 — SB 27	
SB PS 26 — SB 28	
SB PS 27 — SB 30	
SB PS 28 — SB 31	
SB PS 29 — SB 32	
SB PS 30 — SB 33	
SB PS 31 — SB 34	
SB PS 32 — SB 35	
SB PS 33 — SB 36	
SB PS 34 — SB 37	
SB PS 35 — SB 38	
SB PS 36 — SB 39	

96 Signatures in the Plate on Sacred Bible Mixed Media Lithographs

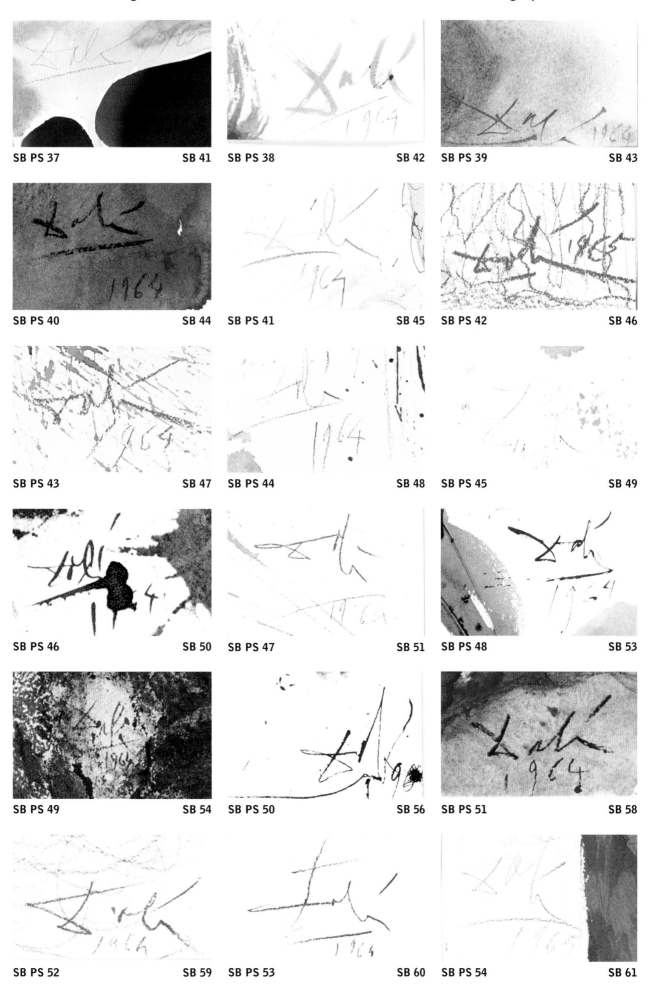

SB PS 37 — SB 41	SB PS 38 — SB 42	SB PS 39 — SB 43
SB PS 40 — SB 44	SB PS 41 — SB 45	SB PS 42 — SB 46
SB PS 43 — SB 47	SB PS 44 — SB 48	SB PS 45 — SB 49
SB PS 46 — SB 50	SB PS 47 — SB 51	SB PS 48 — SB 53
SB PS 49 — SB 54	SB PS 50 — SB 56	SB PS 51 — SB 58
SB PS 52 — SB 59	SB PS 53 — SB 60	SB PS 54 — SB 61

96 Signatures in the Plate on Sacred Bible Mixed Media Lithographs

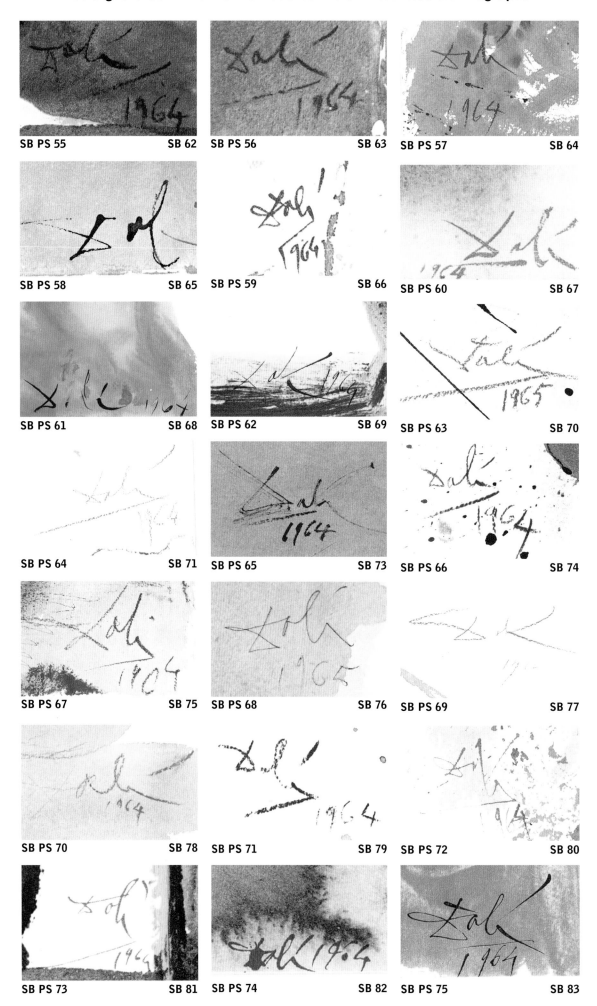

SB PS 55 SB 62	SB PS 56 SB 63	SB PS 57 SB 64
SB PS 58 SB 65	SB PS 59 SB 66	SB PS 60 SB 67
SB PS 61 SB 68	SB PS 62 SB 69	SB PS 63 SB 70
SB PS 64 SB 71	SB PS 65 SB 73	SB PS 66 SB 74
SB PS 67 SB 75	SB PS 68 SB 76	SB PS 69 SB 77
SB PS 70 SB 78	SB PS 71 SB 79	SB PS 72 SB 80
SB PS 73 SB 81	SB PS 74 SB 82	SB PS 75 SB 83

96 Signatures in the Plate on Sacred Bible Mixed Media Lithographs

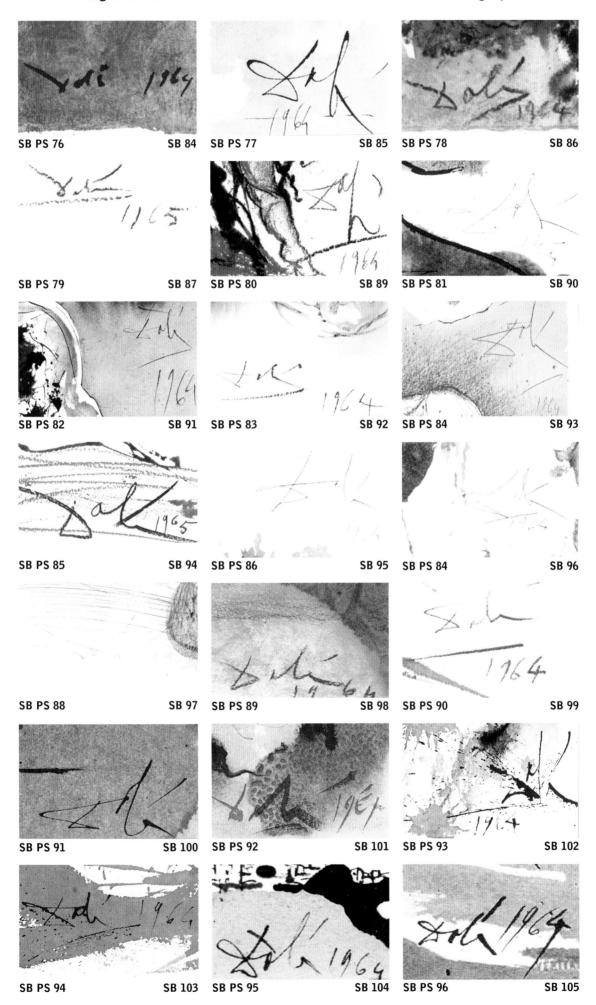

SB PS 76	SB 84
SB PS 77	SB 85
SB PS 78	SB 86
SB PS 79	SB 87
SB PS 80	SB 89
SB PS 81	SB 90
SB PS 82	SB 91
SB PS 83	SB 92
SB PS 84	SB 93
SB PS 85	SB 94
SB PS 86	SB 95
SB PS 84	SB 96
SB PS 88	SB 97
SB PS 89	SB 98
SB PS 90	SB 99
SB PS 91	SB 100
SB PS 92	SB 101
SB PS 93	SB 102
SB PS 94	SB 103
SB PS 95	SB 104
SB PS 96	SB 105

28 EDITIONS

PUBLISHED BY LES HEURES CLAIRES, PARIS
UNDER AGREEMENTS BETWEEN GIUSEPPE ALBARETTO AND DALÍ

After the success of the *Biblia Sacra,* Giuseppe Albaretto in cooperation with Jean Estrade and Les Heures Claires, Paris, continued to work with Dalí on other projects of books illustrated by Dalí. Albaretto commissioned Dalí to paint 10 original watercolor paintings to illustrate the *Our Father*. Albaretto also commissioned Dalí to paint 10 original watercolor paintings to illustrate Shakespeare's *Hamlet*. These paintings were a part of the contract between Dalí and Giuseppe Albaretto for the illustration of the book *A Thousand and One Nights*, where Dalí agreed to paint 500 watercolors. Dalí painted 100 of these watercolors on Arabian themes. These works on Arabian themes are among the most imaginative, colorful and rich watercolors Dalí ever painted. Dalí also created 50 watercolor paintings for the *Odyssey*, 10 for *Romeo and Juliet* and 40 drawings to illustrate *Don Quixote*. Most of these works only exist as watercolor paintings or drawings and have never been published in any other form.

In 1969, Salvador Dalí and Giuseppe Albaretto entered into an agreement allowing Albaretto to publish editions of graphic works based on paintings purchased by Albaretto from Dalí. One of the conditions imposed by Dalí in his agreement with Albaretto regarding publishing graphic editions was that each of the graphic works published by Albaretto be of the highest possible quality.

In order to satisfy this condition, Albaretto made an agreement with Jean Estrade, Director of Editions d'Art Les Heures Claires, Paris, to work directly with Dalí in the publishing and printing of the editions.

In 1971, Dalí created a design for an embossed blind-stamp of his signature with a crown above, which was to be affixed to each example of these published works. A copy of the original letter is reproduced here.

The documentation of the collaboration between Dalí and the Albarettos is without doubt the most complete in existence regarding the work of Dalí. The documentation of Les Heures Claires, Paris regarding the work of Dalí is equally precise in its thoroughness and detail.

Design and authorization by Salvador Dalí for the Albaretto blindstamp.

Translation:

Dr. Giuseppe Albaretto
Port Lligat
I, the undersigned Salvador Dalí, authorize Dr. Giuseppe Albaretto of Turin to manufacture an embossed stamp with my signature below to mark the engravings, the lithographs and the copies of what he will be reproducing and publishing of my works, for which he has been allowed the copyright.
Signature

DR. GIUSEPPE ALBARETTO

CADAQUES 20 AOUT 1970

Je Soussigné Salvador Dali m'éngage à illustrer pour

le Docteur Giuseppe Albaretto de Turin / Italie :

" LES NEUF DEESES DES ARTES "

CLIO - THALIE - ERATO - EUTERPE - POLYMNIE --CALLIOPE -

TERPSICHORE --URANIE --MELPOMENE .

en cuivre de 41 cm. Hauteur et 32 cm. Largeur.
On fera un tirage en Papier Arches limité a 145 exemplaires
et un tirage en Papier Japon limité à XCV exemplaires,
qui seront signées par ma main.

Maître Salvador Dali.

Agreement to create the "Nine Muses" intaglio editions.

Translation:

Letterhead: Dr. Giuseppe Albaretto
Cadaqués (Spain), August 20, 1970
I the undersigned Salvador Dalí promise to illustrate for Dr. Giuseppe Albaretto of Turin, Italy
"THE NINE GODDESSES OF THE ARTS"
CLIO—THALIA—ERATO—EUTERPE—CALLIOPE—
TERPSICHORE—URANUS—MELPOMENE
in copper 41 cm high and 32 cm wide.
There will be an edition on Arches Paper limited to 145 examples and a printing on Japanese paper, limited to 95 (XCV) examples that will be signed by my hand.
Master Salvador Dalí
Signature: Salvador Dalí

In light of the sad chapter that occurred in the later life of Dalí regarding forgeries, Jean Estrade and Dr. Giuseppe Albaretto showed great foresight to have been so clear and thorough in their documentation. Dr. Albaretto, a major collector and close personal friend of Dalí, and Jean Estrade, an astute and experienced editor of illustrated books and long time friend and confidant of Dalí, provided a great service to the Dalinean art world by clearly documenting in writing the contracts, and Dalí's involvement, in all of the projects.

In addition to the aforementioned agreements with Dalí and Estrade for these editions, Albaretto also retained "Bon a tirer" proofs signed and annotated by Dalí for each of the works.

Dalí signing prints published by Les Heures Claires, Paris.

I studied the archives of Les Heures Claires, Paris and Giuseppe Albaretto and have reproduced many documents from them here. They reference the list of editions edited by Jean Estrade and published by Les Heures Claires according to title, medium and edition size. They identify 44 lithograph editions and 24 intaglios, including 10 comprising the "*Hamlet Suite*."

The works were marketed by Les Heures Claires, Paris until 1981. In 1981, the marketing of all remaining examples was transferred to Les Heures Claires, Italy, the Italian company formed by Dr. Giuseppe Albaretto when Jean Estrade authorized Giuseppe Albaretto to use the name of Les Heures Claires.

In the letter of authorization from Les Heures Claires, Paris, it is specified that Albaretto may not cede the name Les Heures Claires to third parties and that the rights are exclusive to the Albaretto family.

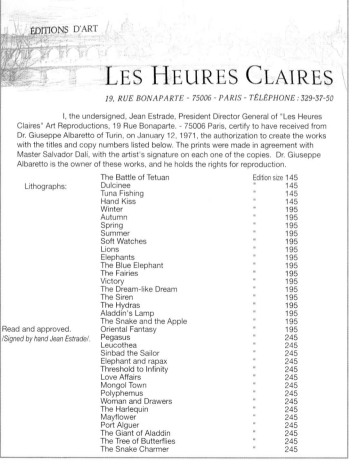

Document prepared by Jean Estrade of Les Heures Claires in 1985 providing details of the lithographs and intaglios that had been purchased by Les Heures Claires, Italy.

ÉDITIONS D'ART

LES HEURES CLAIRES

19, RUE BONAPARTE - 75006 - PARIS - TÉLÉPHONE : 329-37-50

I, the undersigned, Jean Estrade, President Director General of "Les Heures Claires" Art Reproductions, 19 Rue Bonaparte. - 75006 Paris, certify to have received from Dr. Giuseppe Albaretto of Turin, on January 12, 1971, the authorization to create the works with the titles and copy numbers listed below. The prints were made in agreement with Master Salvador Dali, with the artist's signature on each one of the copies. Dr. Giuseppe Albaretto is the owner of these works, and he holds the rights for reproduction.

Lithographs:	The Battle of Tetuan	Edition size	145
	Dulcinee	"	145
	Tuna Fishing	"	145
	Hand Kiss	"	145
	Winter	"	195
	Autumn	"	195
	Spring	"	195
	Summer	"	195
	Soft Watches	"	195
	Lions	"	195
	Elephants	"	195
	The Blue Elephant	"	195
	The Fairies	"	195
	Victory	"	195
	The Dream-like Dream	"	195
	The Siren	"	195
	The Hydras	"	195
	Aladdin's Lamp	"	195
	The Snake and the Apple	"	195
Read and approved.	Oriental Fantasy	"	195
/Signed by hand Jean Estrade/.	Pegasus	"	245
	Leucothea	"	245
	Sinbad the Sailor	"	245
	Elephant and rapax	"	245
	Threshold to Infinity	"	245
	Love Affairs	"	245
	Mongol Town	"	245
	Polyphemus	"	245
	Woman and Drawers	"	245
	The Harlequin	"	245
	Mayflower	"	245
	Port Alguer	"	245
	The Giant of Aladdin	"	245
	The Tree of Butterflies	"	245
	The Snake Charmer	"	245

Translation in English.

LES HEURES CLAIRES

19, RUE BONAPARTE - 75006 - PARIS - TÉLÉPHONE : 329-37-50

Lithographies:			
Orient	Tirage	245	
Homage a Dulcinée	"	245	
Les trois éléphantins	"	245	
Ulysse cubiste	"	245	
Le cheval géologique	"	245	
L'angelus surrealiste de Millet		245	
Montres molles et papillons	"	245	
La métamorphose des Montres Molles		245	
La baie de Port Lligat	"	245	

Gravures a cuivres originaux:

Danse	Tirage	Arches	145	Japon	99
Musique	"	"	145	"	99
Astronomie	"	"	145	"	99
Tragédie	"	"	145	"	99
Thalie	"	"	145	"	95
Clio	"	"	145	"	95
Erato	"	"	145	"	95
Polymnie	"	"	145	"	95
Calliope	"	"	145	"	95
Nu de dos	"	"	145	"	95
Tournoi	"	"	245	"	145
Oursin	"	"	145	"	95
Les chevaux surrealistes			245	"	145
Saint Georges et le dragon			245	"	145
Hamlet 10 sujets		"	145	d'aprés les	
originaux					

Les gravures et les lithographies sont maintenant épuisés, le solde a été vendu à la Société "Les Heures Claires" Italie. Cuivres, typons ayant été détruits, tous les droits de reproduction concernant les oeuvres citées ci-dessous, sont la propriété exclusive du dr. Giuseppe Albaretto.

Fait à Paris le 7 Février 1985

Lu et approuvé

LES HEURES CLAIRES

19, RUE BONAPARTE - 75006 - PARIS - TÉLÉPHONE : 329-37-50

Lithographs:

Orient	Edition size	245
Hommage to Dulcinee	"	245
The Three Elephants	"	245
Cubist Ulysses	"	245
The Geological Horse	"	245
The Surrealist Angelus of Millet	"	245
Soft Watches and Butterflies	"	245
The Metamorphosis of Soft Watches	"	245
The Bay of Port Lligat	"	245

Original engraving plates:

Dance	Edition Size	Arches	145	Japon	99
Music	"	"	145	"	99
Astronomy	"	"	145	"	99
Tragedy	"	"	145	"	99
Comedy	"	"	145	"	95
History	"	"	145	"	95
Poetry of Love	"	"	145	"	95
Sacred Poetry	"	"	145	"	95
Eloquence	"	"	145	"	95
Nude from the Back	"	"	145	"	95
Tournament	"	"	245	"	145
Sea-Urchin	"	"	145	"	95
the Surrealist Horses	"	"	245	"	145
Saint George and the Dragon	"	"	245	"	145
Hamlet - 10 Subjects	"	"	145 off the original.		

The etchings and the lithographs are now sold out, the surplus having been sold to the Association "Les Heures Claires" Italy. The plates, and the patterns have been destroyed, and all the reproduction rights regarding the above mentioned works are the exclusive property of Dr. Giuseppe Albaretto.

Signature de Jean Estrade in Paris on February 7, 1985

Read and approved.
/Signed by hand Jean Estrade./

Translation in English.

Authentic Signatures by Salvador Dalí

28 of the *Editions* published by Les Heures Claires, Paris under publishing agreements between Giuseppe Albaretto and Dalí are illustrated on pages 267 - 277.

Each of the works came from the archives of Giuseppe Albaretto and contain an authentic hand signature of Dalí.

In addition, there are Dalí hand signatures authenticated by Alfredo Ghio on works from the *28 Editions* published by Les Heures Claires, Paris under agreements between Giuseppe Albaretto and Dalí on pages 309 - 312.

Illustrations

Intaglios

The Surrealistic Horses
FO 250

Saint George and the Dragon
FO 251

Intaglios

The Nine Muses

Eloquence
FO 252

History
FO 253

Poetry of Love
FO 254

Intaglios

The Nine Muses

Music
FO 255

Intaglios

The Nine Muses

Tragedy
FO 256

Sacred Poetry
FO 257

Dance
FO 258

Comedy
FO 259

Intaglios

The Nine Muses

Astronomy
FO 260

Lithographs

The Three Elephants
(Three Surrealist Elephants)
FO 262

Victory
FO 261

Soft Watches and Butterflies
FO 263

Lithographs

Don Quixote

The Hand Kiss
FO 264

The Bay of Port Lligat
FO 266

Homage to Dulcinee
FO 265

Lithographs

The Odyssey

The Siren
FO 267

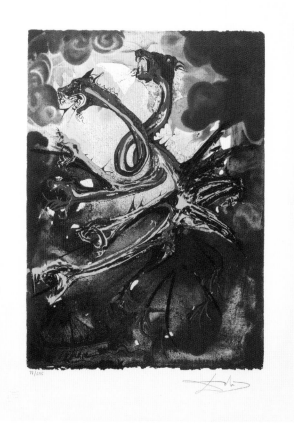

The Hydras
FO 268

Lithographs

A Thousand and One Nights

Aladdin's Giant
FO 269

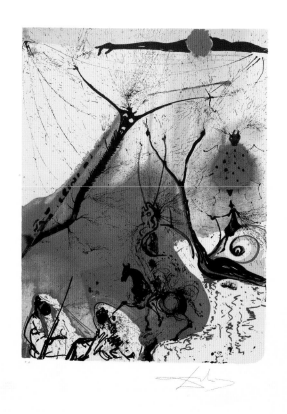

The Dream-like Dream
FO 270

The Snake and the Apple
FO 271

Lithographs

A Thousand and One Nights

The Snake Charmer
FO 272

The Lions
FO 273

Love Affairs
FO 274

Lithographs

A Thousand and One Nights

Mayflower
FO 275

Orient
FO 276

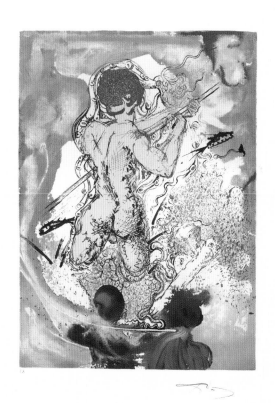

Sinbad the Sailor
FO 277

EXPERT OPINIONS

Expert Opinions

Expert opinions regarding the authenticity of hand signatures
by Salvador Dalí on works
from the Divine Comedy,
the Sacred Bible,
and
Editions published by Les Heures Claires, Paris
under agreements
between Giuseppe Albaretto and Dalí

Expert Opinion of Robert Wittman

I was engaged to evaluate the authenticity of artworks that are the subject of this book. I traveled to four different countries conducting interviews over a period of approximately one year. The below list are the people interviewed:

U.S.

Cyril Boisson, Dalí art dealer
Philippe duNoyer, Dalí art dealer
Bernard Ewell, Dalí expert
Frank Hunter, Dalí expert
Albert Scaglione, Dalí art dealer
Morris Shapiro, Dalí art dealer

Paris, France

Daniel David, publisher Les Heures Claires
Stefaan Delbaere, dealer in *Divine Comedy*
Jean Jacques Biagini, art dealer
Marc Ways, dealer in *Divine Comedy*

Marseilles, France

Christian Branducci, dealer in *Divine Comedy*
Antoine Branducci, dealer in *Divine Comedy*

Barcelona, Spain

Eduard Fornés, Dalí expert

Turin, Italy

Cristiana Albaretto, daughter of Giuseppe and Mara Albaretto
Beniamino Cristini, husband of Cristiana Albaretto
Alfred Ghio, expert document examiner and graphologist

I conducted a completely transparent investigation. No requests for interviews were denied and any and all documents that I requested were produced. Based on my review, requested documents and the interviews conducted, it is my opinion that the documentation in this book specifically as it relates to its Salvador Dalí collections of the *Divine Comedy*, *Sacra Biblia* and the '*Albaretto Prints*' are the most thorough I have ever seen. I have no doubt as to their authenticity.

Curriculum Vitae

ROBERT K. WITTMAN

SPECIAL AGENT (r), FEDERAL BUREAU OF INVESTIGATION

Address: P.O. Box 653
Chester Heights, PA 19017

Email: Robertwittmaninc@live.com
Tel: 610-361-8929 (office)
610-368-1338 (cell)

Website: www.robertwittmaninc.com

Professional Background:

Robert K. Wittman joined the FBI as a Special Agent in 1988 and was assigned to the Philadelphia Field Division. As a result of specialized training in art, antiques, jewelry and gem identification, he served as the FBI's investigative expert in this field. During his 20-year career with the FBI he recovered more than $300 million worth of stolen art and cultural property resulting in the prosecution and conviction of numerous individuals. In 2005, he was instrumental in the creation of the FBI's rapid deployment Art Crime Team. He was named as the ACT's Senior Investigator and instructed the team members in how to conduct cultural property investigations. He has represented the United States around the world conducting investigations and instructing international police and museums in investigation, recovery and security techniques. In 2011, Mr. Wittman was elected as Vice Chairman of the Museum Association Security Committee (MASC), a standing committee of the American Alliance of Museums (AAM).

Investigative Highlights:

- Theft at Pennsbury Manor, the historical home of William Penn, founder of Pennsylvania
  First prosecution and convictions under the federal Theft of Major Artwork Statute
  Recovery: More than 30 historical items valued at more than $100,000

- Theft of one of the original 14 copies of the Bill of Rights stolen by a Union Soldier in 1865
  Recovery: Valued at $30 million

- Theft of numerous paintings at a private estate in Madrid, Spain
  Recovery: comprised of 17 paintings including two by Francisco Goya valued at $50 Million

- Theft from the Swedish National Museum in Stockholm
  Recovery: Rembrandt's 1630 "Self-Portrait" valued at $36 million

- Theft from a private gallery in Minneapolis
  Recovery: 5 Norman Rockwell paintings worth $1 million from a farmhouse in Brazil

- Looting of the Royal Tomb of the Lord of Sipan in Peru
  Recovery: 2,000 year-old golden Pre-Columbian piece of body armor known as a Backflap

- Recovery of Native American Apache medicine man Geronimo's eagle feather war bonnet valued at $1.2 million

- Theft from the U.S. Naval Academy in 1932 of an 1862 Tiffany presentation sword which was awarded to Admiral John Worden, for his heroic command aboard the U.S.S. Monitor during its historic Civil War battle with the C.S.S. Virginia (Merrimac).
  Recovery: The Tiffany presentation sword valued at $650,000

Presentations and Art Community Partnership:

SA Wittman served as a member of the Department of State's Cultural Antiquities Task Force based in Washington, D.C. He has sought to educate others in the cultural property protection community about techniques to avoid becoming a victim of theft or fraud and the importance of prompt reporting. He has been the FBI spokesperson for art theft matters nationally and represented the United States at numerous international conferences regarding cultural property protections. Some of those venues include:

The American Association of Museums (AAM) Annual Conference
J. Paul Getty Museum
Philadelphia Museum of Art
San Diego Museum of Art
Princeton University Art Museum
Museum of Modern Art, New York
Museum of Fine Arts, Boston
Minneapolis Institute of Arts
Cambridge University, Cambridge, U.K.
International conferences in Romania, Poland, Russia, Belgium, and France
United Nations Conference on Art theft and Organized Crime, Courmayer, Italy

Awards and Recognitions:

2000- "Peruvian Order of Merit for Distinguished Service," presented by the President of Peru.

2001- "Outstanding Contributions in Law Enforcement Award," presented by Attorney General John Ashcroft

2003- "White Cross of Law Enforcement Merit Medal" by the Spanish National Police

2004- "Robert Burke Memorial Award for Excellence in Cultural Property Protection" by the Smithsonian Institution at the National Conference on Cultural Property Protection

2010- Saving Antiquities for Everyone (SAFE) "Beacon Award" for recovering stolen art.

2010- Wrote the New York Times Best Seller *Priceless: How I Went Undercover to Rescue the World's Stolen Treasures*

2013- Authored the article *Security Lessons: What can we learn from the Rotterdam Heist?* for Museum Magazine.

SA Wittman is now President of Robert Wittman, Inc. and is available for private and public consultation. His vast knowledge of the customs and practices in the art industry makes him uniquely qualified to assist with fraud prevention and detection, as well as art security and recovery matters.

Expert Opinion of Alfredo Ghio

I am a third generation accredited expert document examiner and graphologist. I was asked in my professional capacity to examine signatures attributed to Salvador Dalí which are the subject of this book. As a result of my examination, using approved and accepted technical procedures performed on the original versions of the signatures presented for verification attributed to the artist Salvador Dalí, I can certify that the signatures on pages 289 - 312 presented for verification are the authentic signatures of the artist Salvador Dalí.

Alfredo Ghio

ALFREDO GHIO
EXPERT DOCUMENT EXAMINER AND GRAPHOLOGIST

Mr. Alfredo Ghio is an expert in signature and art authentication. He was born in Turin, Italy on September 3, 1960, and is domiciled there at Corso Francia 276/2.

Mr. Ghio has been a member of the Italian Association of Technical Experts Collegio Italiano Esperti Consulenti Tecnici since January 1984, and is also registered with the Court of Turin and the local Chamber of Commerce (in Italian, respectively, Albo dei Consulenti Tecnici del Giudice del Tribunale Civile e Penale di Torino and Ruolo Periti ed Esperti della Camera di Commercio, Industria, Artigianato e Agricoltura).

Mr. Ghio is regularly called on as an independent expert by Italian Courts and local counsel. He was awarded a technical diploma in Turin, and in October 1983, joined his family firm specializing in calligraphic expertise and judicial examinations. The firm was founded by Mr. Ghio's grandfather, Prof. Alfredo Ghio, at the beginning of the 20th century.

In his initial years, Mr. Ghio collaborated with Mr. Max Frei Sulzer, a criminologist of international standing, then head of the Scientific Section of the Zurich police, Switzerland. In 1991, Mr. Ghio formed his own company.

1991: Participated at the 9th and 10th International Symposia, Mannheim University (Germany, 1989-1991) organized by the Gesellschaft für Forensische Schriftsuntersuchung (GFS) on *Graphic Identification Techniques and Analysis of Manuscripts.*

1993: Invited by Dr. Peter Bayer of GFS to attend the International Berlin Convention in March-April 1993

1996: National Seminar in Judicial Graphology, Erice (Italy)

1999: Invited by Prof. Fabbiani of the Turin Polytechnic University as speaker to the 7th International Convention SECURITY '99 – *Originality and Anti-falsification in Valuable Documents and Certification.*

1999: Invited as speaker on *The Analysis of Manuscripts* at the International Convention of the GFS, Hamburg (Germany)

2000: Invited by Prof. Fabbiani of Turin Polytechnic University as speaker to the 8th International Convention *SECURITY* MM – *Originality, Anti-falsification, Analysis of Manuscripts.*

2000: Invited to the Convention at the GFS, Bingen (Germany)

2005: Invited as speaker at the Convention on *The Future of Graphology - Problems, Methods and Perspectives*, Bologna (Italy).

2005: Invited as speaker at the Convention on *Technological Support to the Judicial Documents Analysis*, Turin (Italy)

2007: Participated at the Technical Experts Meeting, Milan (Italy)

2008: Invited to the 5th National Convention on *The Judicial Surveys*, Mesagne (Italy)

2009: Participated at the Convention on *Parkinson and Alzheimer Disease, Impacts on the Capacity of Writing*, Milan (Italy)

2010: Participated at the 6th Convention on *The Judicial Exam of Documents,* Mesagne (Italy)

2013: Participated at The National Convention organized by the Istituto Superiore di Grafologia (Superior Institute of Graphology) in Roma on *Continuing Professional Education and Accountability of Consultants and Legal Graphology Experts.*

2014: Participated at a professional Seminar held in Roma on *Psychopathology and Graphopathology of the Testament -* organized by The International Center for Medical Graphology.

2015: Participated at the second professional Seminar held in Roma on *Psychopathology and Graphopathology of the Testament -* organized by International Center for Medical Graphology.

AUTHENTIC SIGNATURES BY SALVADOR DALÍ

Authentic Signatures by Salvador Dalí:

Authentic Signatures by Salvador Dalí on Works from the Divine Comedy

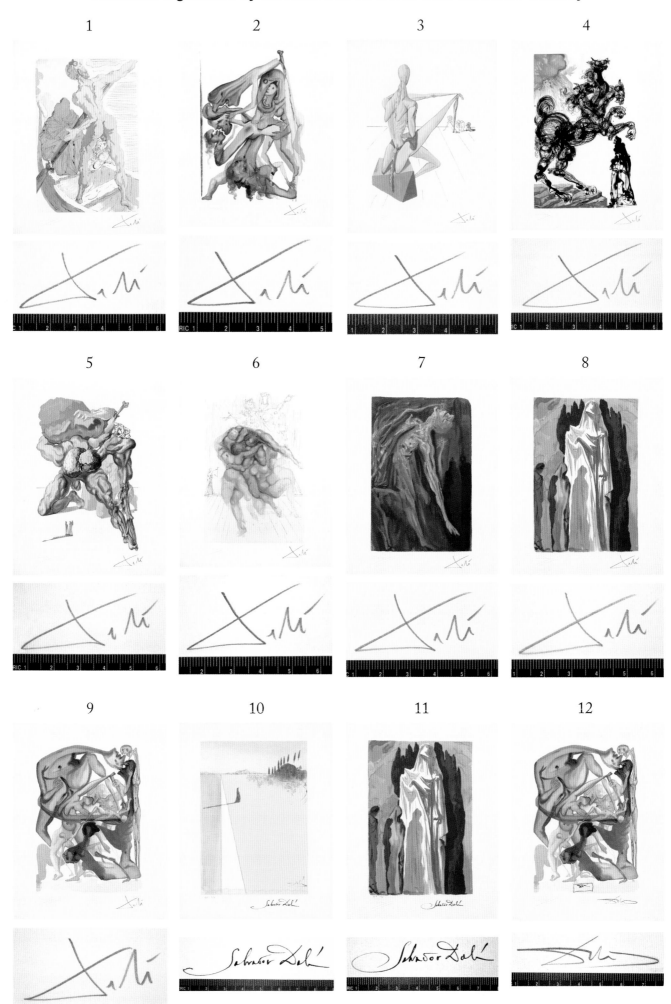

Authentic Signatures by Salvador Dalí on Works from the Divine Comedy

Authentic Signatures by Salvador Dalí on Works from the Divine Comedy

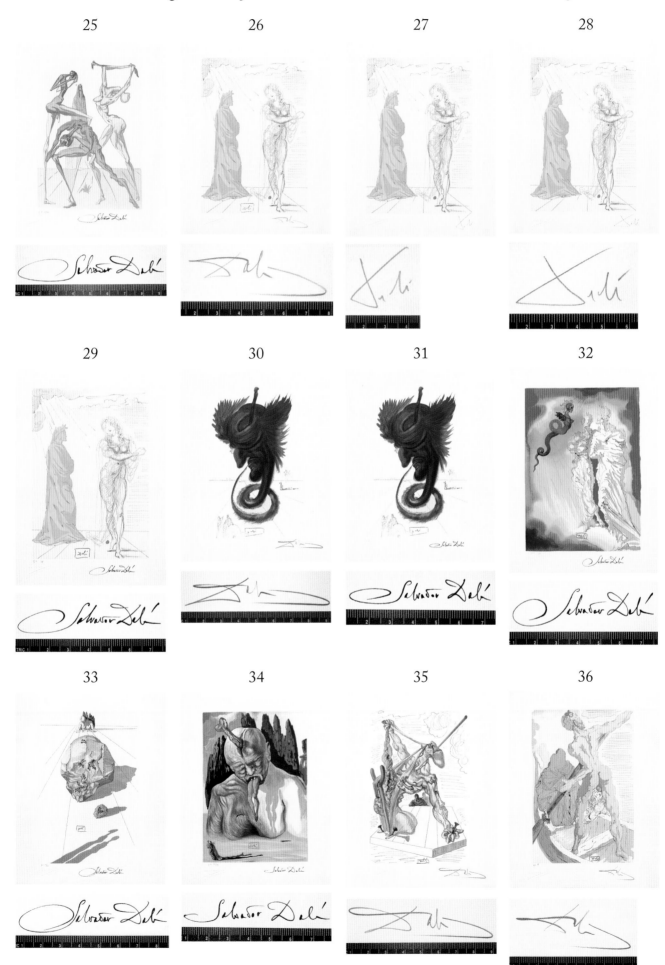

25   26   27   28

29   30   31   32

33   34   35   36

Authentic Signatures by Salvador Dalí on Works from the Divine Comedy

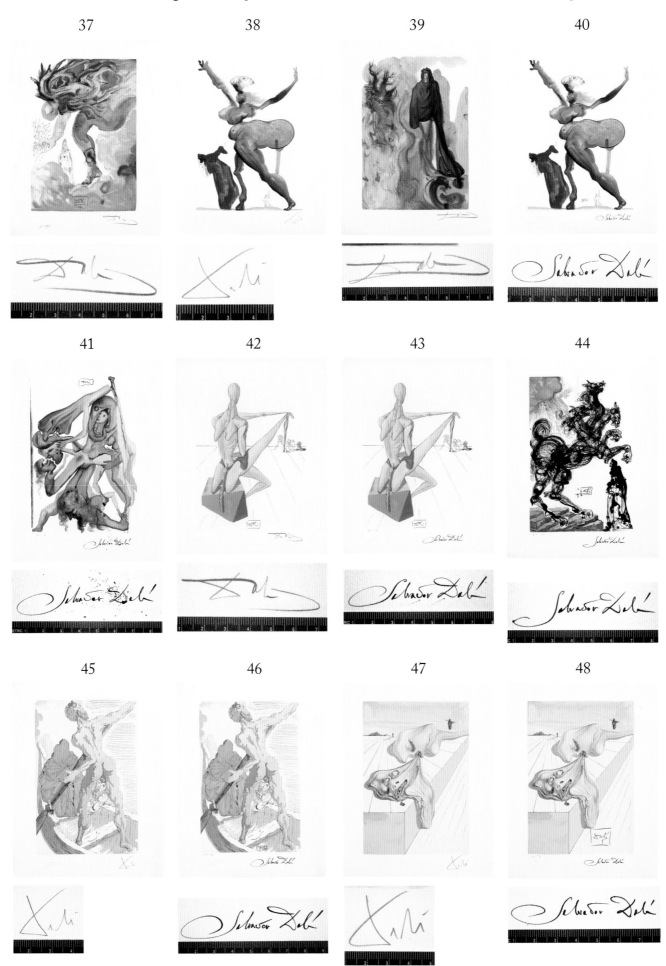

Authentic Signatures by Salvador Dalí on Works from the Divine Comedy

49 50 51 52

53 54 55 56

57 58 59 60

Authentic Signatures by Salvador Dalí on Works from the Divine Comedy

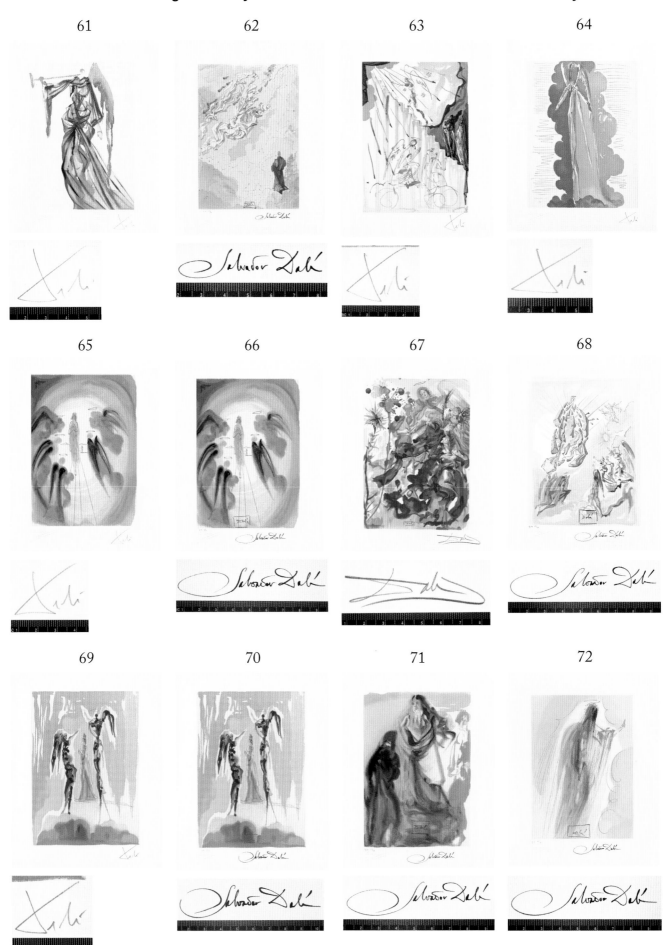

61 62 63 64

65 66 67 68

69 70 71 72

Authentic Signatures by Salvador Dalí on Works from the Divine Comedy

73

74

75

76

77

78

79

80

81

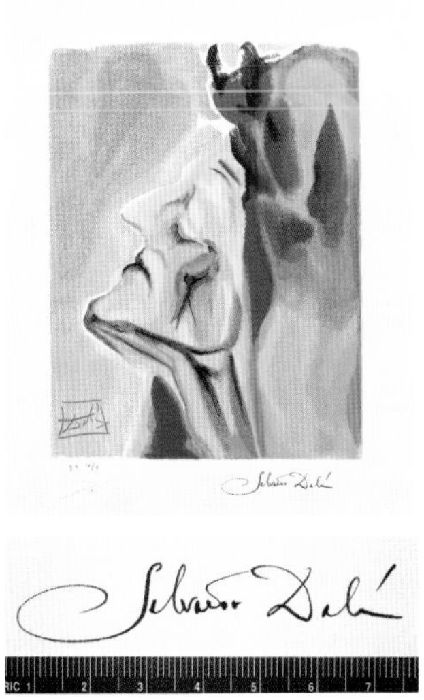

82

83

84

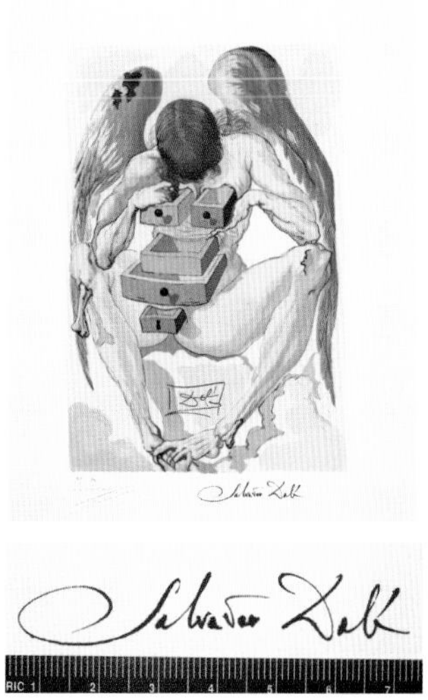

Authentic Signatures by Salvador Dalí on Works from the Divine Comedy

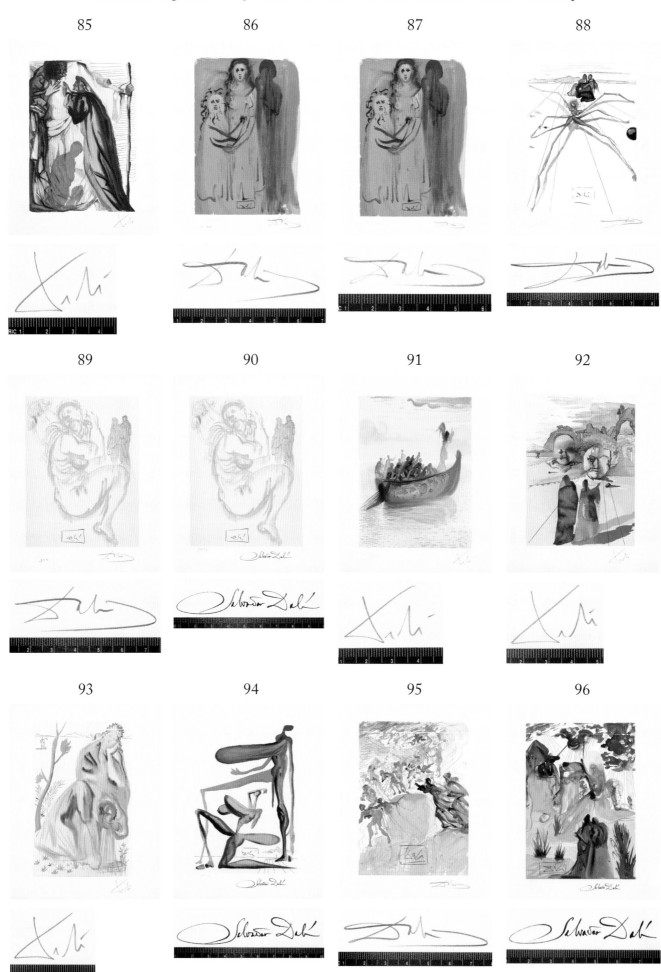

85 86 87 88

89 90 91 92

93 94 95 96

Authentic Signatures by Salvador Dalí on Works from the Divine Comedy

97	98	99	100

101	102	103

LA MAISON D'ÉDITIONS D'ART
«LES HEURES CLAIRES»

a réalisé une édition de la DIVINE COMÉDIE de DANTE illustrée par le MAÎTRE SALVADOR DALI, en dix exemplaires numération romaine de I à X, en trois tomes, sans texte, avec toutes les illustrations encadrées dans un elegant carton noir frisé en or.

Chaque illustration est signée avec signature en entier par le Maître, en encre de chine sépia.

Le MAÎTRE SALVADOR DALI s'engage à ne plus signer aucune autre illustration de la DIVINE COMÉDIE en encre de chine sépia avec signature en entier.

PARIS 1964

Maître
Salvador Dali

Les Heures Claires
Directeur General et Fondateur
Robert Blairon

Translation:

The Art Publishing House LES HEURES CLAIRES has produced an edition of DANTE'S DIVINE COMEDY, illustrated by MASTER SALVADOR DALÍ in ten suites numbered in roman numerals from I to X, in three volumes, without text, with all illustrations matted in elegant black matt-board bordered in gold.

Each illustration is signed with the full signature by the Master, in sepia india ink.

MASTER SALVADOR DALÍ commits to no longer sign any other illustration of the DIVINE COMEDY in sepia ink with a full signature.

Authentic Signatures by Salvador Dalí on certificates from the Divine Comedy

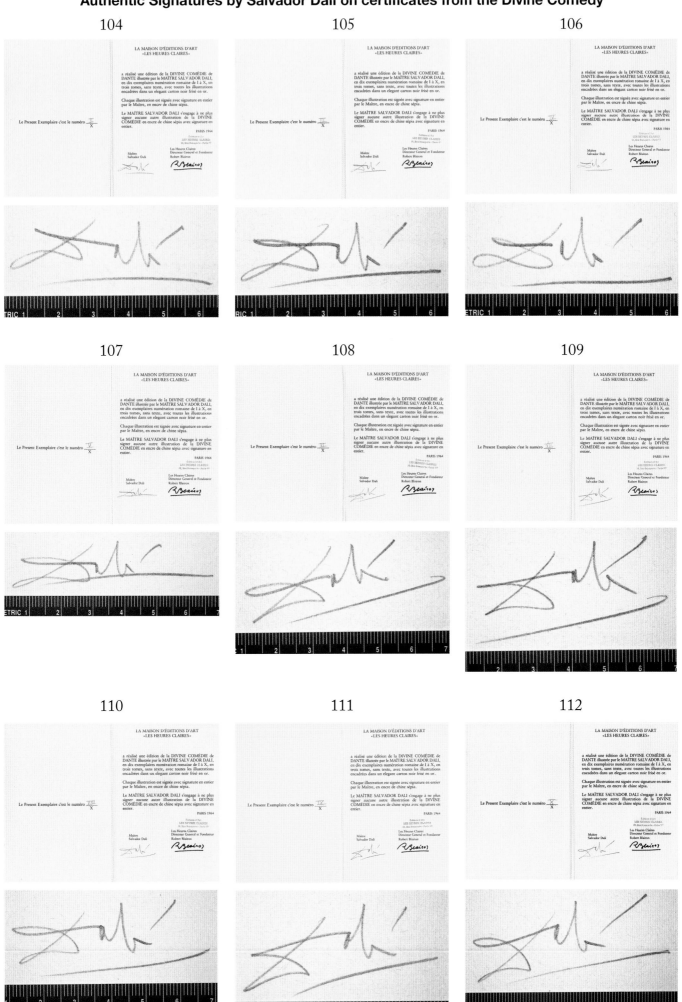

Authentic Signatures by Salvador Dalí on Works from the Sacred Bible

Between 1976 and 1979, Roberto Mastella, a prominent collector of the art work of Salvador Dalí, arranged through Dr. Giuseppe Albaretto to have Dalí hand sign examples of the *Sacred Bible* lithographs. Dalí hand signed individual examples from complete bound sets of the *Sacred Bible*, individual portfolios of six lithographs as issued by Rizzoli and other loose sheet lithographs over this three-year period. All of the individual sheets were stamped with the number "5" on the verso to distinguish these lithographs as coming from the Mastella collection.

In the publication of this book, I contacted the parties involved and in possession of verifiable documentation concerning the hand-signed *Sacred Bible* lithographs and requested their documentation for review and possible inclusion herein. The substantial documentation and independent confirmation of this documentation allow me to state that hand-signed *Sacred Bible* lithographs with a written provenance from Giuseppe Albaretto and Robert Mastella contain authentic signatures of Salvador Dalí.

I am aware of no other collections of *Sacred Bible* lithographs which are described as having hand signatures of Salvador Dalí other than those described herein.

Authentic Signatures by Salvador Dalí on Works from the Sacred Bible

Authentic Signatures by Salvador Dalí on Works from the Sacred Bible

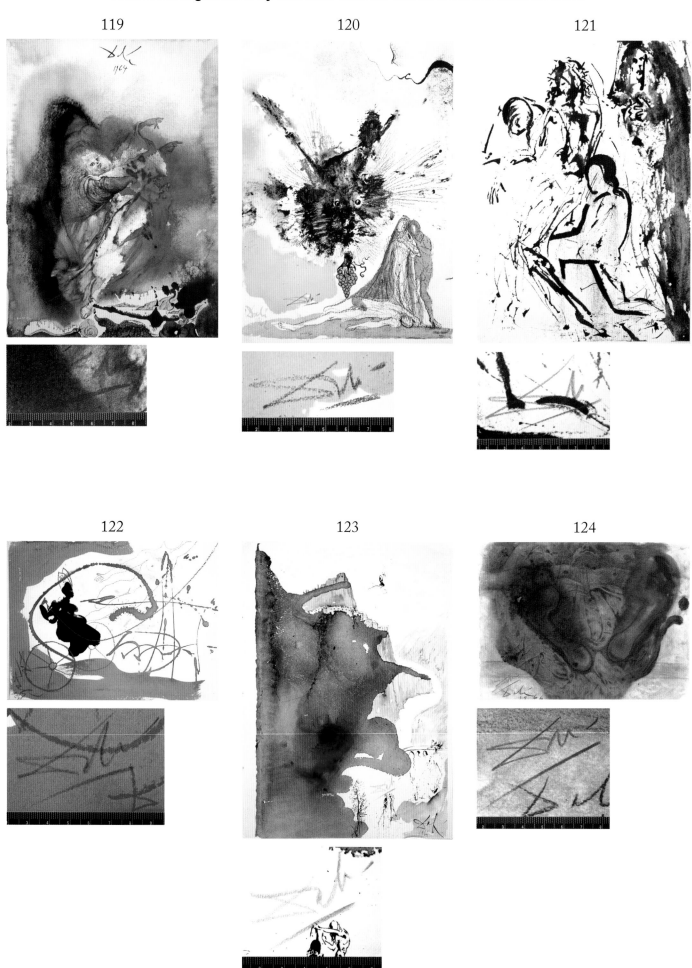

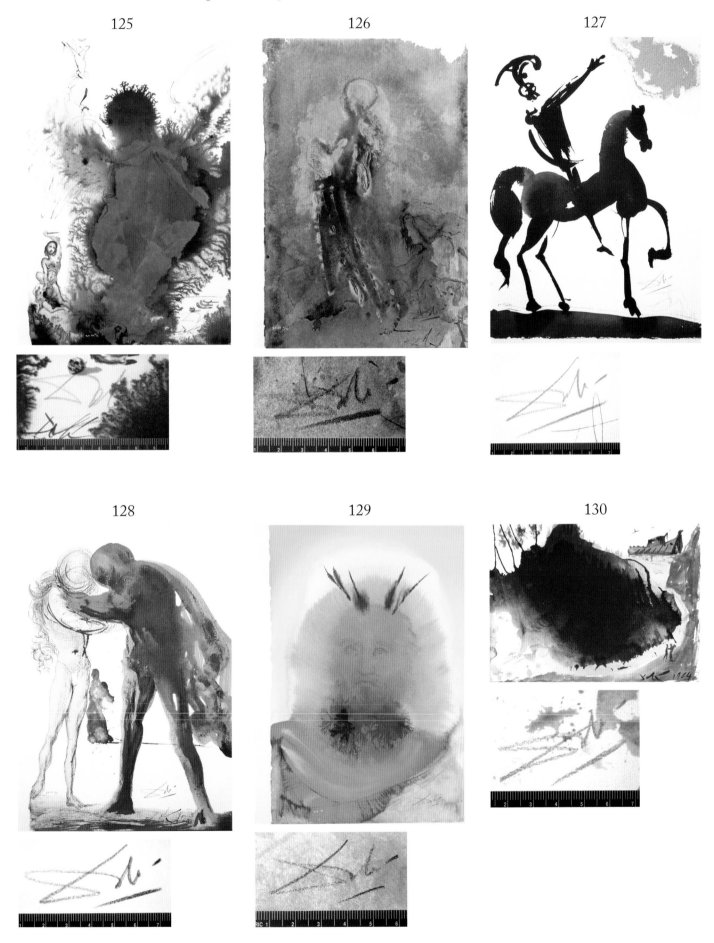

125

126

127

128

129

130

Authentic Signatures by Salvador Dalí on Works from the Sacred Bible

131

132

133

134

135

136

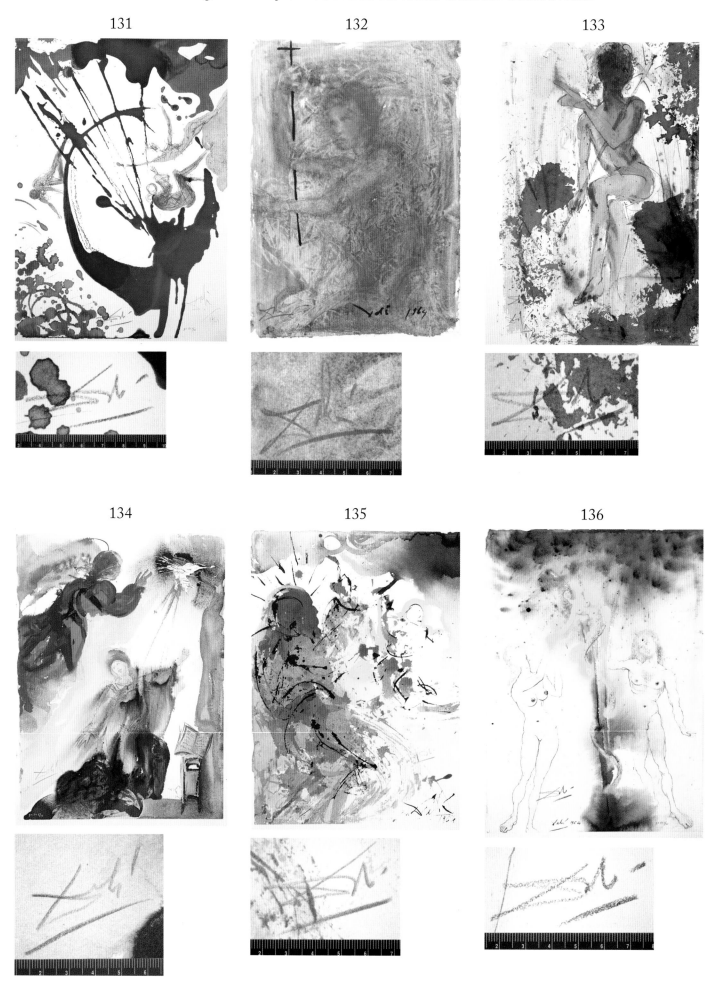

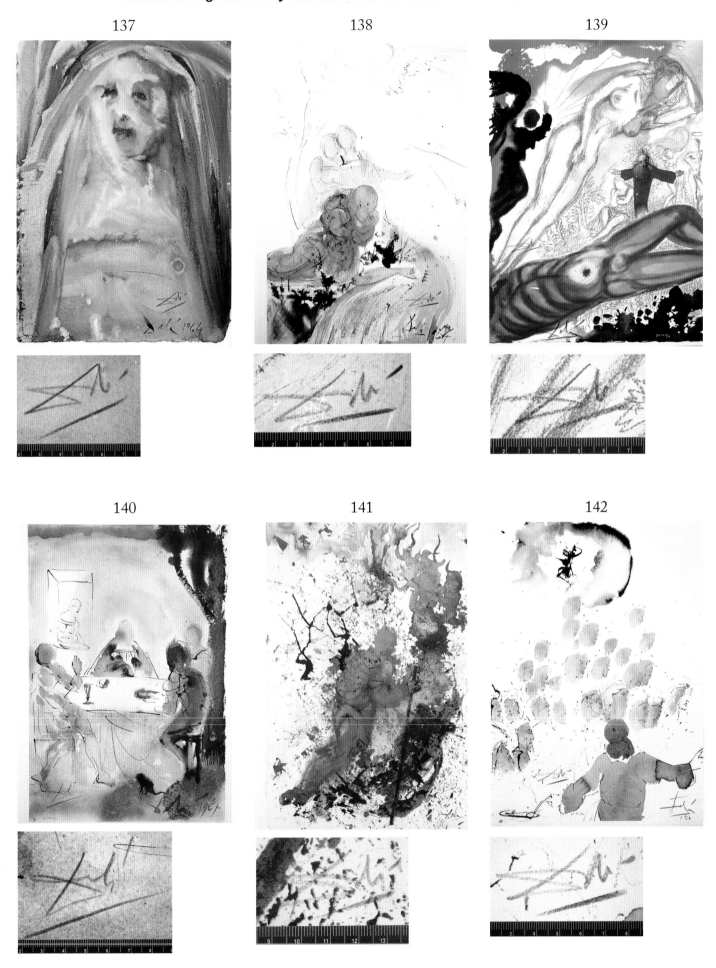

137

138

139

140

141

142

143

144

145

146

147

Authentic Signatures by Salvador Dalí
on Editions
published by
Les Heures Claires, Paris under agreements
between
Giuseppe Albaretto and Dalí

Authentic Signatures by Salvador Dalí on Works from Editions
published by Giuseppe Albaretto and Les Heures Claires

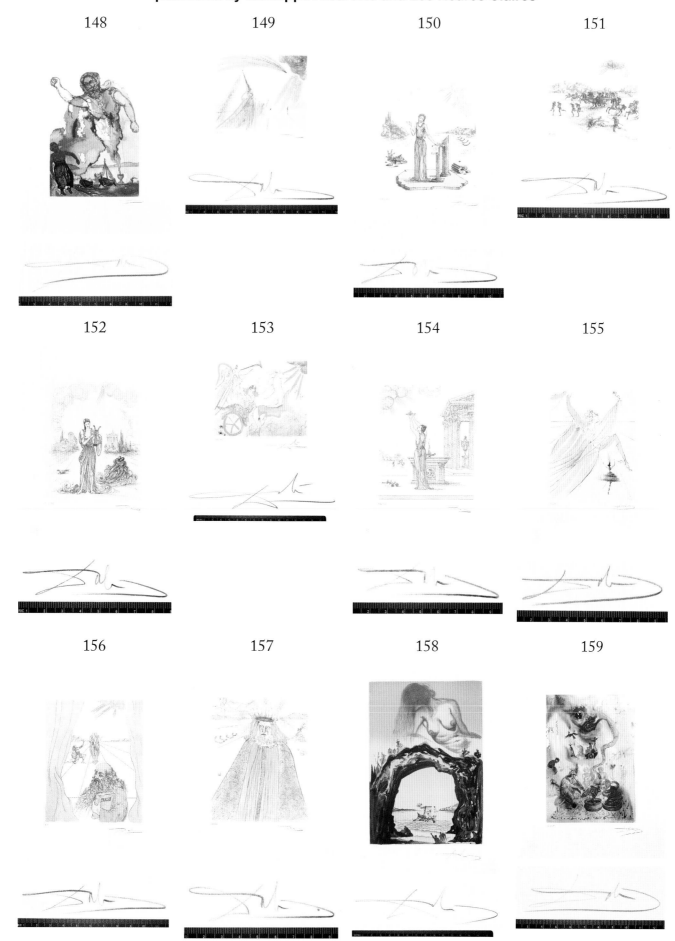

148

149

150

151

152

153

154

155

156

157

158

159

Authentic Signatures by Salvador Dalí on Works from Editions
published by Giuseppe Albaretto and Les Heures Claires

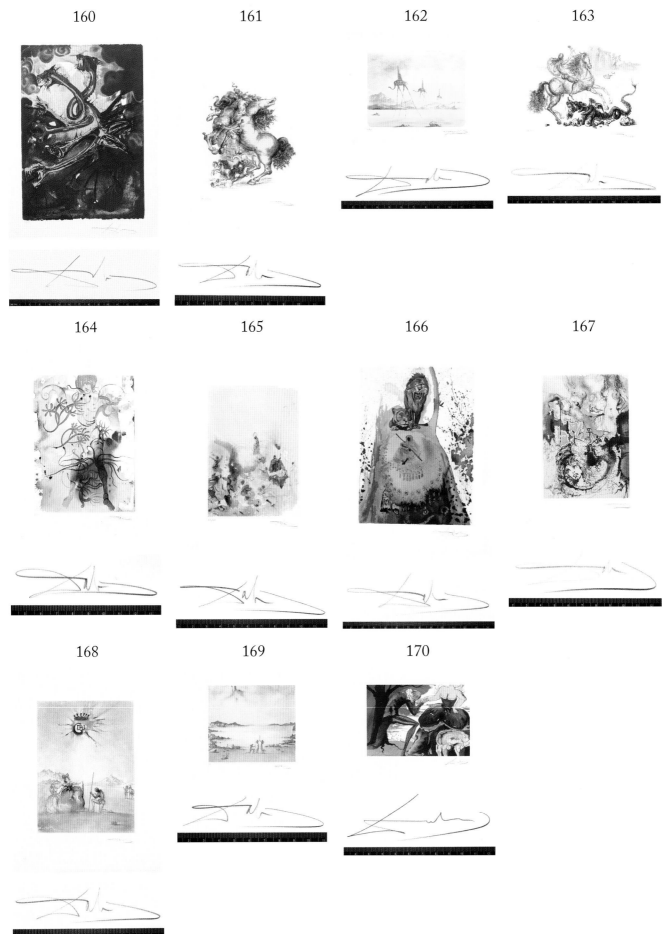

160

161

162

163

164

165

166

167

168

169

170

DOCUMENTATION

THE DIVINE COMEDY, SACRED BIBLE AND 28 EDITIONS PUBLISHED
BY LES HEURES CLAIRES, PARIS UNDER AGREEMENTS BETWEEN
GIUSEPPE ALBARETTO AND DALÍ

Documentation regarding the Divine Comedy

Dalí certificate of authentic hand signatures for a Divine Comedy suite signed for Giuseppe Albaretto

HOTEL MEURICE
228, Rue de Rivoli
75001 PARIS

Je Soussigné Mâitre Salvador Dali

certifie par la presente d'avoir signé
par ma main au Docteur Giuseppe Albaretto
de Turin,un lot de trois series de 100
illustrations de la "DIVINE COMEDIE"
Réalisées en gravure sur bois.

·Fait à Paris le 24 Novembre 1974

Mâitre SALVADOR DALI

Translation:

Hotel Meurice
228, Rue de Rivoli
75001 Paris

I the undersigned Master Salvador Dalí

Hereby certify to have hand-signed for Doctor Giuseppe Albaretto of Turino, three series of 100 wood engravings of the "DIVINE COMEDY" produced in wood engraving.

Done in Paris, November 24, 1974

Master Salvador Dalí

/signed/

Certificate of Jean Estrade, Les Heures Claires, for a hand-signed Divine Comedy suite

ÉDITIONS D'ART

LES HEURES CLAIRES

19, RUE BONAPARTE - PARIS 6ᵉ - TÉLÉPHONE :

329-37-50

CERTIFICAT

Je soussigné Jean ESTRADE, Président Directeur Général des "Editions d'Art les Heures Claires" éditeur et réalisateur de l'édition de "La Divine Comédie" illustrée par Salvador Dali, certifie que les 100 illustrations de cette édition contresignées par moi au crayon au verso, portent au recto, la signature originale de Salvador Dali.

La première illustration de cette série est enrichie d'un dessin original du maître.

Certificat fait à Paris le 5 Avril 1979

J. ESTRADE

Jean ESTRADE

Société Anonyme : Capital 280.000 Frs - R. C. Seine 57 B 13.211 - C. C. P. Paris 5290-61

Translation:

CERTIFICATE

I the undersigned Jean ESTRADE, President General Director of "Editions d'Art Les Heures Claires" editor and publisher of the edition of "The Divine Comedy" illustrated by Salvador Dalí, certify that the 100 illustrations of this edition countersigned by me in pencil on the verso,contains the authentic signature of Salvador Dalí on the recto.

The first illustration of this series is enriched with an original drawing by the master.

Certificate done in Paris April 5, 1979

/signed/

J. ESTRADE

318

Certificate of Jean Estrade and Daniel David, Les Heures Claires, for a hand signed Divine Comedy suite

Translation: ATTESTATION

We the undersigned, Jean Estrade and Daniel David, respectively founding president and Director of Editions d'Art Les Heures Claires attest to the sale :

To GPL Promotions/ PASS 220 Madison Avenue New York USA
The following piece:

1 collection no. 4648 of the Divine Comedy by Dante, illustrated by Salvador Dalí, comprised of 6 volumes of sheets, including the text and 100 illustrations.
The 100 illustrations bear the original signature of Salvador Dalí lower right and are counter signed on the back by Jean Estrade.
This collection edited by Les Editions d'Art Les Heures Claires was repurchased from one of our clients.

Done in Paris January 7, 2005

/signed/

Jean ESTRADE   Daniel DAVID
President and one of the founders   Director
of Les Heures Claires, Paris

Letter from Marc Ways regarding Dalí's hand-signing prints for him

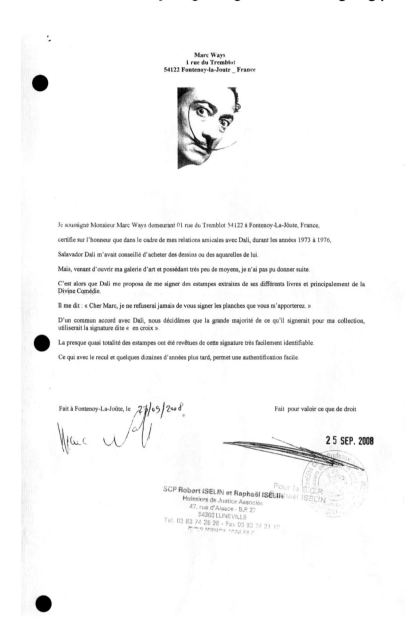

Translation:

I the undersigned Mr. Marc Ways living at 1 Rue de Tremblot 54 122, Fontenay, France, solemnly certify that as a result of my amicable relationship with Dalí, during the years 1973 to 1976, Salvador Dalí recommended that I purchase some drawings and watercolors from him. But, having just opened my art gallery and having little financial means I was unable to.

It was then that Dalí proposed that he would hand-sign some engravings from his different books, mainly the Divine Comedie (the Divine Comedy).

He told me, "Dear Marc, I would never refuse to sign the plates which you bring to me."

In agreement with Dalí, we decided that the majority of what he would sign for me would use the signature referred to as "*en croix*" (in the shape of a cross).

Almost all of these engravings carried this very easily identifiable signature.

In hindsight and several dozen years later, this allows easy certification.

/signed/

JUSTIFICATION DU TIRAGE

15 EXEMPLAIRES SUR VÉLIN PUR CHIFFON DE RIVES
auxquels on a ajouté par volume : un cuivre encré - une suite
du trait gravé sur cuivre - une suite en couleurs des illustrations -
une décomposition des couleurs d'une illustration.
Numérotés de 1 à 15

150 EXEMPLAIRES SUR VÉLIN PUR CHIFFON DE RIVES
auxquels on a ajouté : une suite du trait gravé sur cuivre - une
suite en couleurs des illustrations - une décomposition des couleurs d'une illustration.
Numérotés de 16 à 165

350 EXEMPLAIRES SUR VÉLIN PUR CHIFFON DE RIVES
auxquels on a ajouté : une suite en couleurs des illustrations - une
décomposition des couleurs d'une illustration.
Numérotés de 166 à 515

350 EXEMPLAIRES SUR VÉLIN PUR CHIFFON DE RIVES
auxquels on a ajouté une décomposition des couleurs d'une
illustration.
Numérotés de 516 à 865

3.900 EXEMPLAIRES SUR VÉLIN PUR CHIFFON DE RIVES
Numérotés de 866 à 4.765

EXEMPLAIRE
2965

JOSEPH FORET

ÉDI

LA DIVINE

ILLUSTI

SALVAD

DE 100 AÇ

GRAVÉES SUR BOI

Salvador Dali et Joseph Foret

Dans l'édition monumentale de *La Divine Comédie*, JOSEPH FORET, éditeur d'art, s'est réservé les vingt et un exemplaires de tête, numérotés de I à XXI, sur Japon nacré, enrichis d'aquarelles originales de Salvador Dali.

Un exemplaire sur Japon nacré, avec 9 aquarelles originales.
(Souscrit)
        L'exemplaire, prix : **210.000** NF ou **21** millions.

2 exemplaires sur Japon nacré, avec 6 aquarelles originales.
(Souscrits)
        L'exemplaire, prix : **150.000** NF ou **15** millions.

5 exemplaires sur Japon nacré, avec 3 aquarelles originales.
        L'exemplaire, prix : **90.000** NF ou **9** millions.

13 exemplaires sur Japon nacré, avec une aquarelle originale.
(Souscrits)
        L'exemplaire, prix : **30.000** NF ou **3** millions.

Raymond Jacquet
établissant des essais de couleurs

JOSEPH FORET, Éditeur d'Art

64. RUE LAFAYETTE, PARIS-IXe — Tél. : PRO 34-27

322

LES HEURES CLAIRES

ENT

COMÉDIE

ÉE PAR

OR DALI

UARELLES
PAR R. JACQUET

Salvador Dali et Jean Rivière

Les Editions d'Art LES HEURES CLAIRES éditent les exemplaires sur vélin pur chiffon de Rives, auxquels ont été ajoutés : soit un cuivre, soit des suites sur cuivre, soit des suites en couleurs des illustrations.

15 exemplaires sur vélin pur chiffon de Rives, avec suites et cuivre. (Souscrits)

L'exemplaire, prix : **10.800** NF ou **1.080.000** F

150 exemplaires sur vélin pur chiffon de Rives, avec une suite en couleurs, une décomposition d'une planche et une suite des illustrations gravées sur cuivre.

L'exemplaire, prix : **6.000** NF ou **600.000** F

350 exemplaires sur vélin pur chiffon de Rives, avec suite et décomposition de couleurs.

L'exemplaire, prix : **3.600** NF ou **360.000** F

350 exemplaires sur vélin pur chiffon de Rives, avec décomposition de couleurs.

L'exemplaire, prix : **2.400** NF ou **240.000** F

3.900 exemplaires sur vélin pur chiffon de Rives.

L'exemplaire, prix : **1.800** NF ou **180.000** F

Raymond Jacquet
gravant une des illustrations

Éditions d'Art LES HEURES CLAIRES

19, RUE BONAPARTE, PARIS-VIe — Tél.: DAN 54-75

Printing Specifications for the Les Heures Claires Italian edition

La presente edizione in sei volumi della Divina Commedia
con cento illustrazioni di Salvador Dali è stata stampata in tremila-
quarantaquattro esemplari. Ne sono stati impressi, sotto la direzione
del Maestro tipografo Giovanni Mardersteig, quarantaquattro esemplari nel torchio a mano dell'Officina Bodoni di Verona su carta a
tino del Giappone 'Kaji Torinoko' e tremila esemplari dalla Stamperia
Valdonega di Verona, su carta a mano dei Fratelli Magnani di Pescia.
Le incisioni e le tavole sono state eseguite a Parigi sotto la direzione
del Maestro Raymond Jacquet, su carta di Rives. La confezione
è stata eseguita dalla Legatoria Torriani di Milano.

APRILE MCMLXIV

Translated in English:

This edition, consisting of six volumes of the *Divine Comedy*,
with one hundred illustrations by Salvador Dalí, has been printed in three
thousand forty-four copies. Forty-four copies have been printed under the
supervision of Master Printer Giovanni Mardesteig, with the manual printing press,
by the Bodoni Printers in Verona on Japanese "Kaji Torinoko" refined paper, and
three thousand copies by the Valdonega Printers in Verona, on hand made paper
produced by the Magnani Brothers in Pescia.
The engravings and the tables have been produced in Paris under the direction of
Master Raymond Jacquet, on pure rag vellum paper. The binding has been made by
the Torriani Binders in Milano.

April 1964

RUBRICA DELLA TIRATURA

4 ESEMPLARI fuori commercio « ad personam » impressi nel torchio a mano dell'Officina Bodoni di Verona su carta a tino del Giappone « Kaji Torinoko », arricchiti da una seconda serie di tutte le tavole, una serie di progressive, e da una serie di illustrazioni in bianco e nero da incisioni su rame.

15 ESEMPLARI « ad personam » impressi nel torchio a mano dell'Officina Bodoni di Verona su carta a tino del Giappone « Kaji Torinoko », arricchiti da una seconda serie di tutte le tavole, una serie di progressive, una serie di illustrazioni in bianco e nero da incisioni su rame, e da un acquerello originale di Salvador Dali.

25 ESEMPLARI contraddistinti con lettere da A a Z, impressi nel torchio a mano dell'Officina Bodoni di Verona su carta a tino del Giappone « Kaji Torinoko », arricchiti da una seconda serie di tutte le tavole, una serie di progressive, e da una serie di illustrazioni in bianco e nero da incisioni su rame.

100 ESEMPLARI contraddistinti con numeri romani da I a C, impressi dalla Stamperia Valdonega di Verona su carta a mano dei Fratelli Magnani di Pescia, e arricchiti da una seconda serie di tutte le tavole.

2900 ESEMPLARI numerati da 1 a 2900, impressi dalla Stamperia Valdonega di Verona su carta a mano dei Fratelli Magnani di Pescia.

ESEMPLARE

JEAN ESTRADE

September 6, 1991 letter from Jean Estrade authorizing Park West Gallery Inc. to affix his blind-stamp

Park West Gallery, Inc.,
29469 Northwestern
Southfield, MI 48034
Its Clients,
And other interested parties

I, Jean Estrade, was formerly the Director of Les Heures Claires, 19 Les Bonaporte, Paris, France and the editor of the collection of the 101 Salvador Dali wood engravings which were created for the Divine Comedy.

The stamp affixed hereon is my official stamp:

All wood engravings of the Divine Comedy, bearing this stamp, have passed through my hand and have been authenticated directly by me.

Albert Scaglione, President of Park West Gallery, Inc., is the only person duly authorized by me to cause this stamp to be affixed to works of the Divine Comedy.

Witness:

Denise Arditti, 17 Rue Cepre, Paris, 75015, employee of Les Heures Claires and Mr. Jean Estrade, from 1971 to 1986 hereby witness this signature by Mr. Jean Estrade.	Le editor, Jean Estrade

On this 6TH day of SEPTEMBER, 1991 Le editor, Jean Estrade, known personally to me appeared before me and duly executed this document as his own free act and deed.

Notary Public

Raymond JACQUET   SALVADOR DALÍ   Jean ESTRADE
Le Graveur   *L'Editeur*

Dear Mr. Scaglione:

I hereby authorize Park West Gallery to be the exclusive agent for the sale of my collection of works of the "Divine Comedy" by Salvador Dalí.

The 101 wood engravings for the "Divine Comedy" were executed over a 14 year period from 1951 to 1964. From 1951 to 1960 Dalí painted the 101 watercolors which were used as studies for the wood engravings. From 1960 to 1964 Raymond Jacquet created the 3,000 wood blocks necessary for the complete "Divine Comedy" with the participation and final approval of Salvador Dalí for each of the 101 works.

As the director of "Les Heures Claires", 19 rue Bonaparte, Paris, France, the publishers of the "Divine Comedy", I personally supervised the destruction of the 3,000 wood blocks which were used after a single printing of the editions.

All of the works from this collection bear my stamp, "Jean Estrade, Editor".

Jean Estrade
November 20, 1992

327

Documentation regarding the Sacred Bible

**Attestation of Rafaello Aprili confirming that he witnessed the hand-signing by Dalí
of the Mastella Collection of the Sacred Bible**

DICHIARAZIONE

IL SOTTOSCRITTO SIG. RAFFAELLO APRILI, RESIDENTE A VERONA IN VIA FALCONETTO N°3, DICHIARO DI AVER ACCOMPAGNATO IL GEOM. ROBERTO MASTELLA DAL MAESTRO SALVADOR DALI', A FIGUERAS, IN SPAGNA, NEL PERIODO DAL 24/08/1979 AL 30/08/1979.
IN QUEST'OCCASIONE IL MAESTRO SALVADOR DALI' HA FIRMATO PER IL GEOM. ROBERTO MASTELLA DELLE STAMPE E DEI VOLUMI INTERI DELLA "SACRA BIBBIA", COME RINGRAZIAMENTO DEI REGALI RICEVUTI DAL GEOM. ROBERTO MASTELLA.

VERONA LI, 06/07/1999

IN FEDE
RAFFAELLO APRILI

Translation:

CERTIFICATE

THE UNDERWRITTEN MR. RAFFAELLO APRILI, RESIDENT OF VERONA IN VIA FALCONETTO NUM. 3, DECLARE TO HAVE ACCOMPANIED GEOM. ROBERTO MASTELLA TO VISIT THE MASTER SALVADOR DALI, IN FIGUERAS, SPAIN IN THE PERIOD BETWEEN 08/24/1979 AND 08/30/1979.
IN THIS OCCASION, THE MASTER SALVADOR DALI SIGNED SOME PRINTS AND WHOLE VOLUMES OF THE "SACRED BIBLE" FOR GEOM. ROBERTO MASTELLA TO THANK HIM FOR GIFTS GIVEN TO HIM BY GEOM. ROBERTO MASTELLA.

VERONA, 07/06/1999

IN WITNESS WHEREOF
RAFFAELLO APRILI
[signature]

Attestation of Mara Albaretto that her husband, Giuseppe, arranged to have Dalí sign Sacred Bible lithographs in the Mastella Collection

DR. MARA ALBARETTO BERIO
VIA MICHELE LESSONA, 13 - TEL. 011/771.02.22
10145 TORINO (ITALIA)

Torino 2/2/1999

Mi si richiede certificare di avere conosciuto, insieme a mio marito, il signor Roberto Mastella di Verona.

Sò che il signor Mastella ha acquistato, negli anni passati, alcune opere originali e grafiche di Salvador Dali, direttamente dalle mani di mio marito, dr. Albaretto.

Mi risulta inoltre che mio marito ha confermato l'autenticità della firma del Maestro Salvador Dali su tavole della Sacra Bibbia (edizione Rizzoli), personalizzate con il numero 5 e su certificazioni di volumi della Sacra Bibbia.

Confermo inoltre che mio marito, dr. Giuseppe Albaretto, ha personalmente fatto firmare dal Maestro Dali, per il signor Roberto Mastella, tavole della Sacra Bibbia nel periodo dal 1976 al 1979.

In fede.

Mara Albaretto
(Mara Albaretto)

Translation:

Torino 2/2/1999

This is to certify Mr. Roberto Mastella from Verona was well known by both myself and my husband. And that some years ago, Mr. Mastella acquired originals and graphic art works by Salvador Dalí directly from my husband, Dr. Albaretto.

I am aware that my husband has confirmed the authenticity of the signature of Master Salvador Dalí on loose sheets of the Holy Bible (Rizzoli Edition) marked with the Number 5 for certification and on the sheets contained in the full sets of the Holy Bible.

I also confirm that my husband, Dr. Giuseppe Albaretto, personally had Master Dalí sign tear sheets of the Holy Bible from 1976 till 1979 for Mr. Roberto Mastella.

To whom it may concern,

/signed/
Mara Albaretto

Attestation of Dalí that he hand-signed the Mastella collection and that the collection has been stamped with the number "5". A copy of the certificate was also authenticated by Giuseppe Albaretto

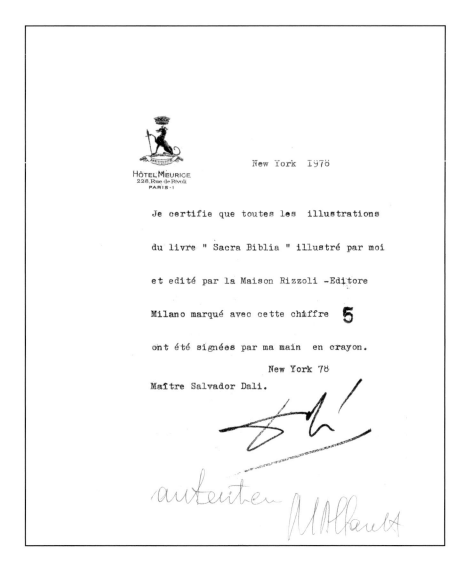

Translation:

Date 10/2/07

Translation letter: S. Dalí - New York 1978

New York 1978

I certify that all the illustrations of the: "Sacred Bible" book illustrated by me and published by the Maison Rizzoli Publisher in Milano stamped with the number 5 were signed by my hand in pencil.

New York 78

Maestro Salvador Dalí
/signed/

Dalí's comments on the Sacred Bible

Port Lligat 4.IO.I964

Estoy perfectamente de acuerdo con que la Biblia illustrada
con mis cien cuadros, de propiedad del Doctor Albaretto, sea
editada por el editor RIZZOLI segun las normas establecidas
en mi contrato con el Doctor José Albaretto.
El Doctor Albaretto deberá cuidarse que sean respetados mis
deseos conforme a dicho contrato y deberá presentarme las
pruebas de la reproducción y eventualmente las de imprenta.
Estoy seguro que la colaboración entre el Doctor Albaretto
y la Casa Rizzoli dara optimo resultado.
Por lo demás confio al Doctor Albaretto, por completo, quanto
se refiere a la propaganda, exposiciones y otras decisiones.

Translation:

Port Lligat, April 10, 1964

I completely agree that the Bible illustrated with 100 of my paintings,
property of Doctor Albaretto, be published by RIZZOLI, according
to the established clauses in my contract with Dr. Jose Albaretto.

Dr. Albaretto shall make sure that my wishes are respected in
accordance with the aforementioned contract, and shall present before
me, the proofs of reproduction and eventually, the printing proofs.

I am sure that the collaboration between Dr. Albaretto and the Rizzoli
Publishing House will bear optimum results.

As a whole, I fully trust Dr. Albaretto with every other decision
regarding all matters that have to do with advertising, exhibits and
other issues.

/Signed by hand and dated 1964 by Salvador Dali/

Certificate from a Sacred Bible volume

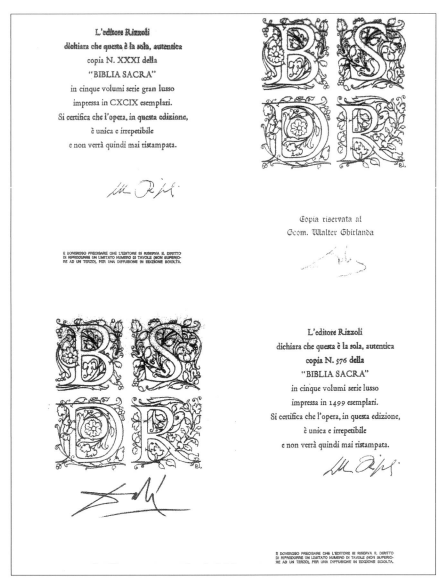

Translation:

The publisher Rizzoli
declares that this is the only one and authentic
Copy Number. XXXI of the
"BIBLIA SACRA",
in the deluxe suite including five volumes,
printed in CXCIX exemplars.
It is certified that the suite, in this edition,
is unique and inimitable
and therefore it will never be reprinted.

/signed/

/signed/

Copy reserved to
Mr. Walter Ghirlanda

/signed/

Rizzoli Publishing
declares that this Copy is the only one and
authentic Copy - Number 576 of the
"BIBLIA SACRA",
in the deluxe suite including five volumes, printed
in 1499 exemplars.
It is certified that the suite, in this edition,
is unique and inimitable
and therefore it will never be reprinted.

/signed/

Insert included in the portfolios of six loose sheets, issued by Rizzoli.

Le sei tavole presentate in questa cartella appartengono al ciclo di 105 appositamente eseguite da Salvador Dalí a illustrazione e interpretazione della Biblia Sacra, che costituisce la più recente e vasta impresa pittorica del geniale maestro catalano.

Superando l'espressione lucidamente surrealista che è più consueta nella sua opera e avvalendosi delle esperienze visionarie di cui sempre il suo spirito s'è nutrito, come della sbalorditiva abilità tecnica servita anche da una sensibilità particolarmente acuta per la materia, Dalí perviene in queste tavole a un linguaggio straordinariamente ricco, di una libertà e ampiezza di respiro a momenti epico, in una pregnanza e scioltezza di colore fluido e duttile di una mobilità e pluralità di accenti da ricondurre alla miglior vena barocca che ha tanta parte nella sua fantasia.

Una tale ricchezza di connotazioni senza precedenti posta dall'artista al servizio del suo commento visuale al sacro testo, non poteva non comportare, sul piano della riproduzione grafica, un impegno tecnico altrettanto severo, tale da conseguire il risultato del più pregevole artigianato d'arte, sia perché condizionato dall'alto livello lirico degli originali di Dalí, sia per la finezza e vastità dei mezzi impiegati al fine di ottenerne la massima fedeltà di riproduzione.

Per raggiungere un risultato così eccezionale — del quale le sei tavole qui presentate offrono un'eccellente testimonianza — si è fatto ricorso, dopo tutta una serie di prove e di esperienze, a tutte le tecniche possibili, moderne e antiche. Sullo speciale cartoncino, appositamente fabbricato per poter ricevere le molte impressioni di colore, sovrapposte l'una all'altra, le diverse tecniche coesistono, le più raffinate e sottili: a restituire intatta, nella sua smagliante ricchezza, la sontuosità materica del linguaggio cromatico che Salvador Dalí ha "inventato" sotto l'ispirazione del "Libro dei Libri".

Translation:

The six illustrations in this portfolio belong to the suite of 105 Prints illustrated by Salvador Dali as his own interpretation of the Sacred Bible, and constitute the most recent and vast pictorial achievement of the brilliant Catalan master.

Going beyond the lucid surreal expression that is most typical of his work, and taking advantage of the visionary experiences which always nurtured his spirit, as well as, of the incredible technical ability complemented by a particularly acute sensibility for the subject, Dali achieves in these illustrations a language extraordinarily rich in freedom and with a scope at time epic, in depth and motion of fluid and malleable colors of such a plurality and vitality of accents to bring back the best Baroque style that took always a big place in his imagination.

Such unprecedented richness of nuances captured by the artist to the service of his visual comment to the sacred text, it entails - on the graphic reproduction level - a technical commitment just as strong, which results in the most exquisite and artistic craftsmanship, influenced by the high lyrical level of the Dali's originals, as well as, of the excellence and amplitude of resources used in order to obtain the highest reproduction accuracy.

To reach such an exceptional result of which the six illustrations here presented are excellent examples, it was resorted to, after a series of tests and experiments, all possible modern and ancient techniques. On special cardstock specifically made to capture the multiple color impressions overlapping one another, the diverse techniques, the most refined and subtle, coexist: to restore intact in its magnificent richness, the textural sumptuousness of Salvador Dali's chromatic language he "invented" under the inspiration of "The Book of the Books".

Documentation regarding 28 Lithographs and Intaglios printed by Les Heures Claires, Paris

Design and authorization by Salvador Dalí for the Albaretto blindstamp

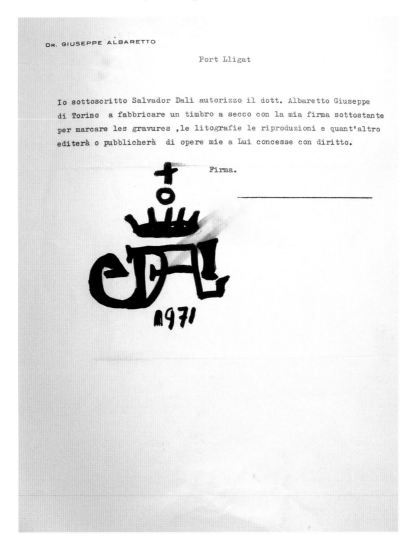

Translation:

Dr. Giuseppe Albaretto

Port Lligat

I, the undersigned Salvador Dalí, authorize Dr. Giuseppe Albaretto of Turin to manufacture an embossed stamp, bearing my signature underneath, to mark the engravings, the lithographs and the copies of what he will be reproducing and publishing of my works, for which he has been granted the copyright.

Signature:

/Hand drawing of seal including Dali's signature and date/

Document prepared by Jean Estrade of Les Heures Claires, Paris in 1985 providing details of the lithographs and intaglios that had been purchased by Les Heures Claires, Italy

Translation:

I, the undersigned, Jean Estrade, President Director General of "Les Heures Claires" Art Reproductions, 19 Rue Bonaparte. - 75006 Paris, certify to have received from Dr. Giuseppe Albaretto of Turin, on January 12, 1971, the authorization to create the works with the titles and copy numbers listed below. The prints were made in agreement with Master Salvador Dalí, with the artist's signature on each one of the copies. Dr. Giuseppe Albaretto is the owner of these works, and he holds the rights for reproduction.

Lithographs:	The Battle of Tetuan	Edition size	145
	Dulcinee	"	145
	Tuna Fishing	"	145
	Hand Kiss	"	145
	Winter	"	195
	Autumn	"	195
	Spring	"	195
	Summer	"	195
	Soft Watches	"	195
	Lions	"	195
	Elephants	"	195
	The Blue Elephant	"	195
	The Fairies	"	195
	Victory	"	195
	The Dream-like Dream	"	195
	The Siren	"	195
	The Hydras	"	195
	Aladdin's Lamp	"	195
	The Snake and the Apple	"	195
	Oriental Fantasy	"	195
	Pegasus	"	245
	Leucothea	"	245
	Sinbad the Sailor	"	245
	Elephant and rapax	"	245
	Threshold to Infinity	"	245
	Love Affairs	"	245
	Mongol Town	"	245
	Polyphemus	"	245
	Woman and Drawers	"	245
	The Harlequin	"	245
	Mayflower	"	245
	Port Alguer	"	245
	The Giant of Aladdin	"	245
	The Tree of Butterflies	"	245
	The Snake Charmer	"	245

Read and approved.
/Signed by hand Jean Estrade/

Translation:

Lithographs:			
	Orient	Edition size	245
	Homage to Dulcinee	"	245
	The Three Elephants	"	245
	Cubist Ulysses	"	245
	The Geological Horse	"	245
	The Surrealist Angelus of Millet	"	245
	Soft Watches and Butterflies	"	245
	The Metamorphosis of Soft Watches	"	245
	The Bay of Port Lligat	"	245

Original engraving plates:

	Edition Size	Arch		Japan	
Dance		Arch	145	Japan	99
Music	"	"	145	"	99
Astronomy	"	"	145	"	99
Tragedy	"	"	145	"	99
Comedy	"	"	145	"	95
History	"	"	145	"	95
Poetry of Love	"	"	145	"	95
Sacred Poetry	"	"	145	"	95
Eloquence	"	"	145	"	95
Nude from the Back	"	"	145	"	95
Tournament	"	"	245	"	145
Sea-Urchin	"	"	145	"	95
Surrealist Horses	"	"	245	"	145
Saint George and the Dragon	"	"	245	"	145
Hamlet - 10 Subjects	"	"	145 off the original.		

The etchings and the lithographs are now sold out, the surplus having been sold to the Association "Les Heures Claires" Italy. The plates, and the patterns have been destroyed, and all the reproduction rights regarding the above mentioned works are the exclusive property of Dr. Giuseppe Albaretto.

Issued in Paris on February 7, 1985.
Read and approved.
/Signed by hand Jean Estrade/

1981 Authorization by Jean Estrade for the Albaretto family to use the name of Les Heures Claires for their Italian publishing house

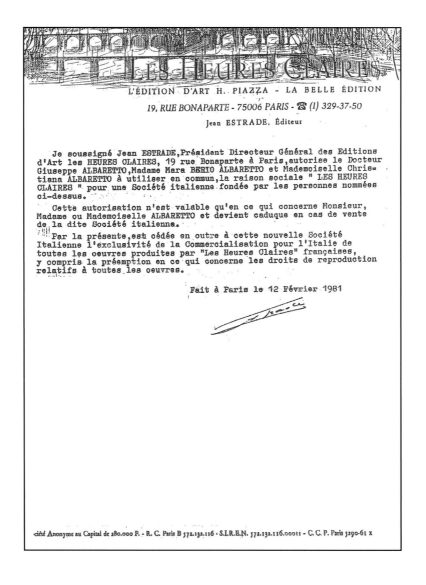

Translation:

I, the undersigned, Jean ESTRADE, President, General Director of HEURES CLAIRES Art Editions, 19 rue Bonaparte in Paris, authorize Dr. Giuseppe ALBARETTO, Mrs. Mara BERIO ALBARETTO and Miss Christiana ALBARETTO to mutually use the corporate name "LES HEURES CLAIRES" for an Italian Corporation established by the aforementioned.

This authorization is not valid unless it concerns Mr., Mrs. or Miss ALBARETTO and becomes null and void in case the aforementioned Italian Corporation is sold.

Hereby, it is ceded, in addition, to this new Italian Corporation, the Commercialization exclusivity in Italy of all the French works produced by "Les Heures Claires", inclusive of the preemption which concerns the reproduction rights of all the works.

Paris February 12, 1981

/Signed by hand by Jean Estrade/

338

1978 Affidavit of Dalí for the creation of the 68 lithographs and intaglios published by Les Heures Claires, Paris

DR. GIUSEPPE ALBARETTO

Paris 7 Novembre 1978

Je Soussigné Maître Salvador Dali, declare avoir realisées pour le docteur Albaretto - via Lessona 13 - Turin, en collaboration avec la Maison d'Editions d'Art "Les Heures Claires" - 19 rue Bonaparte - Paris, lithographies de mes oeuvres, de propriété du cocteur Albaretto, dont les titres et les tirages sont énumérés ci-dessous.
Il est bien entendu que les lithographies ont été signées par moi même.

Lithographies: La bataille de Tétouan 145 - Dulcinée 145 - La pêche au thon 145 - Le baisemain 145 - L'hiver 195 - L'automne 195 - Le printemps 195 - L'été 195 - Les montres molles 195 - Les lions 195 - Les éléphants 195 - L'éléphant bleu 195 - Lés fées 195 - La victoire 195 - Le rêve onirique 195 - La siréne 195 - Le hydres 195 - La lampe d'Aladin 195 - Le serpent e la pomme 195 - La fantasie orientale 195 - Pégase 245 - Leucothée 245 - Sindbad le marin 245 - L'éléphant et le rapax 245 - La porte de l'infinie 245 - Liaisons d'amour 245 - La ville mongole 245 - L'Arlequin 245 - Orient 245 - Montres molles et papillons 245 - La baie de Port Lligat 245 - Nu de dos 245 - Enchanteurs de serpents 245 - Mayflower 245 - Géant d'Aladin 245 - Trois éléphantins surrealistes 245 - Homage a Dulcinée 245 - La giraffe et chameau 245 -

Gravures a cuivres originaux:

Danse	Arches	145	Japon	99
Musique	Arches	145	Japon	99
Astronomie	Arches	145	Japon	99
Tragédie	Arches	145	Japon	99
Thalie	Arches	145	Japon	99
Clio	Arches	145	Japon	99
Erato	Arches	145	Japon	99
Polymnie	Arches	145	Japon	99
Calliope	Arches	145	Japon	99
Tournoi	Arches	245	Japon	145
Oursin	Arches	145	Japon	95
Les chevaux surrealistes	Arches	245	Japon	145
Saint Georges et Dragon	Arches	245	Japon	145
Hamlet 10 sujets	Arches	145	d'apres les originaux.	

Fait a Paris le 7 novembre 1978

Maître Salvador Dali

Translation:

PARIS, November 7, 1978

I, the undersigned Master Salvador Dalí, declare to have created for Dr. Albaretto, in collaboration with the Maison d'Editions D'Art "Les Heures Claires, 19 Bonaparte Street, Paris (France), lithographs of my works, with ownership rights to Dr. Albaretto, of which the titles and selections are numbered below.

It is understood that the lithographs have been signed by myself.

Lithographs: *The Battle of Tetouan* 145 - *Dulcinee* 145 - *Tuna Fishing* 145 - *The Hand Kiss* 145 - *Winter* 195 - *Autumn* 195 - *Spring* 195 - *Summer* 195 - *Soft Watches* 195 - *The Lions* 195 - *The Elephants* 195 - *The Blue Elephant* 195 - *The Fairies* 195 - *Victory* 195 - *The Dream-like Dream* 195 - *The Siren* 195 - *The Hydras* 195 - *The Lamp of Aladdin* 195 - *The Snake and the Apple* 195 - *Oriental Fantasy* 195 - *Pegasus* 245 - *Leucothea* 245 - *Sinbad the Sailor* 245 - *The Elephant and the Rapax* 245 - *The Threshold Infinity* 245 - *Love Affairs* 245 - *The Mongol Village* 245 - *The Harlequin* 245 - *Orient* 245 - *Soft Watches and Butterflies* 245 - *The Bay of Port Lligat* 245 - *The Nude from Back* 245 - *The Snake Charmers* 245 - *Mayflower* 245 - *Aladdin's Giant* 245 - *Three Surrealist Elephants* 245 - *Homage to Dulcinee* 245 - *The Giraffe and Camel* 245

Original Engravings:

Dance	Arches 145	Japon 99
Music	Arches 145	Japon 99
Astronomy	Arches 145	Japon 99
Tragedy	Arches 145	Japon 99
Comedy	Arches 145	Japon 99
History	Arches 145	Japon 99
Poetry of Love	Arches 145	Japon 99
Sacred Poetry	Arches 145	Japon 99
Eloquence	Arches 145	Japon 99
Tournament	Arches 145	Japon 99
Sea Urchin	Arches 145	Japon 99
The Surrealist Horses	Arches 145	Japon 99
Saint George and the Dragon	Arches 145	Japon 99
Hamlet 10 subjects	Arches 145 after the originals	

Paris, November 7, 1978
Master Salvador Dalí
/Signed by hand with the full signature of Salvador Dalí/

THE SALVADOR DALI ARCHIVES

2025 29TH STREET ASTORIA, NEW YORK 11105
PHONE & FAX (718) 274-0407
e-mail dallarch ⌐ nyc.pipeline.com
internet http://dallarchives.com

Archives
Registry
Catalog

ALBERT FIELD
ARCHIVIST

PERIZIA

Io sottoscritto Albert Field, Esperto d'Arte e titolare

de "The Salvador Dali Archives", con questa mia dichiarazione,

affermo e certifico che le seguenti opere grafiche di

Salvador Dali sono autentiche e firmate dallo stesso

Maestro, editate dalla società Les Heures Claires.

Estate	Autunno	Inverno
Primavera	Leoni	Vittoria
Baciamano	Sindbad il marinaio	Sirene
Idre	Serpente e la mela	Leucotea
Fate	Elefanti	Pegaso
Sogno onirico	Elefantini bleu	Danseuses
Nu de dos	Terpsicore	Thalia
Clio	Melpomene	Euterpe
Uranie	Erato	Calliope
Polymnie	Ville Mongole	Oursin
Cavalli surrealisti	Oriente	Baia di Port Lligat
Elefante e rapax	Homage a Ducinea	Torneo
San Giorgio e drago	Battaglia di Tetouan	Pesca dei tonni
Lampada d'Aladino	Fantasia orientale	Porta dell'infinito
Liaisons d'amour	Tre elefanti surrealisti	Gigante d'Aladino
Mayflower	Incantatore di serpenti	Giraffa e Cammello
Orologi Molli	Montres molles papillons	

Le dieci gravures appartenenti all'opera Hamlet.

Ho preso visione di vari documenti originale di Salvador DALI e
dell'editore francese che certificano l'avvenuta realizzazione
di dette opere grafiche.

Di tutto ciò ho conoscenea da molti anni per la lunga amicizia
che mi lega alla famiglia Albaretto.

In fede.

Albert Field

Albert Field

Translation: on page 341

Albert Field authentication of lithographs and intaglios published by Les Heures Claires, Paris, under rights granted by Salvador Dalí to Giuseppe Albaretto (Translation)

Translation:

THE SALVADOR DALI ARCHIVES
2025 29th Street Astoria, New York 11105
PHONE & FAX (718) 274-0407
email daliarch@nyc.pipeline.com
internet http:// daliarchives.com

Archives
Registry
Catalog

ALBERT FIELD
ARCHIVIST

EXPERT REPORT

The underwritten Albert Field, Art Expert and owner of

the "Salvador Dalí Archives", with this document

certifies and affirms that the following works of art by

Salvador Dalí are authentic and have been signed by the

Master himself, and printed by the LES HEURES CLAIRES Company.

Summer	Autumn	Winter
Spring	Lions	Victory
Hand Kiss	Sinbad the Sailor	Siren
The Hydras	The Snake and the Apple	Leucothea
Fairies	Elephants	Pegasus
Dream-like Dream	The Blue Elephant	Dancers
Nude From Back	Dance	Comedy
History	Tragedy	Music
Astronomy	Poetry of Love	Eloquence
Sacred Poetry	Mongolian Town	The Sea Urchin
Surrealistic Horses	The Orient	The Bay of Port Lligat
Elephant and rapax	Homage to Dulcinee	Tournament
Saint George and the Dragon	Battle of Tetuan	Tuna Fishing
Aladdin's Lamp	Oriental Fantasy	Threshold to Infinity
Love Affairs	Three Surrealistic Elephants	Aladdin's Giant
Mayflower	The Snake Charmer	Giraffe and Camel
Soft Watches	Soft Watches and Butterflies	

The ten ENGRAVINGS belonging to the Hamlet work.

I have examined the true original documents by Salvador Dalí and
the French editor certifying that the above mentioned graphic works
are originals.

I have had direct knowledge of all the above due to the long time
friendship that binds me to the Albaretto family.

In trust.

/Signed by hand by Albert Field/
Albert Field

Translation: from page 340

THE SALVADOR DALI ARCHIVES

2025 29TH STREET ASTORIA, NEW YORK 11105
PHONE & FAX (718) 274-0407
e-mail daliarch@nyc.pipeline.com
internet http://daliarchives.com

Archives
Registry
Catalog

ALBERT FIELD
ARCHIVIST

3 September 96

Giuseppe and Mara Albaretto
via Lessona 13
10143 Torino Italia

Dear Friends,

Here is s leather-bound copy of my catalog of the graphic
works of Salvador Dalí.

Some of the listings of your estampes are not correct,
because I did not have accurate information from you
about them.

Corrections will be made as soon as I have the complete
information. These will be published in the Collectors
Newsletter, and perhaps as a separate supplement.

Many thanks for the postcard from San Remo.

I am sorry to hear of Mara's injury. I hope you are
back in good health very soon.

Albert

* Dr. Albaretto died in 1997

28 Lithographs and Intaglios printed by Les Heures Claires
Bon A Tirer Proofs

Before publishing the Les Heures Claires, Paris editions, Dalí provided a signature on a "bon a tirer" (good to pull) proof showing that he was satisfied with the proofing process and signifying his approval for the printing of the edition.

The Siren

The Three Elephants

The Hand Kiss

28 Lithographs and Intaglios printed by Les Heures Claires
Bon A Tirer Proofs

Homage to Dulcinee

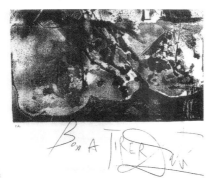

The Snake and the Apple

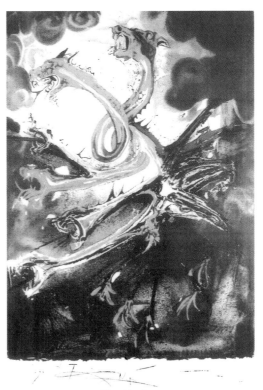

The Hydras

The Surrealist Horses

The Dream-like Dream

The Snake Charmer

The Lions

28 Lithographs and Intaglios printed by Les Heures Claires
Bon A Tirer Proofs

The Bay of Port Lligat

Love Affairs

Mayflower

Soft Watches and Butterflies

Orient

28 Lithographs and Intaglios printed by Les Heures Claires
Bon A Tirer Proofs

Victory

St. Georges and the Dragon

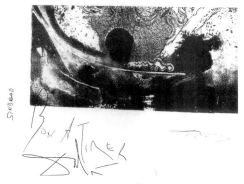

Sinbad the Sailor

History

Aladdin's Giant

28 Lithographs and Intaglios printed by Les Heures Claires
Bon A Tirer Proofs

Eloquence

Poetry of Love

Music

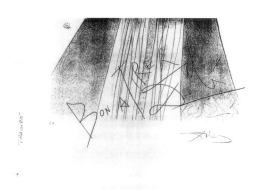

Tragedy

Sacred Poetry

Dance

Comedy

Astronomy

DALÍ GRAPHICS CATALOGS

The Michler and Lopsinger Catalog

The first volume of the *Salvador Dalí Catalog Raisonné of Etchings and Mixed-Media Prints 1924-1980* was edited by Ralf Michler and Lutz Lopsinger and published in 1994 by Prestel-Verlag, Munich. The second volume *Catalog Raisonné of Prints II, Lithographs and Wood Engravings 1956-1980* was published in 1995. Volume I included research from Charles Sahli's *Salvador Dalí—257 Editions Originales 1964-1985* published by J.P. Schneider.

These catalogs, which preceded the publication of Albert Field's catalog, generally provide more detailed information than the Field catalog which was published in one volume with a single printing in 1996. The M/L catalog information is presented in an organized and clear manner. Numerous works are identified therein as fakes or bearing forged signatures. The Field catalog on the other hand documents certain works as fake or bearing forged signatures, but the two catalogs are not in complete agreement in this regard.

In this book, we recognize the existence of numerous fakes of Dalí prints, but do not deal with the difference between the two catalogs regarding fakes. We limit our work to the subjects of this book and state that there are no known forgeries of the etchings of *Les Chants de Maldoror,* the lithographs of the *Sacred Bible* or the wood engravings of *The Divine Comedy.*

Both the Field catalog and the M/L catalog were incomplete. There are documented hand-signed Dalí graphic editions which were not included. Both of the catalogs were printed in single editions without any updates or addenda.

Unfortunately, the M/L catalog must forever live under the cloud of its author. Michler was charged and convicted on 108 counts for forging Dalí prints from 2001-2004 and sentenced to three years and nine months in prison in 2006. However, in spite of this, the M/L catalog remains widely in use by galleries, auction houses and museums as one of only two (until now) resources available for researching Dalí graphic works.

The Divine Comedy wood engravings (M/L 1039-1138) are referenced as 'Edition for Forêt' and 'Edition for Les Heures Claires'. In contrast to Field's catalog which identifies only two images in the six volume suites with text as having signatures in the blocks, and states, "a print without a printed signature is from the book edition," the M/L catalog contains the following accurate text: "With few exceptions all editions (a) to (i) (all Editions for Les Heures Claires, including the book editions) bear engraved signatures in the design itself." With reference to hand-signed Divine Comedy suites it incorrectly includes the following text: "Only a few of the prints were hand-signed for friends and associates. Editions (j) and (k) (Orangerie-Reinz editions) bear no engraved signatures but were hand-signed by Dalí in crayon." There are substantially more than "a few of the prints" signed by Salvador Dalí which have been documented by eye-witnesses to the signatures, including Jean Estrade and Giuseppe Albaretto who had significant relationships with Salvador Dalí, and former gallery owner Marc Ways who had a personal relationship with Dalí and worked closely with him.

The Albert Field Catalog

The Albert Field catalog was something that Dalí, Reynolds Morse and the Dalí art world looked forward to seeing published. Sadly, Dalí died seven years before Albert Field was able to publish it. Albert Field and the art world looked forward to Field's planned revisions to the first edition. Unfortunately, as a result of his death in 2003, those revisions, if completed, were never published.

In *Dalí Illustrator*, through the extensive documentation contained in the archives of Les Heures Claires, the publisher of *The Divine Comedy* and the *Albaretto Editions*, we are able to accurately add to the body of knowledge in both the Field catalog and the M/L catalog regarding *The Divine Comedy*, authentic signatures, annotations and other related information.

Jean Estrade (left), Salvador Dalí (center) and Joseph Forêt (right) discuss a work at the installation of *The Divine Comedy* inaugural exhibition.

There are numerous authentic Dalí hand signatures in black pencil on wood engravings of *The Divine Comedy* which do not contain "signatures in the block," where Dalí's signing was witnessed by the editor of *The Divine Comedy*, Jean Estrade and by Dr. Giuseppe Albaretto. Examples of these hand-signed wood engravings are contained in the archives of Les Heures Claires, Paris. When the Field catalog was published in 2003 Field was not aware of these Dali signatures and as a result the Field catalog is inaccurate regarding the statement: "A print without a printed signature within the image is from the book editions. Since Dalí did not sign any of these prints in black pencil, a pencil signature on one must be a 'forgery.'"

Most six volume sets of *The Divine Comedy* contain various numbers of images with "signatures in the block." Examples are contained in the archives of Les Heures Claires, Paris. When Les Heures Claires began to release volumes of *The Divine Comedy* wood engravings to collectors who had subscribed to purchasing the complete suites with text, the first two volumes comprised the Paradise wood engravings with text that did not have block signatures (except Paradise 1, which had a block signature).

After release of these first volumes, Les Heures Claires received numerous requests from collectors to add printed signatures to the individual illustrations. Responding to this demand from collectors, in 1963 Les Heures Claires applied block signatures to the wood engravings where the trimming had not yet been completed (due to the complex printing and registration process involved, another block could not be added to trimmed examples). As a result, suites assembled and released for sale after 1963 were assembled in a random manner and contained examples with and without signatures in the block. The Field catalog incorrectly states that: "the six volume set contains only two of the engravings with 'signatures in the block.'"

Fifty-nine different block signatures were used. The signatures were added at different times to the remaining inventory of *Divine Comedy* wood engravings. Fifty-two of the images have the same block signature on each image. Seven images have two different block signatures for the same image. The chart on page 184 provides a quick reference to *The Divine Comedy* block signatures. The block signatures are illustrated on pages 185-197.

After 1964, Les Heures Claires released three-volume sets of the illustrations only (without text) and each image contained a block signature. The Field catalog accurately reflects this information. The archives of Les Heures Claires also provided the information that there were 950 full sets of *The Divine Comedy* with each engraving containing a "signature in the block."

The Field catalog is somewhat inconsistent in the description of *Divine Comedy* block signatures. It refers to them variously as a, "boxed signature in color," "plate-signed" and a "printed signature within the image." While there is a distinction in the way the block signature appears, in that since some of the block signatures contain a box around them and some do not, there is essentially no difference between "plate-signed" and a "printed signature within the image." The underling characteristic of all of them is that they are signed in the block.

The Field catalog accurately shows the Jean Estrade blind-stamp, but does not state how or why the stamp was applied to certain *Divine Comedy* engravings. Park West Gallery of Southfield Michigan, in 1992, purchased almost all of the remaining stock of *Divine Comedy* wood engravings from Les Heures Claires, Paris. The blind-stamp was created by Jean Estrade for Park West Gallery as part of this purchase so that only authentic engravings from *The Divine Comedy* would bear this stamp. Estrade and Les Heures Claires gave the rights to Park West Gallery to apply the blind-stamp to authentic engravings from *The Divine Comedy* as part of this transaction. All engravings bearing this stamp will have passed through the hands of Jean Estrade as editor, Les Heures Claires as publisher and printer, and Park West Gallery, providing collectors with a clear provenance for these engravings.

Albert Field was extremely dedicated to the mission of archiving the graphic works of Dalí. Mr. Field with the cooperation of his then assistant Frank Hunter did an exceptional job of creating this first catalog. The documents, which were the basis of the catalog, remain intact in The Salvador Dalí Archives. Frank Hunter, who worked alongside Albert Field for many years, is the current director of The Salvador Dalí Archives and continues to be a highly respected resource for Dalí studies and authentication.

1991 Declaration of Jean Estrade for his blind-stamp.

Estrade Blindstamp.

1992 Authorization of U.S. gallery, Park West Gallery, to be the exclusive agent of Jean Estrade's *Divine Comedy* collection.

WHO WAS SALVADOR DALÍ?

HISTORY OF A LAST WILL AND TESTAMENT

During his life, Dalí drew up seven different wills and testaments. What was thought to be his Last Will and Testament was the one that coincided with the construction of the Gala Salvador Dalí Foundation in Figueres, duly signed in Cadaqués in front of a notary from Llançà, Mr. Ramon Coll Figa, on December 12, 1980. Prior to that, Dalí had dictated a Last Will and Testament to Mr. Raimundo Negre Balet, a notary in Figueres, on three occasions, namely on November 12, 1954, December 3, 1959 and November 8, 1960. He had also drawn up Last Wills and Testaments with the notary, Mr. José Gómez de la Serra on June 1, 1974 and on August 17, 1976, after which he signed the above mentioned Last Will and Testament which was thought to be his Last Will and Testament on December 12, 1980. However, on September 20, 1982, following the death of Gala in June, Dalí, likely unknowingly if at all, signed a Last Will and Testament in Púbol in front of the notary of La Bisbal de l'Empordà, Mr. José María Foncillas Casaus.

The will and testament drawn up in 1980 was prepared by Dalí and Gala together in conjunction with the notary Mr. Ramon Coll Figa, and two originals were signed at the same time. This will bequeathed all personal belongings to the Spanish State and to the Catalan people through the Generalitat of Catalonia in equal parts. In the second clause, Dalí explains in writing: "On my death, I bequeath half of all my artistic and pictorial art (irrelevant of the nature) to the Spanish State, and the other half also without exception to the people of Catalonia through the Generalitat of Catalonia or the body which represents it." Mr. Jaime Teno Junca and Mr. Tomás Estévez Andres, both then residing in Llançà, signed as witnesses.

Once the text was read to the couple by the notary, to his surprise as well as to the two witnesses, Dalí asked to add two extra points, so there is written proof of the following: "1) I recommend that Generalitat of Catalonia takes into account the special love I have for my Museum of Figueres; 2) I expressly declare that since I have never had any secretary or other person that I validly trust..." This is followed by the signatures of the two witnesses and the notary. On the same day and at the same time, Gala signed a parallel testament in Cadaqués, in front of the same notary and the same witnesses.

In June 1982, Gala died, and on the following September 20, associates of Dalí claimed that Dalí signed a new testament under circumstances which cloud the legality of the document. Dalí had been living in the Púbol castle since the death of Gala and was suffering from a severe progressive deterioration of his physical and mental faculties. Due to this fact, very few people were able to approach him as he could no longer make public appearances, not even for the new constitution of the Theatre Museum Foundation when it became private. The privatization of the Foundation drew protests from many artists and intellectuals who viewed this change as a maneuver on the part of some people to control the work of Dalí after his death.

Every Wednesday afternoon, associates of Dalí would visit him, and often during this time have documents for Dalí to sign. Dalí signed without reading the contents of the documents he was signing. He would be given reasons for signing such as: "the document was the agreement for the anthological exhibition of Madrid and Barcelona; or, *The 400 Works by Dalí Exhibition*, which allowed the works from the retrospective exhibition at the Beaubourg in Paris to be kept in Geneva; or, for the works from New York, which did not have an inventory, to enter the country." The King of Spain bestowed the title of Marquis of Dalí and Púbol, when in reality Dalí's focus was mainly on Port Lligat.

On September 20, 1982, at a quarter past six in the afternoon before the notary of La Bisbal, Mr. José María Foncillas, Dalí signed a new will and testament by which he named the Spanish state as the heir to all his property and goods, rights and artistic creations with the duty of conserving, divulging and protecting his works of art. Two days later, Mr. Joaquín Chicot Cebrià and Mr. Narciso Vila Vila were asked to sign as witnesses.

This will and testament had been typed by Miguel Domenech, a Madrid lawyer who was one of the three administrators of the Dalí Foundation. Domenech's approach had always been that of accommodating those whom he thought could protect or help him. Dalí's heritage was considered 'a matter of the state' and because of this, once more, the centralism that characterized the cultural policy of the Spanish state adapted itself perfectly to the maneuver of changing the will and testament. We will never know whether Dalí was conscious of this change.

On his death, representatives from the magazine *Cambio 16* offered me a considerable sum of money if I could get them a copy of the Last Will and Testament. I told them they could get it if they offered that sum of money to the lawyer Miguel Domenech. Effectively, Domenech sent them the text he had drawn up of the Last Will and Testament by fax – you can see his name and number at the head of the fax – and consequently, logically, *Cambio 16* published it. What they did not know was that the notary of La Bisbal, Mr. Foncillas, had already made 11 amendments to that Last Will and Testament. Therefore what they published did not include any of the corrections. For example, in the new text where Domenech said "of Catalan civil nationality," Mr. Foncillas had put "of Catalan civil regionalism," or the addition of the identity numbers of the new signatories as witnesses to these changes.

The surprise was even greater when, after the date of the Last Will and Testament, the president of Catalonia and the Central Judicial Services of the Catalan Government received letters signed by the lawyer Miguel Domenech in which he stated in writing: "The destiny of this future heritage as decided by S. Dalí in a notarial will and its addressees, and according to his repeated public declarations, are the Spanish State and the Generalitat of Catalonia." The letter addressed to the Honorable Jordi Pujol, dated Madrid, April 14, 1986 states: "The decision of Mr. Dalí to leave his artistic heritage, his cultural legacy and the rest of his assets is public and notarial; this is what he has stated on many occasions to the media, and it is reflected in the instructions of his Last Will and Testament."

Another conflicting letter by Domenech was sent to the Judicial Department of the Government of Catalonia, dated Madrid, April 9, 1986 stating that the Spanish state was the only heir. In these letters written five days apart, it is clear that Domenech was inconsistent regarding Dalí's wishes to leave his heritage both to the Spanish state and the Generalitat of Catalonia. Independently of Domenech's written statement that Dalí wished his art to be shared by both the Spanish state and the Generalitat of Catalonia, this Last Will and Testament (which it is highly likely Dalí was never aware of) bequeathed all of Dalí's art to the Spanish state.

When the Last Will and Testament was made public a few days after the death of Dalí, President Pujol appointed a committee to pursue what had happened with this changing of wills. This committee was formed by the Honorable Mr. Max Canher, former advisor of culture and deputy of the Catalonian Parliament; Mr. Ramon Maria Llevadot, the general manager of the Judicial Department of Central Services of the Government of Catalonia; Mr. Antonio Perramon, the general director of the National Heritage of the Government of Catalonia; Josep A. Blázquez, assistant general manager of Property Heritage; as secretary, Mr. Lluís Inglada, consultant of successions of the Government of Catalonia, and myself Eduard Fornés, publisher and confidant of Dalí.

In the report of the committee, the first thing analyzed was a decree in the execution of Gala's will dated April 21, 1983, whereby the generalitat cedes the rights and assets for Dalí art in favor of Dalí. This decree had the intention of protecting any works of Dalí art which might be out of Spain and ensure their return.

Two members of the committee interviewed over 40 people – among them Cecile Eluard (Gala's daughter) – as well as witnesses to the Last Will and Testament including Mr. Joaquín Chicot Cebrià, who stated that he was offered a contract for life in exchange for his signature. We also interviewed family members, secretaries, etc., connected to Dalí in order to discover their knowledge of the Last Will and Testament of Dalí.

The committee provided all the documentation it gathered to the notary, Mr. Josep Maria Puig Salellas, who presented a report. In his report, he stated, after having taken into consideration different judgements based on jurisprudence on the interpretation of a will and testament and the last will, that there are contradictions between the contents of the will of Dalí and the texts signed by him. Salellas declared that in a text signed by Dalí, Dalí declared his wishes that at least part of his works be at the Museum in Figueres.

On September 23, 1983, once the will and testament after the death of Gala had been signed, the new Foundation was created (from public to private): the latter was created to "promote, foster, divulge, give prestige to, protect and defend... the artistic, cultural and intellectual work" of the founder.

Even if one accepts that the Spanish state was the only heir, its obligation is to comply with the will of the testator as declared in multiple texts and manuscripts, as well as in the minutes of the meetings of the Patrons of the Foundation, where Dalí mentions concrete works and their placing at the Museum of Figueres. However, works have been moved to the National Museum Centro Reina Sofia in Madrid without respect to the expressed written wishes of the artist.

The following are but two examples of the Spanish state not following the wishes of Dalí. The records show that in 1984 Dalí directed that the painting *The Great Masturbator* be exhibited in the Sala de Pescaderias (Fishmonger's Room) of the Theater-Museum. The records show that on May 7, 1987 (preserved in the minutes of the artistic commission), Dalí expressed his wishes in writing that *The Invisible Man* and *Imperial Monument to the Child-Woman* be exhibited facing each other in the Sala del Tesoro (Treasure Room). Why are these works of art at the National Museum Centro Reina Sofia of Madrid, not hanging where or how Dalí requested? The unintended consequence is that many of the works at the Museum of Figueres are cataloged as belonging to the National Museum Centro Reina Sofia of Madrid on deposit to the Theatre Museum Dalí of Figueres when they travel to exhibitions, leaving no assurance that the works will even be returned to the Museum of Figueres as Dalí wished.

On February 6, 1989 and January 29, 1990, Mr. Marià Lorca i Bard, the mayor of Figueres who is also a member of the Gala-Salvador Dalí Foundation, sent letters to the Minister of Culture of Spain, Mr. Jorge Semprún y Maura, stating the need of the presence of the foundation in the execution of the Last Will and Testament of Dalí. These letters were to no avail.

The following are excerpts from those letters: "In my capacity as a member of the patronage of the Gala-Salvador Dalí Foundation, I am addressing you in your dual capacity as receiver and as trustee of the will and testament of the Master Dalí of the Gala-Salvador Dalí Foundation, on behalf of the Central Government of the Spanish State, to vindicate the convenience of co-protagonism of said Foundation in the execution of the Dalínian will..." (February 6, 1989) "...c) that the city of Figueres be the Dalínian Mecca as Dalí himself expounded in the written public preamble of the constitution of the Foundation when he pointed out that: 'it has always been my intention and my express wish to convert Figueres, the city of my birth and to which I feel so deeply attached, into a cultural center and museum of Spain and a world Mecca.'" (January 29, 1990).

On February 3, 1990, Mr. Marià Lorca, the mayor of Figueres, summoned a plenary meeting of the City Council of Figueres to discuss certain decisions taken by the Spanish state where the wishes of Dalí were not respected. At the meeting, the mayor presented a report stating that the Gala-Salvador Dalí Foundation was excluded in the execution of the Last Will and Testament of Dalí and the report also went into detail regarding incidents where Dalí's wishes had not been respected.

The City Council, with the support of the mayor, then commenced with legal actions in order to enforce the wishes that Dalí had declared regarding his art. As a result of this action, some work stayed in the Figures museum, but these works still are only on deposit and remain the property of the Reina Sophia Museum in Madrid. This was not the wish of Dalí.

WHO WAS SALVADOR DALÍ?

Much has been written about Dalí and while the eulogies about Dalí have multiplied, so have the slander and attacks on his reputation. But who, in fact, was Salvador Dalí?

There is no doubt that he was an artistic genius, a multifaceted person with an amazing creative capacity in multiple areas, and at the extreme upper echelon of the entire 20th century art world. He was constantly in the public eye and the subject of abundant praise. Despite everything that has been published, and even to those who best knew him, there are many gray areas that cause us to see Dalí as an enigma and prevent us from being capable of answering the very questions we raise. The visible Dalí is Dalí the painter, illustrator, writer, lecturer, sculptor, filmmaker, actor, designer, choreographer, publicist, connoisseur of the history of art, self-taught, avid reader, studious learner, etc.

Behind the exterior image lies the man. The man who, I believe, was always searching to find himself in the contradictory circumstances in which he lived and as a result, adopted different and contradictory positions which he then had to justify to himself. This can be evidenced in his book *Secret Life*. On July 30, 1940 in Caresse Crosby's house, in Hampton Manor, New York, he finished writing his *Secret Life*, where he manipulates facts and judgments to justify his point of view. This supposed autobiography is in reality a part of his continuous search to adapt and justify his contradictory and often bizarre positions.

On a first analysis of the book, where reality is mixed with fiction, we are allowed to follow a series of real events lived during his first 36 years where he had to adopt an attitude and decide who he was: Dalí must face the rejection of Gala by his family, and the tentative reconciliation with his father in June 1940. He has gone through the break up with André Breton and the Surrealist movement to which he had given himself wholeheartedly. It was in fact as a result of this very Surrealist moment that Dalí gained international recognition and consequentially was forced to take a stand as he states: " The only difference between me and the Surrealists is that I am a Surrealist." He suffered through the collapse of the world of his youth, both in his school period in Figueres as well as in Madrid, ending with the Spanish civil war, the assassination (or execution) of García Lorca, and the internal strife that divided his native land of Catalonia which was repressed and sanctioned because of the Franco regime.

In Paris, he identifies with the Surrealist movement, but has to escape to America due to the dismantling of a Europe that had welcomed him and was now facing WWII – another escape. Dalí needs to maintain his own identity and he does it by looking for a reference. In *Secret Life,* this reference is centred in the person of Gala, whom he wants to mystify (like Beatrice in Dante) and to whom history must pay homage, even if it means his own destruction.

Throughout his life, Dalí demonstrates to us the objectives he is proposing through his art. Gala is the muse immortalized in many of his paintings. In other paintings, we see the metamorphosis of his own contradictions that are kept in the darkest parts of his soul, which realize the enigma that is Dalí and which provoke such great admiration, and yet at the same time, great contempt.

In *The Secret Life,* Dalí describes how Gala once again is the one to save him from destruction:

"For like a chrysalis, I had wrapped myself in the silk shroud of my imagination, and this had to be pierced and torn to enable the paranoiac butterfly of my spirit to emerge, transformed-living and real. My 'prisons' were the conditions of my metamorphosis, but without Gala they threatened to become my coffins, and again it was Gala who with her very teeth came to tear away the wrappings patiently woven by the secretion of my anguish, and within which I was beginning to decompose.

"'Arise and walk!'...

"'You have accomplished nothing yet! It is not time for you to die!'

"My Surrealist glory was worthless; I must incorporate Surrealism in tradition. My imagination must become classic again. The rest of my life would not suffice for the work I would have to accomplish and which Gala convinced me I still had to do. Instead of stagnating in the anecdotal mirage of my success, I had now to begin to fight for a thing that was 'important.' This important thing was to render the experience of my life 'classic,' to endow it with a form, a cosmogony, a synthesis, an architecture of eternity."

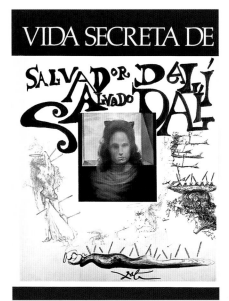

The Secret Life of Salvador Dalí. Spanish edition.

BIBLIOGRAPHY

The magnitude of the work which Dalí illustrated in books and articles can be appreciated in the following bibliography which, while not claiming to be complete, contains more than 130 references.

1924 **Fages de Climent**, **C.** *Les bruixes de Llers*, Bacelona: Políglota, 1924 // Olot: Aubert, 1977.

López Vieira Alfonso. *La vida.* La Coruña: Alfar, 1924, No.36.

1926 **Foix, J.V.** *Conte de Nadal*. Sitges: *L'Amic de les Arts,* December 1926, No. 9 p.10-11.

Residéncia, *Madrid, 1926, year I, No. 3 / 1928, year III No. 2.*

Pujades, Josep P. *L'oncle Vicents* / Barcelona: Políglota, 1926.

1927 **Plana, Alexandra**. *Del cinema dins el sistema de les Belles Arts*. Barcelona: La Nova Revista, July 1927 vol. II, No. 7.

1928 **Buendía, Rogelio**. *Naufragio en tres cuerdas de guitarra*. Sevilla: Imprenta de Manuel Carmona, 1928.

1930 **Breton, André, Éluard, Paul.** *L'Immaculée Conception*. Paris: José Corti, 1930.

Dalí, Salvador. *La femme visible*. Paris: Éditions Surréalistes, 1930.

Breton, André. *Second manifeste du Surréalisme*. Paris: Simon Kra, 1930.

Benoit, Pierre-Andre, Char, René. *Artine*. Paris: Éditions Surréalistes, 1930.

1931 **Crevel, René.** *Dalí ou l'anti-obscurantisme*. Paris: Éditions Surréalistes, 1931.

1932 **Breton, André.** *Le révolver à cheveux blancs.* Paris: Editions des Cahiers Livres, 1932.

1933 **Breton, André**, **Char, René and Éluard, Paul**. *Violette Nozières*. Paris: Nicolas Flamel, 1933.

Ducasse, Isidore, Comte de Lautréamont. *Les chants de Maldoror.* Paris: *Minotaure*, 1933 No. 3-4.

Miravitlles, Jaume. *El ritme de la revolució.* Barcelona: Documents, 1933.

1934   **Ducasse, Isidore, Comte de Lautréamont**. *Les chants de Maldoror.* Paris: Albert Skira, 1934 (the odd numbers of the edition). Paris: Argillet, 1979 (the even numbers of the edition).

Hugnet, George. *Onan*, Paris: Grou-Radenez pour Éditions Surréalistes,1934.

Hugnet, George and Peret, Benjamin. *De derrière les fagots.* Paris: Éditions Surréalistes, 1934.

1935   **Dalí, Salvador**. *La conquête de l'irrationnel.* Paris: Éditions Surréalistes, 1935.

"New York as seen by the 'Super-Realist' Artist, M. Dalí." American Weekly, February 24, 1935, p.3.

"How Super-Realist Dalí saw Broadway." American Weekly, March 17, 1935, p.5.

"The American City Night-and-Day by Dalí." American Weekly, March 31, 1935, p.5.

"American Country Life interpreted by M. Dalí." American Weekly, April 24, 1935, p.7.

"Gangsterism and Goofy Visions of New York by M. Dalí Super Realist Artist." American Weekly, May 19, 1935, p.11.

"Crazy movie Scenario of M. Dalí, the Super Realist Artist." American Weekly, Feb. 24, 1935.

Éluard, Paul. *Nuits partagées.* Paris: *G.L.M. collection* « Repères », 1935, cahier 1.

Tzara, Tristan. *Grains et issues*. Paris: Denöel et Steele, 1935.

1936   Paris: *Minotaure*, June 15, 1936, No. 8, cover.

James, Edward. *Trois sècheresses.* Paris: *Minotaure*, June the 15th. 1936, No. 8, p. 53-56.

Parrot, Louis. *Federico García Lorca.* Paris: Cahiers G.L.M., November 1936, No. 3.

Breton, André and Éluard, Paul. *Notes sur la poésie.* Paris: *Cahiers G.L.M.*, Paris 1936.

1937   *"M. Dalí Sur-realist Artist, at Night-club."* New York American, January 3, 1937, p.7.

"American 50 years from you." American Weekly, January 24, 1937, p. 9.

"Conquest by the Air from Dalí." American Weekly, November 7, 1937, p.1.

1938   **Blanchard, Maurice**. *Trajectoire du Rêve.* Paris: *Cahiers G.L.M.*,1938 No. 7.

Ducasse, Isidore, Jaloux, Edmond, Comte de Lautréamont. *Oeuvres Complètes.* Paris: José Corti, 1938.

Éluard, Paul. *Cours naturel* Paris: Éditions Sagittaire, 1938.

1939 New York: *Vogue*, June 1, 1939, cover.

The underwater dream house (at New York World's Fair) New York: *Town and Country*, June 1939, vol. 94, p. 48-49. May 1941, vol. 96 p. 54-57. New York: *Vogue*, June 1939, vol. 93, No. 11, p. 56-57.

1942 **Dalí, Salvador**. *The Secret Life of Salvador Dalí*. New York: Dial Press, 1942. *Vida secreta de Salvador Dalí*. Buenos Aires: Poseidón,1944. *The Secret Life of Salvador Dalí*. London: Vision Press, 1948. *La mia Vita segreta.* Milano: Longanesi, 1949. *La vie Secrete de Salvador Dalí/* Paris: La Table Ronde, 1952; Paris: Le Club Français du Livre, 1954. *The Secret Life of Salvador Dalí,* new enlarged edition. New York: Dial Press, New York, 1951. *La vie Secrete de Salvador Dalí.* Paris: Gallimard, 1979. *La vida Secreta de Salvador Dalí per Salvador Dalí* / Barcelona: Dasa edicions, 1981. *Das Geheime Leben des Salvador Dalí.* Munchen: Shirmer Mosel, Munchen, 1984. *The Secret Life of Salvador Dalí.* Barcelona: Dasa edicions, 1986, edition specially printed for the Salvador Dalí Foundation, St. Petersburg, Florida. *La vida secreta de Salvador Dalí. Textos autobiogràfics 1.* Barcelona: Edicions Destino – Fundació Gala-Salvador Dalí, Obra Completa volum I, 2003, Catalan and Spanish editions.

1942 *Ballet russe de Montecarlo* / New York: Hurok Attractions, season 1941-1942, cover.

Gram Swing, Raymond. *Nativity of a New World.* New York: *Esquire,* vol. XVIII, No. 6, December, 1942, p. 41-42.

1944 New York: *Vogue,* vol. 103, No. 7, April 1, 1944, cover.

Sandoz, Maurice. *Fantastic Memories*. New York: Doubleday, Doran and Co., 1944.

"Dream vs. Reality" New York: *Vogue*, February 15, 1944, p.48-49.

"Nightmare Journey," *Life*, vol.16, No. 10, March 3, 1944.

"Schiaparelli Red 'Shocking Radiance,'" *Vogue*, vol. 103, No. 10, May 15, 1944, p. 112.

Dalí, Salvador. *Hidden Faces.* New York: The Dial Press, New York, 1944. London: Nicholson and Watson, London, 1947. *Rostros ocultos*. Barcelona: Luís de Caralt, 1952. *Visages cachés.* Paris: Stoch, 1973. *Hidden Faces* / London: Peter Owen, 1973. *Rostros ocultos*. Barcelona: Planeta, 1974.

1945 **North, Sterling**. *Speak of the Devil.* New York: Doubleday, Doran and Co.,1945.

Sandoz, Maurice. *The Maze.* New York: Doubleday, Doubleday, Doran and Co. New York, 1945. *El Laberinto*. Barcelona: Comtalia, 1948. *Le Labyerinthe.* Geneva: Kunding, 1949.

Dalí, Salvador. *Dalí News Monarch of the Dailies.* New York, November 20, 1945.

1946 **Cervantes Saavedra, Miguel de.** *El ingenioso Hidalgo Don Quijote.* New York: Randon House, 1946. Buenos Aires: Emecé Editores S.A., Buenos Aires, 1957. *Don Quijote de la Mancha.* Barcelona: Mateu, 1945. New York: Abeville Press, 1979.

New York: *Vogue,* vol. 108, No. 10, December 1, 1946, cover.

Rose, Billy. *Wine, Women and Words.* New York: Simon and Shuster, 1946. London: Reinhardt and Evans, 1949.

Shakespeare, William. *Macbeth.* New York: Doubleday, 1946.

1947 **Dalí, Salvador.** *Dalí News Monarch of the Dailies.* New York, November 25, 1947.

Montaigne, Michel de. *Essays of Michel de Montaigne.* New York: Doubleday, 1947.

New York: *Vogue,* vol. 110, No. 9, November 1, 1947, p.91.

1948 **Dalí, Salvador.** *Fifty Secrets of Magic Craftsmanship.* New York: Dial Press, 1948. *50 Secretos Mágicos para Pintar.* Barcelona: Luís de Caralt, Barcelona 1951. *Dalí, Cinquante Secrets Magiques.* Paris: Lausanne Edita, 1974.

Cellini, Benvenuto. *The Autobiography of Benvenuto Cellini.* New York: Doubleday, 1948.

Éluard, Paul: *Voir, Poèmes, Pintures, Dessins.* Geneva-Paris: Éditions des Trois Collines, 1948.

Shakespeare, William. *As You Like It.* Roma, Bestetti, 1948. London: The Folio Society, 1953.

Sandoz, Maurice. *Das Haus ohne Fenster.* Zurich: Morgarten, 1948. *La Maison sans Fenêtre.* Paris: Pierre Seghers, 1949.

1950 **Sandoz, Maurice**. *On the Verge.* New York: Doubleday, New York, 1950. *La Limite.* Paris: Table Ronde, Paris, 1951. *Am Rande.* Zurich: Diogenes, 1954.

1951 **Dalí, Salvador.** *Manifeste Mystique.* Paris: Robert J. Godet, 1951.

1952 Souvenir programme du Voyage Inaugural de SS. United States. *Arrault Tours,* 1952, cover.

1954 **d'Ors, Eugeni**. *La Verdadera Historia de Lidia de Cadaqués.* Barcelona: José Janés, 1954.

Fages de Climent, Carles. *Balada del sabarer d'Ordis.* Barcelona: Pérgamo, 1954.

1956 **Dalí, Salvador.** *Les Cocus du vieil art modern*, Paris: Fasquelle, 1956.

1957 **Cervantes, Miguel de**. *Pages choisies de Don Quichotte de la Manche.* Paris: Joseph Forêt, 1957.

Dalí, Salvador and Déon, Michel. *Histoire d'un grand livre « Don Quichotte de Cervantes ».* Paris: Joseph Forêt, 1957.

Program for the Summer Children Fund. Benefit recital. New York: Museum of Modern Art, 1957, cover.

1958 **Goll, Yvan and Claire**. *Nouvelles petites fleurs de Saint François d'Assise*. Paris: Émile Paul, 1958.

Alarcon, Pedro A. de. *Le Tricorne*. Monaco: Éditions du Rocher, 1958. Paris: Nouveau Cercle Parisien du Livre, 1958.

1959 **Dalí, Salvador**. *Anti-matter Manifesto* / New York: Carstairs Gallery, December 1958 – January 1959.

1960 *L'Apocalypse de Saint Jean.* Paris: Joseph Forêt, 1960.

Alighieri, Dante. *La Divine Comédie*. Paris: Les Heures Claires pour Joseph Forêt, 1960.

1961 **Fages de Climent, Carles**. *El triomf i el rodolí de la Gala i en Dalí.* Figueres: Llibreria Canet, 1961.

1962 Souvenir programme "La nuit de France." New York, 1962, cover.

Argillet, Pierre. *Les Rois Mages.* Paris: Graphik Europa, 1962.

1963 **Alighieri, Dante**. *La Divine Comédie, Enfer, Purgatoire, Paradis*. Paris: Les Heures Claires, 1963. Paris: Les Heures Claires and Milan: Rizzoli, 1965.

Valette, Robert D. *Deux Fatrasies*. Cannes: Robert de Valette, 1963.

Dalí, Salvador. *Le Mythe Tragique de l'Angélus de Millet : interprétation « paranoïque-critique »*. Paris: Jean-Jacques Pauvert, 1963. *El mito tragico del « Angelus « de Millet.* Barcelona: Tusquets, 1978.

1964 **Cervantes Saavedra De, Miguel.** *Don Chisciotte della Mancia*. Milan: Palazzi, published in the weekly "Time" from September 16, 1964, to April 14, 1965.

Walpole, Horace. *Le Château d'Otrante*. Paris: Club Français du Livre, 1964.

Dalí, Salvador. *Journal d'un Génie*, Paris: La Table Ronde, 1964.

1966 **Dalí, Salvador**. *Lettre ouverte à Salvador Dalí*. Paris: Albin Michel, 1966.

Huit péchés capitaux. Cadaqués, 1966.

Tauromachies. Paris: Argillet, 1966-1967, 1969.

Paternoster. Milan: Rizzoli, 1966.

1967 **Apollinaire, Guillaume**. *Lettres à Marie*. Paris: Éditions Argillet, 1967.

Tse-Tung, Mao. *Poèmes de Mao Tse-Tung*. Paris: Argillet, 1967.

Biblia Sacra. Milan: Rizzoli, 1967-1969.

Dalí illustre Casanova. Paris: Cercle du Livre Précieux, 1967.

Apollinaire, Guillaume. *Poèmes secrets*. Paris: Argillet, 1967.

Dalí, Salvador. *Hommage à Meissonier*, Paris: Hôtel Meurice, 1967.

1968 **Ronsard, Pierre de**: *Les Amours de Cassandre*. Paris: Argillet, 1968.

El Crist de la Tramuntana. VP, any XXXIX, No. 1,500, Figueres: December 21, 1968, cover.

Dalí, Salvador. *Flora Dalínae.* Paris: Jean Schneider, Basel and Michèle Broutta, 1968.

Dalí, Salvador. *Ma Révolution Culturelle*, Paris, 1968.

Dalí, Salvador; Pauwels, Louis. *Les Passions selon Dalí, Paris*: Denoël, 1968.

1969 **Dalí, Salvador.** *Les métamorphosis érotiques.* Lausanne: Edita, 1969.

Carrol, Lewis. *Alice's Adventures in Wonderland*. New York: Maecenas Press, 1969.

Cassou, Jean. *Bonheur du jour. Cantique d'un ouvrier nègre. Sur la côte. L'air de la séduction*. Paris: Les impénitents, 1969.

Goethe, J. Wolfgang. *Faust: La nuit des Walpurgis*. Paris: Graphic-Europa Anstalt, 1969.

Les mille et une nuits. Milan: Rizzoli, 1969.

Le Marquis de Sade. New York: Shorewood, 1969.

Argillet, Pierre. *Les Rois Mages.* Paris: Graphic-Europa, 1969.

1970 **Sacher-Masoch, Leopold von**: *La Vénus aux fourrures*. Paris: Graphic-Europa Anstalt, 1970.

Carmen. New York: Shorewood, 1970.

Goll, Yvan, Goll, Claire. *La septième rose*. Paris: Émile Paul, 1970.

Jouhandeau. *Fleurs revées*. Paris: Bibliophiles de l'Union française, 1970.

Tristan et Iseult. Paris: Michèle Broutta, 1970.

1971 Paris: *Vogue,* December, 1971, No. 522.

Album Scarab, Brussels: Scarab, 1971, No. 1.

Yourcenar, Margueritte. *Alexis ou le traité du vain combat*. Paris: Les Cent Une, 1971.

Dalí, Salvador. *Procès en diffamation*, Paris: Belfond, 1971.

1972 **Bocaccio, Giovanni**. *Decameron*. New York-Fribourg: Transworld Art, 1972.

1973 *Les douze tribus d'Israel.* New York-Fribourg: Transworld Art, 1973.

Malraux, André. *Roi, je t'attends à Babylone.* Genève: Albert Skira, 1973.

Dalí, Salvador. *Dix recettes d'immortalité*. Paris: Audoin-Descharnes, 1973.

Dalí, Salvador; Parinaud, André. *Comment on deviant Dalí*, Paris: Robert Laffont, 1973.

1974   **Corbière, Tristan.** *Les amours jaunes de Tristan Corbière*. Paris: Pierre Belfond, 1974.

Homenatage al Futbol Club Barcelona, 75 aniversari. Barcelona: Edicions Dronte, 1974.

Freud, Sigmund, Berman, Anne. *Moïse et le Monothéisme*. Paris: Art et valeur, 1974.

Hemingway, Ernest. *Der alte mann und das meer*. Stuttgart: Manus Press, Stuttgart, 1974. *El viejo y el mar*. Barcelona: Circulo de lectores, 1984.

Milton, John. *Paradis perdu: quatrième chant*. Paris: Les bibliophiles de l'Automobile Club de France, 1974.

1975   *La quête du Graal*. Paris: Oeuvres Graphiques Contemporanies, 1975.

Shakespeare, William. *Roméo et Juliette*. Milan: Rizzoli, 1975.

Barca, Calderón de la, Ynduráin, Domingo. *La vida es sueño.* Barcelona: Editorial Subirana, 1975.

1976   **Romero, Luís.** *Todo Dalí en un rostro.* Barcelona: Blume, 1975. *Tout Dalí en un visage.* Paris: Éditions du Chéne, 1976. *All Dalí in a Face.* New Jersey: Chartwell Books, 1978.

Komberg, A., Horecker, B.L., Cornudella, L., and Oro, J. *Reflections on Biochemistry, in Honour of Severo Ochoa.* Oxford: Pergamon Press, 1976

Alchimie des philosophes. Paris-Nice: Art et valeur, 1976.

1977   **Dalí, Salvador.** *Les vins de Gala.* Paris: Draeger, 1977.

Les caprices de Goya par Salvador Dalí. Paris: Heinz Berggruen, 1977.

1978   *Cadaqués i l'art*. Figueres: Art – 3, 1978.

1979   **Ovide**. *L'art d'aimer.* Centre culturel de Paris, 1979.

Dalí, Salvador. *Babaouo*. Paris: Dasa editions, Centre culturel de Paris, 1979. Barcelona: Labor, 1979.

1980   **Pla, Josep**. *Obres de Museu.* Barcelona: Dasa editions, 1980.

1981   **Descharnes, Robert**. *Neuf paysages*. Paris: Michaele Broutta, 1981.

1983   **Decaux, Alain** and **Zitrone, Léon**. *Les chevaux de Dalí.* Paris: Armand et Georges Israël, 1983.

1984   *Tarot Universal Dalí.* Barcelona: Distribucions d'art surrealista, 1984.

2014   *Dali and the Thousand and One Nights.* Barcelona, Spain: Catalan Encyclopedia SAU, 2014. Print.

DALÍ BOOKS PUBLISHED BY OR EDITED BY EDUARD FORNÉS/EDITORIAL MEDITERRÀNIA

1978   *Babaouo*
Author: Salvador Dalí
Publisher: Editorial Labor
Published in Spanish, French

1979   *Obres de Museu*
Authors: Josep Pla, Salvador Dalí
Publisher: DASA editions, S.A.
Bibliophile edition with 22 etchings

1981   *Obres de Museu*
Regular edition
150,000 copy's in Catalan
100,000 copy's in Spanish

1981   *Vida secreta de Salvador Dalí per Salvador Dalí*
Author: Salvador Dalí
Publisher: DASA editions, S.A.
Text introduction by Eduard Fornés
Published in Catalan and Spanish

1982   *Dalí and His Books*
Author: Eduard Fornés
Publisher: Editorial Mediterrània
Catalan edition, 1982
Italian edition, 1982 and 1984
Germany edition, 1983
French edition, 1984 - 1991
Spanish edition 1985
English edition, 1987
Japanese edition, 1987
Suede edition, 1989
Slovak edition, 1992

1984   *The Little Story of Dalí*
Author: Eduard Fornés
Publisher: Editorial Mediterrània, 1984
Editions in Catalan, Spanish, English,
French, Italian, Germany, Japanese, Chinese, Russian

1984   *400 Obres de Salvador Dalí*
Catalog exhibition in Barcelona
Publisher: Editorial Mediterrània

1984   *Salvador Dalí corresponsal de J.V. Foix, 1932 -1936*
Author: Rafael Santos Torroella
Publisher: Editorial Mediterrània
Published Catalan and Spanish

1985   *Opera-Poeme Être Dieu*
Author: Salvador Dalí, Manuel Vázquez Montalban
Music by Igor Wakhévitch
Conducting the polyphonic orchestra of Paris, Boris de Vinogradow
Publisher: Editorial Mediterrània – Distribucions d'Art Surrealista

1985   *Tarot Universal Dalí*
Author: Rachel Pollack
Publisher: Spanish edition Editorial Mediterrània
English edition: Salem House

1986   *The secret Life of Salvador Dalí by Salvador Dalí*
Author: Salvador Dalí
Publisher: Editorial Mediterrània with copy right DASA editions, S.A.

1986   *Sant Narcís Dalí i les Mosques*
Several Authors
Publisher: Editorial Mediterrània

1988   *Torero Al•lucinogen*
Author: Luis Romero
Publisher: Editorial Mediterrània

1989   *Les Contradiccions del cas Dalí*
Author: Eduard Fornés
Publisher: Premsa Catalana, S.A.
60.000 copies

1989   *Salvador Dalí l'Obra Literaria*
Author: Annemieke van de Pas
Publisher: Editorial Mediterrània

1990   *Salvador Dalí, Dedicatòries*
Author: Eduard Fornés
Publisher: Editorial Mediterrània

1991   *Les Morts et Moi*
Authors: Salvador Dalí, Joaquim Molas
Photographer & illustrator: Carles Fontserè
Publisher: Editorial Mediterrània

1991   *Psicodalico Dalí*
Author: Luis Romero
Publisher: Editorial Mediterrània

1992   *Dalí Vision*
Author: Eduard Fornés
Publisher: Editorial Mediterrània
Catalog Exhibition in Hamm Germany

2008   *Dali et Dieu un rendez-vous manqué ?*
Author: Bernard Durand
Preface: Eduard Fornés
Publisher: Editorial Mediterrània

2016   *Dalí illustrator*
Authors: Eduard Fornés and others.
Publisher: Éditions d'Art Les Heures Claires, Paris

INDEX OF IMAGES

LES CHANTS DE MALDOROR:
Pages 107 – 121 (FO 1-FO 44)

All illustrations from *Les Chants de Maldoror* bear the following description:

The 87 etching illustrations shown are from the extremely rare complete suite of 87 engravings, heliogravures and drypoint remarques in and before text. 31 heliogravures without remarques; 31 heliogravures with remarques in drypoint, 13 drypoint remarques before text, and 13 drypoint remarques in text. Signed in pencil and numbered on the colophon. From the first edition of 40 with the accompanying suite, as published by Albert Skira in 1934.

THE DIVINE COMEDY: Handsigned
Pages 139 – 183 (FO 45-FO 144)
Titles in English and French

All illustrations from *The Divine Comedy* bear the following description:

Wood engraving in color on wove paper after a watercolor. One of 100 illustrations from Dante's *Divine Comedy*, published by Les Heures Claires, Paris. Hand-signed in pencil. *The Divine Comedy* suite consists of 100 color wood engravings created between 1960 and 1964 after 100 watercolors painted between 1951 and 1960. The 100 *Divine Comedy* engravings were created from over 3,000 blocks.

While frequently referred to as 'wood' blocks in reference literature and catalogs documenting *The Divine Comedy*, the actual blocks used in the creation were not wood but a resin-based composite material. Between 1959 and 1962 Salvador Dalí directly supervised the creation of the blocks and worked closely with the engraver, Raymond Jacquet, Joseph Forêt and the Editor and Artistic Director of Les Heures Claires, Jean Estrade. Salvador Dalí gave final approval for each of the more than 3,000 blocks used in *The Divine Comedy* project.

Note: For information and details regarding hand signatures and annotations see pages 205 - 207.

For information and details regarding block-signatures see pages 184 - 197.

**Departure on the Grand Voyage
(Départ pour le grand voyage)
(FO 45) IN 1**......................................pg 139
1960, 9¾" x 7"
Signed in the block lower right.

**Virgil Comforts Dante
(Virgile réconforte Dante)
(FO 46) IN2**....................................pg 140
1960, 9¾" x 7"
Signed in the block lower right.

**Sharon and the Passage of Acheron
(Charon et le passage de l'Achéron)
(FO 47) IN 3**....................................pg 140
1960, 9¾" x 7"

**Legs
(Les limbes)
(FO 48) IN 4**....................................pg 140
1960, 9¾" x 7"

**Minos
(Minos)
(FO 49) IN 5**....................................pg 141
1960, 9¾" x 7"

**Cerberus
(Cerbère)
(FO 50) IN 6**....................................pg 142
1960, 9¾" x 7"

**Misers and Squanderers
(Les Avares et les prodigues)
(FO 51) IN 7**....................................pg 142
1960, 9¾" x 7"

**Choleric People
(Les coléreux)
(FO 52) IN 8**....................................pg 143
1960, 9¾" x 7"

**Erinnyes
(Les erinnyes)
(FO 53) IN 9**....................................pg 143
1960, 9¾" x 7"

**Heretics
(Les hérétiques)
(FO 54) IN 10**....................................pg 143
1960, 9¾" x 7"

**At the Edge of the Seventh Bolge
(Au bord du 7e bolge)
(FO 55) IN 11**....................................pg 143
1960, 9¾" x 7"

**Minotaur
(Le minotaure)
(FO 56) IN 12**....................................pg 144
1960, 9¾" x 7"

**The Forest of Those Who Committed Suicide
(La forêt des suicidés)
(FO 57) IN 13**....................................pg 145
1960, 9¾" x 7"

**Blasphemers
(Les blasphemateurs)
(FO 58) IN 14**....................................pg 145
1960, 9¾" x 7"

**The Borders of Phlegethon
(Les margelles du Phlégéton)
(FO 59) IN 15**....................................pg 145
1960, 9¾" x 7"

**The Climb of Geryon
(La montée de Géryon)
(FO 60) IN 16**....................................pg 146
1960, 9¾" x 7"

**Usurers
(Les usuriers)
(FO 61) IN 17**....................................pg 146
1960, 9¾" x 7"

**Imposter
(Les trompeurs)
(FO 62) IN 18**....................................pg 146
1960, 9¾" x 7"

**Simoniacs
(Les simoniaques)
(FO 63) IN 19**....................................pg 147
1960, 9¾" x 7"

**Soothsayers and Sorcerers
(Devins et sorciers)
(FO 64) IN 20**....................................pg 148
1960, 9¾" x 7"

**The Black Devil
(Le diable noir)
(FO 65) IN 21**....................................pg 148
1960, 9¾" x 7"
Signed in the block lower center.

**The Dishonest
(Les prévaricators)
(FO 66) IN 22**....................................pg 149
1960, 9¾" x 7"
Signed in the block upper center.

The Mystical Ladder
(L'échelle mystique)
(FO 132) PA 21 ....…pg 178
1960, 9¾" x 7"

The Angel Of The Seventh Heaven
(L'ange du 7e ciel)
(FO 133) PA 22 ....…pg 178
1960, 9¾" x 7"
Signed in the block lower center.

The Triumph of Christ and the Virgin
(Le triomphe du Christ et de la Vierge)
(FO 134) PA 23 ....…pg 178
1960, 9¾" x 7"

The Joy of the Blessed
(La joie des bienheureux)
(FO 135) PA 24 ....…pg 178
1960, 9¾" x 7"

Saint John and Hope
(Saint Jacques et l'espérance)
(FO 136) PA 25 ....…pg 179
1960, 9¾" x 7"

Meeting of the Forces of Luxury
(Dante Recovers his Sight)
(Dante recouvre la vue)
(FO 137) PA 26 ....…pg 179
1960, 9¾" x 7"
Signed in the block lower center.

Gloria Patri
(Gloria Patri)
(FO 138) PA 27 ....…pg 180
1960, 9¾" x 7"

The March Towards God
(La marche vers Dieu)
(FO 139) PA 28 ....…pg 182
1960, 9¾" x 7"

The Creation of Angels
(La création des anges)
(FO 140) PA 29 ....…pg 181
1960, 9¾" x 7"

At the Empyrean
(A l'empyrée)
(FO 141) PA 30 ....…pg 182
1960, 9¾" x 7"

The Archangel Gabriel
(L'archange Gabriel)
(FO 142) PA 31 ....…pg 182
1960, 9¾" x 7"

Preparation of the Last Prayer
(Preparation à la prière finale)
(FO 143) PA 32 ....…pg 183
1960, 9¾" x 7"

Prayer of Saint Bernard
(Prière de Saint Bernard)
(FO 144) PA 33 ....…pg 182
1960, 9¾" x 7"
Signed in the block lower center.

THE SACRED BIBLE
Pages 219 – 251 (FO 145 - FO 249)
Titles in English and Latin

All illustrations from the *Sacred Bible* bear the following description:

Lithograph in color, combining offset lithography, continuous tone lithography, and serigraphy on thick paper-board specially fabricated by the publisher for this project, after a watercolor. Signed in colored pencil. One of one hundred and five illustrations of the *Sacred Bible* by Salvador Dalí, published by Rizzoli Editions, Milan, Italy, 1969 under rights granted to Giuseppe Albaretto by Salvador Dalí.

Saint Jerome
(Sanctus Hieronymus)
(FO 145) SB 1 ....…pg 219
1964, 19" x 13¾"
Signed in colored pencil and signed in the plate. Six examples numbered in Roman and annotated "g.a. EA.", nine examples numbered in Roman and annotated "g.a."; 56 examples numbered in Arabic and annotated "g.a."; 15 examples numbered in Arabic and annotated "g.a." and "EA".

In the Beginning God Created Heaven and Earth
(In Principio creavit Deus caelum et Tennam)
(FO 146) SB 2 ....…pg 219
1964, 19" x 13¾"
Signed in colored pencil and signed in the plate. Six examples numbered in Roman and annotated "g.a. EA.", nine examples numbered in Roman and annotated "g.a.", one example numbered in Arabic and annotated "g.a. EA."

The Creation of Earthly and Sea Animals
(Creatio animalium terrae et maris)
(FO 147) SB 3 ....…pg 219
1964, 19" x 13¾"
Signed in colored pencil and signed in the plate. Six examples numbered in Roman and annotated "g.a. EA.", nine examples numbered in Roman and annotated "g.a."

The Creation of Flying Things
(Creatio volatilium)
(FO 148) SB 4 ....…pg 219
1964, 19" x 13¾"
Signed in colored pencil and signed in the plate. Six examples numbered in Roman and annotated "g.a. EA.", nine examples numbered in Roman and annotated "g.a."; 55 examples numbered in Arabic and annotated "g.a."; three examples lettered (A-C) and annotated "g.a."; 13 examples numbered in Arabic and annotated "g.a. EA".

Let Us Make Man in Our Image and Likeness
(Faciamus Hominem ad imaginem e)
(FO 149) SB 5 ....…pg 220
1964, 19" x 13¾"
Signed in colored pencil and signed in the plate. Six examples numbered in Roman and annotated "g.a." and "EA.", nine examples numbered in Roman and annotated "g.a."; 56 examples numbered in Arabic and annotated "g.a."; three examples lettered (A-C) and annotated "g.a."; 14 examples numbered in Arabic and annotated "g.a. EA".

Woman from the Side of Man
(Mulier e latere viri)
(FO 150) SB 6 ....…pg 220
1964, 19" x 13¾"
Signed in colored pencil and signed in the plate. Six examples numbered in Roman and annotated "g.a. EA", nine examples numbered in Roman and annotated "g.a."; 1 example numbered in Arabic and annotated "g.a. EA".

Man and Woman in the Garden of Pleasure
(Vir et mulier in paradiso voluptatis)
(FO 151) SB 7 ....…pg 220
1964, 19" x 13¾"
Signed in colored pencil and signed in the plate. Six examples numbered in Roman and annotated "g.a." and "EA.", nine examples numbered in Roman and annotated "g.a.".

Original Sin
(Peccatum originis)
(FO 152) SB 8...........................pg 220
1964, 19" x 13¾"
Signed in colored pencil and signed in the plate. Six examples numbered in Roman and annotated "g.a. EA.", nine examples numbered in Roman and annotated "g.a."; 14 examples numbered in Arabic and annotated "g.a. EA."; 35 examples numbered in Arabic and annotated "g.a."

Flood Waters Over the Earth
(Aquae diluvii super terram)
(FO 153) SB 9...........................pg 221
1964, 13¾" x 19"
Signed in colored pencil and signed in the plate. Six examples numbered in Roman and annotated "g.a. EA.", nine examples numbered in Roman and annotated "g.a.", one example numbered in Arabic and annotated "g.a. EA."

Noah Who Planted the First Vineyard
(Noe qui primus plantavit vinea)
(FO 154) SB 10...........................pg 221
1964, 19" x 13¾"
Signed in colored pencil and signed in the plate. Six examples numbered in Roman and annotated "g.a. EA.", nine examples numbered in Roman and annotated "g.a."; 52 examples in Arabic and annotated g.a.; 2 examples lettered (A,B); 13 examples in Arabic annotated "g.a. EA."

The Tower of Babel
(Turris Babel)
(FO 155) SB 11...........................pg 221
1964, 19" x 13¾"
Signed in colored pencil and signed in the plate. Six examples numbered in Roman and annotated "g.a. EA.", nine examples numbered in Roman and annotated "g.a."

Abraham, the Father of Many Nations
(Abraham, pater multarum gentium)
(FO 156) SB 12...........................pg 222
1964, 19" x 13¾"
Signed in colored pencil and signed in the plate. Six examples numbered in Roman and annotated "g.a. EA.", nine examples numbered in Roman and annotated "g.a."; 53 examples numbered in Arabic and annotated "g.a."; 15 examples numbered in Arabic and annotated "g.a. EA."

Lot's Wife, Turned Into a Statue of Salt
(Uxor Lot in statuam salis conversa)
(FO 157) SB 13...........................pg 222
1964, 19" x 13¾"
Signed in colored pencil and signed in the plate. Six examples numbered in Roman and annotated "g.a. EA.", nine examples numbered in Roman and annotated "g.a."

Abraham, Abraham!
(Abraham, Abraham!)
(FO 158) SB 14...........................pg 222
1964, 19" x 13¾"
Signed in colored pencil and signed in the plate. Six examples numbered in Roman and annotated "g.a. EA.", nine examples numbered in Roman and annotated "g.a."; 55 examples numbered in Arabic and annotated "g.a."; one example lettered (A) and annotated "g.a."; 16 examples numbered in Arabic and annotated "g.a. EA."

Joseph and His Brothers in Egypt
(Ioseph et fratres in Egypto)
(FO 159) SB 15...........................pg 222
1964, 19" x 13¾"
Signed in colored pencil and signed in the plate. Six examples numbered in Roman and annotated "g.a. EA.", nine examples numbered in Roman and annotated "g.a."

The Bush That Was Not Burnt
(Rubus incombustus)
(FO 160) SB 16...........................pg 223
1964, 19" x 13¾"
Signed in colored pencil and signed in the plate. Six examples numbered in Roman and annotated "g.a. EA.", nine examples numbered in Roman and annotated "g.a."; 34 examples numbered in Arabic and annotated "g.a."; one example lettered (A) and annotated "g.a."; 15 examples numbered in Arabic and annotated "g.a. EA."

Water Came Out of the Rock
(De petra exivit aqua)
(FO 161) SB 17...........................pg 223
1964, 19" x 13¾"
Signed in colored pencil and signed in the plate. Six examples numbered in Roman and annotated "g.a. EA.", nine examples numbered in Roman and annotated "g.a."

I Am the Lord Your God
(Ego sum Dominus Deus tuus...)
(FO 162) SB 18...........................pg 223
1964, 19" x 13¾"
Signed in colored pencil and signed in the plate. Six examples numbered in Roman and annotated "g.a. EA.", nine examples numbered in Roman and annotated "g.a."; 35 examples numbered in Arabic and annotated "g.a."; 14 examples numbered in Arabic and annotated "g.a. EA."

The Glory of Moses' Face
(The glory of Moses' face)
(FO 163) SB 19...........................pg 223
1964, 19" x 13¾"
Signed in colored pencil. Six examples numbered in Roman and annotated "g.a. EA.", nine examples numbered in Roman and annotated "g.a."; 42 examples numbered in Arabic and annotated "g.a."; 43 examples lettered (A-Z and AA-QQ) and annotated "g.a."; 109 examples numbered in Arabic and annotated "g.a. EA."

Joshua, Brave in War
(Iosue fortis in bello)
(FO 164) SB 20...........................pg 224
1964, 19" x 13¾"
Signed in colored pencil and signed in the plate. Six examples numbered in Roman and annotated "g.a. EA.", nine examples numbered in Roman and annotated "g.a.", one example numbered in Arabic and annotated "g.a. EA."

The Family of Ruth, The Moabite
(Familia Ruth moabitidis)
(FO 165) SB 21...........................pg 224
1964, 19" x 13¾"
Signed in colored pencil and signed in the plate. Six examples numbered in Roman and annotated "g.a. EA.", nine examples numbered in Roman and annotated "g.a."; 11 examples numbered in Arabic and annotated "g.a."; 36 examples lettered (A-Z and AA-JJ) and annotated "g.a."; 2 examples numbered in Arabic and annotated "g.a. EA."

David and the Philistine
(David et Philistaeus)
(FO 166) SB 22...........................pg 224
1964, 19" x 13¾"
Signed in colored pencil and signed in the plate. Six examples numbered in Roman and annotated "g.a. EA.", nine examples numbered in Roman and annotated "g.a.", one example numbered in Arabic and annotated "g.a. EA."

David's Mourning At the Death of Saul
(Planctus David in mortem Saul)
1964, 19" x 13¾"
Signed in colored pencil and signed in the plate. Six examples numbered in Roman and annotated "g.a. EA.", nine examples numbered in Roman and annotated "g.a.", one example numbered in Arabic and annotated "g.a. EA."

The Ark of the Covenant
(Arca foederis)
1964, 19" x 13¾"
Signed in colored pencil. Six examples numbered in Roman and annotated "g.a. EA.", nine examples numbered in Roman and annotated "g.a."

A Cherub Over the Threshold of the Lord
(Cherub super limen domus)
1964, 19" x 13¾"
Signed in colored pencil. Six examples numbered in Roman and annotated "g.a. EA.", nine examples numbered in Roman and annotated "g.a."

Locust and Grasshopper
(Locusta et bruchus)
1964, 19" x 13¾"
Signed in colored pencil and signed in the plate. Six examples numbered in Roman and annotated "g.a. EA.", nine examples numbered in Roman and annotated "g.a."

Elijah by Means of Whirlwind On a Chariot of Fire
(Elias per turbinem super curru)
1964, 13¾" x 19"
Signed in colored pencil and signed in the plate. Six examples numbered in Roman and annotated "g.a. EA.", nine examples numbered in Roman and annotated "g.a.", a single example in Arabic and annotated "g.a. EA"

A Corpse in the Tomb of Elijah
(Cadaver in sepulchro Elisei)
1964, 19" x 13¾"
Signed in colored pencil and signed in the plate. Six examples numbered in Roman and annotated "g.a. EA.", nine examples numbered in Roman and annotated "g.a."

Josiah Buried in the Mausoleum of His Fathers
(Iosias sepultus in mausoleo patrum)
1964, 19" x 13¾"
Signed in colored pencil. Six examples numbered in Roman and annotated "g.a. EA.", nine examples numbered in Roman and annotated "g.a.", one example in Arabic annotated "g.a. EA"

Jeremiah's Prophecy Against King Joachim
(Ieremiae prophetia contra rege)
1964, 19" x 13¾"
Signed in colored pencil. Six examples numbered in Roman and annotated "g.a. EA.", Nine examples numbered in Roman and annotated "g.a."

Lonely Sits the City That Was Full of People
(Sedet sola civitas plena populo)
1964, 19" x 13¾"
Signed in colored pencil and signed in the plate. Six examples numbered in Roman and annotated "g.a. EA.", nine examples numbered in Roman and annotated "g.a.", one example in Arabic annotated "g.a. EA"

Nebuchadnezzar King of Babylon
(Nabuchodonosor rex Babylonis)
1964, 19" x 13¾"
Signed in colored pencil and signed in the plate. Six examples numbered in Roman and annotated "g.a. EA.", nine examples numbered in Roman and annotated "g.a."

Saint Raphael And Tobias
(Sanctus Raphael et Tobias)
1964, 19" x 13¾"
Signed in colored pencil and signed in the plate. Six examples numbered in Roman and annotated "g.a. EA.", nine examples numbered in Roman and annotated "g.a."; 34 examples numbered in Arabic and annotated "g.a."; 15 examples numbered in Arabic and annotated "g.a. EA."

May He Himself Join You in Marriage
(Ipse coniungat vos)
1964, 13¾" x 19"
Signed in colored pencil and signed in the plate. Six examples numbered in Roman and annotated "g.a. EA.", nine examples numbered in Roman and annotated "g.a.", one example numbered in Arabic and annotated "g.a. EA."

And Immediately Tobit Recovered His Sight
(Statimque Tobias visum recepit)
1964, 13¾" x 19"
Signed in colored pencil and signed in the plate. Six examples numbered in Roman and annotated "g.a. EA.", nine examples numbered in Roman and annotated "g.a.", seven examples numbered in Arabic and annotated "g.a. EA."

The Liturgy of Penance
(Liturgia poenitentiae)
1964, 19" x 13¾"
Signed in colored pencil and signed in the plate. Six examples numbered in Roman and annotated "g.a. EA.", nine examples numbered in Roman and annotated "g.a."

Judith Beheads Holofernes
(Cadaver in sepulchro Elisei)
1964, 19" x 13¾"
Signed in colored pencil and signed in the plate. Six examples numbered in Roman and annotated "g.a. EA", nine examples numbered in Roman and annotated "g.a"

Ahasuerus Loved Esther Greatly
(Assuerus adamavit Esther)
1964, 19" x 13¾"
Signed in colored pencil and signed in the plate. Six examples numbered in Roman and annotated "g.a. EA", nine examples numbered in Roman and annotated "g.a"

Lament, Virgin, Girded with Sackcloth
(Plange, virgo, accincta sacco)
1964, 19" x 13¾"
Signed in colored pencil and signed in the plate. Six examples numbered in Roman and annotated "g.a. EA", nine

examples numbered in Roman and annotated "g.a."; 31 examples numbered in Arabic and annotated "g.a. EA"; nine lettered examples (A-I) annotated "g.a"; 34 examples numbered in Arabic and annotated "g.a."

I Give Up My Body and Life for the Laws of Our Fathers
(Animam et corpus trado pro patriis legibus)
(FO 184) SB 40............................pg 230
1964, 13¾" x 19"
Signed in colored pencil. Six examples numbered in Roman and annotated "g.a. EA", nine examples numbered in Roman and annotated "g.a.", one example numbered in Arabic and annotated "g.a. EA"

And Satan Also Was Present Among the Sons of God
(Inter filios Dei affuit etiam Satan)
(FO 185) SB 41............................pg 231
1964, 19" x 13¾"
Signed in colored pencil and signed in the plate. Six examples numbered in Roman and annotated "g.a. EA", nine examples numbered in Roman and annotated "g.a.", one example numbered in Arabic and annotated "g.a. EA"

Leviathan
(Leviathan)
(FO 186) SB 42............................pg 231
1964, 13¾" x 19"
Signed in colored pencil and signed in the plate. Six examples numbered in Roman and annotated "g.a. EA", nine examples numbered in Roman and annotated "g.a".; one example numbered in Arabic and annotated "g.a. EA"

Blessed the Poor, Blessed the Meek… Blessed…
(Beati pauperes... Beati mites... beati...)
(FO 187) SB 43............................pg 232
1964, 19" x 13¾"
Signed in colored pencil and signed in the plate. Six examples numbered in Roman and annotated "g.a. EA", nine examples numbered in Roman and annotated "g.a."

Who Will Go Up to the Mountain of the Lord
(Quis ascendet in montem Domini?)
(FO 188) SB 44............................pg 232
1964, 19" x 13¾"
Signed in colored pencil and signed in the plate. Six examples numbered in

Roman and annotated "g.a. EA", nine examples numbered in Roman and annotated "g.a.", one example numbered in Arabic and annotated "g.a. EA"

You Will Sprinkle Me With Hyssop And I Will Be Cleansed
(Asperges me hyssopo et mundabor)
(FO 189) SB 45............................pg 232
1964, 19" x 13¾"
Signed in colored pencil and signed in the plate. Six examples numbered in Roman and annotated "g.a. EA", nine examples numbered in Roman and annotated "g.a"; 13 examples numbered in Arabic and annotated "g.a."; 33 lettered examples (A-Z and AA-GG) annotated "g.a."; 95 examples numbered in Arabic and annotated "g.a. EA"

And After the Morsel, Satan Entered Into Him
(Et post buccellam introivit in cum satanas)
(FO 190) SB 46............................pg 232
1964, 19" x 13¾"
Signed in colored pencil and signed in the plate. Six examples numbered in Roman and annotated "g.a." and "EA", nine examples numbered in Roman and annotated "g.a."

Behold the Man
(Ecce homo)
(FO 191) SB 47............................pg 233
1964, 19" x 13¾"
Signed in colored pencil and signed in the plate. Six examples numbered in Roman and annotated "g.a." and "EA", nine examples numbered in Roman and annotated "g.a."; one example numbered in Arabic and annotated "g.a" and "EA"

Away With Him, Away With Him, Crucify Him
(Tolle, tolle, crucifige eum)
(FO 192) SB 48............................pg 233
1964, 19" x 13¾"
Signed in colored pencil and signed in the plate. Six examples numbered in Roman and annotated "g.a." and "EA", nine examples numbered in Roman and annotated "g.a."; 19 examples numbered in Arabic and annotated "g.a"; 35 lettered examples (A-Z and AA-II) annotated "g.a"; 251 examples numbered in Arabic and annotated "g.a." and "EA"

He Uttered A Loud Cry and Breathed His Last
(Emissa voce magna expiravit)
(FO 193) SB 49............................pg 233
1964, 19" x 13¾"
Signed in colored pencil and signed in the plate. Six examples numbered in Roman and annotated "g.a" and "EA", nine examples numbered in Roman and annotated "g.a."; one example numbered in Arabic and annotated "g.a" and "EA"

…And Took the Body of Jesus Away
(…et tulit corpus Iesu)
(FO 194) SB 50............................pg 233
1964, 19" x 13¾"
Signed in colored pencil and signed in the plate. Six examples numbered in Roman and annotated "g.a." and "EA", nine examples numbered in Roman and annotated "g.a." ; one example numbered in Arabic and annotated "g.a" and "EA"

And They Bound the Body of Jesus in Linen Cloths with the Spices
(Et ligaverunt corpus Iesu linteis cum aromatibus)
(FO 195) SB 51............................pg 234
1964, 13¾" x 19"
Signed in colored pencil and signed in the plate. Six examples numbered in Roman and annotated "g.a" and "EA", nine examples numbered in Roman and annotated "g.a."

Jesus Walking on the Sea
(Iesus super mare ambulans)
(FO 196) SB 52............................pg 234
1964, 19" x 13¾"
Signed in colored pencil. Six examples numbered in Roman and annotated "g.a." and "EA", nine examples numbered in Roman and annotated "g.a."; one example numbered in Arabic and annotated "g.a" and "EA"

Blow the Trumpet in Zion
(Canite tuba in Sion)
(FO 197) SB 53............................pg 234
1964, 19" x 13¾"
Signed in colored pencil and signed in the plate. Six examples numbered in Roman and annotated "g.a" and "EA", nine examples numbered in Roman and annotated "g.a."

Vanity of Vanities
(Vanitas vanitatum)
(FO 198) SB 54............................pg 235
1964, 19" x 13¾"
Signed in colored pencil and signed in the plate. Six examples numbered in Roman and annotated "g.a" and "EA", nine examples numbered in Roman and annotated "g.a."; 56 examples numbered in Arabic and annotated "g.a"; 13 examples numbered in Arabic and annotated "g.a" and "EA"

I Will Betroth You to Me Forever
(Sponsabo te mihi in sempiternum)
(FO 199) SB 55............................pg 235
1964, 19" x 13¾"
Signed in colored pencil. Six examples numbered in Roman and annotated "g.a" and "EA", nine examples numbered in Roman and annotated "g.a."

All the Nations in the Valley of Jehoshaphat
(Omnes gentes in valle Iosaphat)
(FO 200) SB 56............................pg 235
1964, 19" x 13¾"
Signed in colored pencil and signed in the plate. Six examples numbered in Roman and annotated "g.a" and "EA", nine examples numbered in Roman and annotated "g.a."

A Mason's Trowel in the Hand of the Lord
(Trulla caementarii in manu Domini)
(FO 201) SB 57............................pg 235
1964, 19" x 13¾"
Signed in colored pencil. Six examples numbered in Roman and annotated "g.a" and "EA", nine examples numbered in Roman and annotated "g.a."

Jonah in the Belly of the Fish
(Ionas in ventre piscis)
(FO 202) SB 58............................pg 236
1964, 13¾" x 19"
Signed in colored pencil and signed in the plate. Six examples numbered in Roman and annotated "g.a" and "EA", nine examples numbered in Roman and annotated "g.a."

The Foolish and Wise Maidens
(Stultae et prudentes filiae)
(FO 203) SB 59............................pg 236
1964, 13¾" x 19"
Signed in colored pencil and signed in the plate. Six examples numbered in Roman and annotated "g.a" and "EA", nine examples numbered in Roman and annotated "g.a."

The Money changers Thrown Out of the Temple
(Nummularii de Templo eiecti)
(FO 204) SB 60............................pg 237
1964, 19" x 13¾"
Signed in colored pencil and signed in the plate. Six examples numbered in Roman and annotated "g.a" and "EA", nine examples numbered in Roman and annotated "g.a."; 90 examples numbered in Arabic and annotated "g.a" and "EA"

Give Me a Drink
(Da mihi bibere)
(FO 205) SB 61............................pg 237
1964, 19" x 13¾"
Signed in colored pencil and signed in the plate. Six examples numbered in Roman and annotated "g.a" and "EA", nine examples numbered in Roman and annotated "g.a."; one example numbered in Arabic and annotated "g.a" and "EA"

The Chosen Vineyard
(Vinea electa)
(FO 206) SB 62............................pg 237
1964, 13¾" x 19"
Signed in colored pencil and signed in the plate. Six examples numbered in Roman and annotated "g.a" and "EA", nine examples numbered in Roman and annotated "g.a."; one example numbered in Arabic and annotated "g.a" and "EA"

Behold, A Virgin Shall Conceive
(Ecce virgo concipiet)
(FO 207) SB 63............................pg 238
1964, 19" x 13¾"
Signed in colored pencil and signed in the plate. Six examples numbered in Roman and annotated "g.a." and "EA", nine examples numbered in Roman and annotated "g.a."; one example numbered in Arabic and annotated "g.a" and "EA"

The Lion Eating Straw Like the Ox
(Leo quasi bos comedens paleas)
(FO 208) SB 64............................pg 238
1964, 19" x 13¾"
Signed in colored pencil and signed in the plate. Six examples numbered in Roman and annotated "g.a." and "EA", nine examples numbered in Roman and annotated "g.a."; one example numbered in Arabic and annotated "g.a" and "EA"

The Voice of One Crying Out
(Vox clamantis)
(FO 209) SB 65............................pg 238
1964, 19" x 13¾"
Signed in colored pencil and signed in the plate. Six examples numbered in Roman and annotated "g.a". and "EA", nine examples numbered in Roman and annotated "g.a."; 55 examples numbered in Arabic and annotated "g.a."; 16 examples numbered in Arabic and annotated "g.a" and "EA"

They Will All Come from Saba
(Omnes de Saba venient)
(FO 210) SB 66............................pg 239
1964, 13¾" x 19"
Signed in colored pencil and signed in the plate. Six examples numbered in Roman and annotated "g.a" and "EA", nine examples numbered in Roman and annotated "g.a."; one example numbered in Arabic and annotated "g.a" and "EA"

Before You Came Out from the Womb I Sanctified You
(Antequam exires de vulva sanctificavi te)
(FO 211) SB 67............................pg 239
1964, 19" x 13¾"
Signed in colored pencil and signed in the plate. Six examples numbered in Roman and annotated "g.a." and "EA", nine examples numbered in Roman and annotated "g.a."; one example numbered in Arabic and annotated "g.a" and "EA"

O Lord, You Have Deceived Me
(Seduxisti me, Domine)
(FO 212) SB 68............................pg 239
1964, 19" x 13¾"
Signed in colored pencil and signed in the plate. Six examples numbered in Roman and annotated "g.a" and "EA" and nine examples numbered in Roman and annotated "g.a."

The Prodigal Son
(Filius prodigus)
(FO 213) SB 69............................pg 240
1964, 19" x 13¾"
Signed in colored pencil and signed in the plate. Six examples numbered in Roman and annotated "g.a" and "EA", nine examples numbered in Roman and annotated "g.a."; one example numbered in Arabic and annotated "g.a" and "EA"

The Blood of the New Covenant
(Sanguis novi testamenti)
(FO 214) SB 70............................pg 240
1964, 19" x 13¾"
Signed in colored pencil and signed in the plate. Six examples numbered in Roman and annotated "g.a" and "EA", nine examples numbered in Roman and annotated "g.a."; one example numbered in Arabic and annotated "g.a" and "EA"

Behold, One As The Son of Man In the Clouds of Heaven
(Ecce quasi filius hominis in nubibus caeli)
(FO 215) SB 71............................pg 240
1964, 19" x 13¾"
Signed in colored pencil and signed in the plate. Six examples numbered in Roman and annotated "g.a" and "EA", nine examples numbered in Roman and annotated "g.a."

An Idol By the Name of Baal
(Idolum nomine Bel)
(FO 216) SB 72............................pg 240
1964, 19" x 13¾"
Signed in colored pencil and signed in the plate. Six examples numbered in Roman and annotated "g.a." and "EA", nine examples numbered in Roman and annotated "g.a."; one example numbered in Arabic and annotated "g.a." and "EA"

The Angel Drove Out the Fiery Flame
(Angelus excussit flammam ignis)
(FO 217) SB 73............................pg 241
1964, 13¾" x 19"
Signed in colored pencil and signed in the plate. Six examples numbered in Roman and annotated "g.a." and "EA", nine examples numbered in Roman and annotated "g.a."; one example numbered in Arabic and annotated "g.a." and "EA"

Mene, Tekel, Parsin
(Mane, Thecel, Phares)
(FO 218) SB 74............................pg 241
1964, 19" x 13¾"
Signed in colored pencil and signed in the plate. Six examples numbered in Roman and annotated "g.a." and "EA", nine examples numbered in Roman and annotated "g.a."

The He-Goat of the Wild She-Goats On the Face of the Earth
(Hircus caprarum super faciem terrae)
(FO 219) SB 75............................pg 241
1964, 19" x 13¾"
Signed in colored pencil and signed in the plate. Six examples numbered in Roman and annotated "g.a." and "EA", nine examples numbered in Roman and annotated "g.a.".

The Beauty of Susanna
(Susannae pulchritudo)
(FO 220) SB 76............................pg 242
1964, 19" x 13¾"
Signed in colored pencil and signed in the plate. Six examples numbered in Roman and annotated "g.a." and "EA", nine examples numbered in Roman and annotated "g.a.".

Out of Egypt I Have Called My Son
(Ex Egpto vocavi filium meum)
(FO 221) SB 77............................pg 242
1964, 13¾" x 19"
Signed in colored pencil and signed in the plate. Six examples numbered in Roman and annotated "g.a." and "EA", nine examples numbered in Roman and annotated "g.a.".

Is It Lawful to Pay Taxes to Caesar?
(Licet tributum dare Caesari?)
(FO 222) SB 78............................pg 243
1964, 19" x 13¾"
Signed in colored pencil and signed in the plate. Six examples numbered in Roman and annotated "g.a." and "EA", nine examples numbered in Roman and annotated "g.a.".

The Spotless Offering
(Oblatio munda)
(FO 223) SB 79............................pg 243
1964, 19" x 13¾"
Signed in colored pencil and signed in the plate. Six examples numbered in Roman and annotated "g.a." and "EA", nine examples numbered in Roman and annotated "g.a.".

He Himself Was Elijah
(Ipse erat Elias)
(FO 224) SB 80............................pg 243
1964, 19" x 13¾"
Signed in colored pencil and signed in the plate. Six examples numbered in Roman and annotated "g.a. EA.", nine examples numbered in Roman and annotated "g.a."; 35 examples numbered in Arabic and annotated "g.a."; 38 examples lettered (A-Z and AA-LL) and annotated "g.a."; 22 examples numbered in Arabic and annotated "g.a." and "EA".

The Annunciation To Mary
(Mariae Annunciatio)
(FO 225) SB 81............................pg 243
1964, 19" x 13¾"
Signed in colored pencil and signed in the plate. Six examples numbered in Roman and annotated "g.a." "EA", nine examples numbered in Roman and annotated "g.a."; 52 examples numbered in Arabic and annotated "g.a"; 14 examples numbered in Arabic and annotated "g.a" and "EA"

The Birth of Jesus
(Iesu nativitas)
(FO 226) SB 82............................pg 244
1964, 13¾" x 19"
Signed in colored pencil and signed in the plate. Six examples numbered in Roman and annotated "g.a." and "EA", nine examples numbered in Roman and annotated "g.a.".

Mary Gathering Within Her Heart
(Maria conferens in corde suo)
(FO 227) SB 83............................pg 244
1964, 19" x 13¾"
Signed in colored pencil and signed in the plate. Six examples numbered in Roman and annotated "g.a." and "EA", nine examples numbered in Roman and annotated "g.a."; 14 examples numbered in Arabic and annotated "g.a"; 29 lettered examples (A-Z and AA-CC) annotated "g.a".

And You, Child, The Prophet of the Most High
(Et tu, puer, propheta Altissimi)
(FO 228) SB 84............................pg 244
1964, 19" x 13¾"
Signed in colored pencil and signed in the plate. Six examples numbered in Roman and annotated "g.a." and "EA", nine examples numbered in Roman and annotated "g.a."; 33 examples numbered in Arabic and annotated "g.a"; 38 lettered examples (A-Z and AA-LL) annotated "g.a"; 23 examples in Arabic and annotated "g.a." EA".

And He Was Baptized by John in the Jordan (Et baptizatus est a Ioanne in Iordane)
(FO 229) SB 85.............................pg 245
1964, 19" x 13¾"
Signed in colored pencil and signed in the plate. Six examples numbered in Roman and annotated "g.a." and "EA", nine examples numbered in Roman and annotated "g.a."; 141 examples numbered in Arabic and annotated "g.a." and "EA".

Jesus Is Tempted By Satan (Iesus a satana tentatur)
(FO 230) SB 86.............................pg 245
1964, 19" x 13¾"
Signed in colored pencil and signed in the plate. Six examples numbered in Roman and annotated "g.a." and "EA", nine examples numbered in Roman and annotated "g.a."; 14 examples numbered in Arabic and annotated "g.a"; 33 lettered examples (A-Z and AA-GG) annotated "g.a"; two examples numbered in Arabic and annotated "g.a" and "EA".

The Dance of Herodias' Daughter (Filiae Herodiadis saltatio)
(FO 231) SB 87.............................pg 245
1964, 19" x 13¾"
Signed in colored pencil and signed in the plate. Six examples numbered in Roman and annotated "g.a." and "EA", nine examples numbered in Roman and annotated "g.a."; 14 examples numbered in Arabic and annotated "g.a"; 37 lettered examples (A-Z and AA-KK) annotated "g.a"; 4 examples numbered in Arabic and annotated "g.a" and "EA".

Many Sins Are Forgiven to the Sinful Woman (Mulieri peccatrici remittuntur peccata multa)
(FO 232) SB 88.............................pg 245
1964, 19" x 13¾"
Signed in colored pencil. Six examples numbered in Roman and annotated "g.a." and "EA", nine examples numbered in Roman and annotated "g.a."; one example numbered in Arabic and annotated "g.a." and "EA".

The Transfiguration of Jesus (Iesu transfiguratio)
(FO 233) SB 89.............................pg 246
1964, 19" x 13¾"
Signed in colored pencil and signed in the plate. Six examples numbered in

Roman and annotated "g.a." and "EA", nine examples numbered in Roman and annotated "g.a.".

You Are Peter (Tu es Petrus...)
(FO 234) SB 90.............................pg 246
1964, 19" x 13¾"
Signed in colored pencil and signed in the plate. Six examples numbered in Roman and annotated "g.a." and "EA"; nine examples numbered in Roman and annotated "g.a."; 21 examples numbered in Arabic and annotated "g.a"; 43 lettered examples (A-Z and AA-QQ) annotated "g.a"; 251 examples numbered in Arabic and annotated "g.a" and "EA".

Lazarus, Come Forth (Lazare, veni foras)
(FO 235) SB 91.............................pg 246
1964, 19" x 13¾"
Signed in colored pencil and signed in the plate. Six examples numbered in Roman and annotated "g.a." and "EA", nine examples numbered in Roman and annotated "g.a.".

The Spirit is Willing, But the Flesh is Weak (Spiritus promptus est, caro vero infirma)
(FO 236) SB 92.............................pg 246
1964, 19" x 13¾"
Signed in colored pencil and signed in the plate. Six examples numbered in Roman and annotated "g.a." and "EA", nine examples numbered in Roman and annotated "g.a.".

Jesus, Scourged (Iesus flagellatus)
(FO 237) SB 93.............................pg 247
1964, 19" x 13¾"
Signed in colored pencil and signed in the plate. Six examples numbered in Roman and annotated "g.a." and "EA", nine examples numbered in Roman and annotated "g.a." and seven complete sets are known to exist in private collections.

He Went Out Carrying His Own Cross (Baiulans sibi crucem, exivit...)
(FO 238) SB 94.............................pg 247
1964, 19" x 13¾"
Signed in colored pencil and signed in the plate. Six examples numbered in Roman and annotated "g.a." and "EA",

nine examples numbered in Roman and annotated "g.a.".

It Is Finished! (Consummatum est!)
(FO 239) SB 95.............................pg 247
1964, 19" x 13¾"
Signed in colored pencil and signed in the plate. Six examples numbered in Roman and annotated "g.a." and "EA", nine examples numbered in Roman and annotated "g.a."; one example numbered in Arabic and annotated "g.a." and "EA".

Truly, This Was Just a Man (Vere, hic homo iustus erat)
(FO 240) SB 96.............................pg 247
1964, 19" x 13¾"
Signed in colored pencil and signed in the plate. Six examples numbered in Roman and annotated "g.a." and "EA", nine examples numbered in Roman and annotated "g.a.".

The Taking Down From the Cross (De cruce depositio)
(FO 241) SB 97.............................pg 248
1964, 19" x 13¾"
Signed in colored pencil and signed in the plate. Six examples numbered in Roman and annotated "g.a." and "EA", nine examples numbered in Roman and annotated "g.a."; 53 examples numbered in Arabic and annotated "g.a"; one lettered example (A) annotated "g.a"; 14 examples numbered in Arabic and annotated "g.a" and "EA".

And They Placed Him In A Tomb (Et posuerunt eum in monumento)
(FO 242) SB 98.............................pg 248
1964, 13¾" x 19"
Signed in colored pencil and signed in the plate. Six examples numbered in Roman and annotated "g.a." and "EA", nine examples numbered in Roman and annotated "g.a.".

On the Third Day He Rose From the Dead (Tertia die resurrexit)
(FO 243) SB 99.............................pg 249
1964, 13¾" x 19"
Signed in colored pencil and signed in the plate. Six examples numbered in Roman and annotated "g.a." and "EA", nine examples numbered in Roman and annotated "g.a.".

Don't Touch Me!
(Noli me tangere!)
(FO 244) SB 100 ....…pg 249
1964, 19" x 13¾"
Signed in colored pencil and signed in the plate. Six examples numbered in Roman and annotated "g.a." and "EA", nine examples numbered in Roman and annotated "g.a."; 33 examples numbered in Arabic and annotated "g.a"; 40 lettered examples (A-Z and AA-NN) annotated "g.a"; six examples numbered in Arabic and annotated "g.a" and "EA".

And They Recognized Him In the Breaking of the Bread
(Et cognoverunt eum in fractio panis)
(FO 245) SB 101 ....…pg 249
1964, 19" x 13¾"
Signed in colored pencil and signed in the plate. Six examples numbered in Roman and annotated "g.a." and "EA", nine examples numbered in Roman and annotated "g.a."; 55 examples numbered in Arabic and annotated "g.a"; one lettered example (A) annotated "g.a"; 16 examples numbered in Arabic and annotated "g.a" and "EA".

There Appeared To Them Separated Tongues
(Apparuerunt illis dispertitae)
(FO 246) SB 102 ....…pg 250
1964, 19" x 13¾"
Signed in colored pencil and signed in the plate. Six examples numbered in Roman and annotated "g.a." and "EA", nine examples numbered in Roman and annotated "g.a.".

A Woman Clothed With the Sun
(Mulier amicta sole)
(FO 247) SB 103 ....…pg 250
1964, 19" x 13¾"
Signed in colored pencil and signed in the plate. Six examples numbered in Roman and annotated "g.a." and "EA", nine examples numbered in Roman and annotated "g.a."; 56 examples numbered in Arabic and annotated "g.a"; three lettered examples (A-C) annotated "g.a";12 examples numbered in Arabic and annotated "g.a" and "EA".

A Great Battle in Heaven
(Proelium magnum in caelo)
(FO 248) SB 104 ....…pg 250
1964, 19" x 13¾"
Signed in colored pencil and signed in the plate. Six examples numbered in Roman and annotated "g.a." and "EA", nine examples numbered in Roman and annotated "g.a.".

Come, Lord Jesus
(Veni, Domine Iesu)
(FO 249) SB 105 ....…pg 251
1964, 19" x 13¾"
Signed in colored pencil and signed in the plate. Six examples numbered in Roman and annotated "g.a." and "EA", nine examples numbered in Roman and annotated "g.a."; one example numbered in Arabic and annotated "g.a." and "EA".

LITHOGRAPHS AND INTAGLIOS PUBLISHED BY LES HEURES CLAIRES, PARIS
Pages 267 – 277 (FO 250-FO 233)
Titles in English, French, and Italian

INTAGLIOS

The Surrealistic Horses
(Les chevaux surrealistes)
(Cavalli surrealisti)
(FO 250).....…....................……pg 267
1975, 18¼" x 14⅝"
Etching and engraving with hand-coloring. Signed in pencil lower right and annotated. An edition of 145 examples on Japon Nacre and numbered in Roman, an edition of 245 examples on Arches wove paper and numbered in Arabic, and an epreuve d'artiste (artist proof) edition on both papers and annotated "EA" exist. Published by La Societe d'Editions d'Art Les Heures Claires, Paris under rights granted to Giuseppe Albaretto by Salvador Dalí.

Saint George and the Dragon
(Saint Georges et Dragon)
(San Giorgio e drago)
(FO 251) ....pg 267
1975, 16¼" x 22½"
Etching and engraving with hand-coloring. Signed in pencil lower right and annotated. An edition of 145 examples on Japon Nacre and numbered in Roman, an edition of 245 examples on Arches wove paper and numbered in Arabic and an eprueve

d'artiste (artist proof) edition on both papers annotated "EA" exist. Published by La Societe d'Editions d'Art Les Heures Claires, Paris under rights granted to Giuseppe Albaretto by Salvador Dalí.

ETCHINGS FROM THE NINE MUSES

Eloquence (Calliope)
(FO 252) ....pg 268
1971, 15½" x 13⅛"
Engraving with hand-coloring. Signed in pencil and annotated. An edition of 95 examples on Japon Nacre and numbered in Roman, an edition of 145 examples and numbered in Arabic and an epreuve d'artiste (artist proof) edition on both papers and annotated "EA" exist. Published by La Societe d'Editions d'Art Les Heures Claires, Paris under rights granted to Giuseppe Albaretto by Salvador Dalí.

History (Clio)
(FO 253) 268
1971, 12½" x 16"
Engraving with hand-coloring. Signed in pencil and annotated. An edition of 95 examples on Japon Nacre and numbered in Roman, an edition of 145 examples and numbered in Arabic and an epreuve d'artiste (artist proof) edition on both papers and annotated "EA" exist. Published by La Societe d'Editions d'Art Les Heures Claires, Paris under rights granted to Giuseppe Albaretto by Salvador Dalí.

Poetry of Love (Erato)
(FO 254) ....pg 269
1971, 15⅜" x 13"
Engraving with hand-coloring. Signed in pencil and annotated. An edition of 95 examples on Japon Nacre and numbered in Roman, an edition of 145 examples and numbered in Arabic and an eprueve d'artiste (artist proof) edition on both papers and annotated "EA" exist. Published by La Societe d'Editions d'Art Les Heures Claires, Paris under rights granted to Giuseppe Albaretto by Salvador Dalí.

Music (Musique) (Euterpe)
(FO 255) ....pg 269
1971, 12½" x 16"
Engraving with hand-coloring. Signed in pencil and annotated. An edition of 95 examples on Japon Nacre and numbered in Roman, an edition of 145 examples and

numbered in Arabic and an eprueve d'artiste (artist proof) edition on both papers and annotated "EA" exist. Published by La Societe d'Editions d'Art Les Heures Claires, Paris under rights granted to Giuseppe Albaretto by Salvador Dalí.

Tragedy (Melpomene) (Tragédie)
(FO 256) .... pg 270
1971, 16⅜" x 13"
Engraving with hand-coloring. Signed in pencil and annotated. An edition of 95 examples on Japon Nacre and numbered in Roman, an edition of 145 examples and numbered in Arabic and an eprueve d'artiste (artist proof) edition on both papers and annotated "EA" exist. Published by La Societe d'Editions d'Art Les Heures Claires, Paris under rights granted to Giuseppe Albaretto by Salvador Dalí.

Sacred Poetry (Polymnie)
(FO 257) .... pg 270
1971, 15½" x 13⅛"
Engraving with hand-coloring. Signed in pencil and annotated. An edition of 95 examples on Japon Nacre and numbered in Roman, an edition of 145 examples and numbered in Arabic and an eprueve d'artiste (artist proof) edition on both papers and annotated "EA" exist. Published by La Societe d'Editions d'Art Les Heures Claires, Paris under rights granted to Giuseppe Albaretto by Salvador Dalí.

Dance (Danse) (Terpsicore)
(FO 258) .... pg 270
1971, 16" x 13"
Engraving with hand-coloring. Signed in pencil and annotated. An edition of 95 examples on Japon Nacre and numbered in Roman, an edition of 145 examples and numbered in Arabic and an eprueve d'artiste (artist proof) edition on both papers and annotated "EA" exist. Published by La Societe d'Editions d'Art Les Heures Claires, Paris under rights granted to Giuseppe Albaretto by Salvador Dalí.

Comedy (Thalie) (Thalia)
(FO 259) .... pg 271
1971, 16" x 12¾"
Engraving with hand-coloring. Signed in pencil and annotated. An edition of 95 examples on Japon Nacre and numbered in Roman, an edition of 145 examples and numbered in Arabic and

an eprueve d'artiste (artist proof) edition on both papers and annotated "EA" exist. Published by La Societe d'Editions d'Art Les Heures Claires, Paris under rights granted to Giuseppe Albaretto by Salvador Dalí.

Astronomy (Uranie) (Astronomie)
(FO 260) .... pg 271
1971, 13" x 16"
Engraving with hand-coloring. Signed in pencil and annotated. An edition of 95 examples on Japon Nacre and numbered in Roman, an edition of 145 examples and numbered in Arabic and an eprueve d'artiste (artist proof) edition on both papers and annotated "EA" exist. Published by La Societe d'Editions d'Art Les Heures Claires, Paris under rights granted to Giuseppe Albaretto by Salvador Dalí.

LITHOGRAPHS

Victory (La victoire) (Vittoria)
(FO 261) .... pg 272
1975, 22¼" x 16½"
Lithograph in color. Signed in pencil and annotated. An edition of 195 examples numbered in Arabic and an edition of eprueve d'artiste (artist proof) examples annotated "EA" exist. Published by La Societe d'Editions d'Art Les Heures Claires, Paris under rights granted to Giuseppe Albaretto by Salvador Dalí.

The Three Elephants
Three Surrealist Elephants
(Les trois éléphantins)
(Trios éléphantins surrealistes)
(Tre elefanti surrealisti)
(FO 262) .... pg 272
1974, 14½" x 19¾"
Lithograph in color. Signed in pencil and annotated. An edition of 245 examples numbered in Arabic and an edition of eprueve d'artiste (artist proof) examples annotated "EA" exist. Published by La Societe d'Editions d'Art Les Heures Claires, Paris under rights granted to Giuseppe Albaretto by Salvador Dalí.

Soft Watches and the Butterflies
(Montres molles et papillons)
(FO 263) .... pg 272
1974, 14¼" x 19¾"
Lithograph in color. Signed in pencil and annotated. An edition of 245 examples numbered in Arabic and an eprueve d'artiste (artist proof) edition and annotated "EA" exist. Published by

La Societe d'Editions d'Art Les Heures Claires, Paris under rights granted to Giuseppe Albaretto by Salvador Dalí.

LITHOGRAPHS FROM DON QUIXOTE

The Hand Kiss
(Le baisemain) (Baciamano)
(FO 264) .... pg 273
1971, 13" x 19⅝"
Lithograph in color. Signed in pencil and annotated. An edition of 145 examples numbered in Arabic and an eprueve d'artiste (artist proof) edition and annotated "EA" exist. Published by La Societe d'Editions d'Art Les Heures Claires, Paris under rights granted to Giuseppe Albaretto by Salvador Dalí.

Homage to Dulcinee
(Homage a Dulcinée)
(Homage a Ducinea)
(FO 265) .... pg 273
1974, 20³⁄₁₆" x 15½"
Lithograph in color. Signed in pencil and annotated. An edition of 245 examples numbered in Arabic and an eprueve d'artiste (artist proof) edition and annotated "EA" exist. Published by La Societe d'Editions d'Art Les Heures Claires, Paris under rights granted to Giuseppe Albaretto by Salvador Dalí.

The Bay of Port Lligat
(La baie de Port Lligat)
(Baia di Port Lligat)
(FO 266) .... pg 273
1974, 15⅝" x 18¼"
Lithograph in color. Signed in pencil and annotated. An edition of 245 examples numbered in Arabic and an eprueve d'artiste (artist proof) edition and annotated "EA" exist. Published by La Societe d'Editions d'Art Les Heures Claires, Paris under rights granted to Giuseppe Albaretto by Salvador Dalí.

LITHOGRAPHS FROM THE ODYSSEY

The Siren
(La siréne)
(Sirene)
(FO 267) .... pg 274
1974, 22" x 16"
Lithograph in color. Signed in pencil and annotated. An edition of 195 examples

numbered in Arabic and an eprueve d'artiste (artist proof) edition and annotated "EA" exist. Published by La Societe d'Editions d'Art Les Heures Claires, Paris under rights granted to Giuseppe Albaretto by Salvador Dalí.

The Hydras
(Les hydres)
(Idre)
(FO 268) .... **pg 274**
1974, 22" x 16"
Lithograph in color. Signed in pencil and annotated. An edition of 195 examples numbered in Arabic and an eprueve d'artiste (artist proof) edition and annotated "EA" exist. Published by La Societe d'Editions d'Art Les Heures Claires, Paris under rights granted to Giuseppe Albaretto by Salvador Dalí.

LITHOGRAPHS FROM 1001 NIGHTS

Aladin's Giant
(Le Géant d'Aladin) (Géant d'Aladin)
(Gigante d'Aladino)
(FO 269) .... **pg 275**
1974, 19" x 13¾"
Lithograph in color. Signed in pencil and annotated. An edition of 245 examples numbered in Arabic and an eprueve d'artiste (artist proof) edition and annotated "EA" exist. Published by La Societe d'Editions d'Art Les Heures Claires, Paris under rights granted to Giuseppe Albaretto by Salvador Dalí.

The Dream-like Dream
(Le rêve onirique)
(Sango onirico)
(FO 270) .... **pg 275**
1974, 22¼" x 16¾"
Lithograph in color. Signed in pencil and annotated. An edition of 195 examples numbered in Arabic and an eprueve d'artiste (artist proof) edition and annotated "EA" exist. Published by La Societe d'Editions d'Art Les Heures Claires, Paris under rights granted to Giuseppe Albaretto by Salvador Dalí.

The Snake and the Apple
(Le serpent e la pomme)
(Serpente e la mela)
(FO 271) .... **pg 275**
1977, 21½" x 16"
Lithograph in color. Signed in pencil and annotated. An edition of 195 examples numbered in Arabic and an eprueve d'artiste (artist proof) edition and annotated "EA" exist. Published by La Societe d'Editions d'Art Les Heures Claires, Paris under rights granted to Giuseppe Albaretto by Salvador Dalí.

The Snake Charmer
(Enchanteurs de serpents)
(Incantatore di serpenti)
(FO 272) .... **pg 276**
1974, 19½" x 14¼"
Lithograph in color. Signed in pencil and annotated. An edition of 245 examples numbered in Arabic and an eprueve d'artiste (artist proof) edition and annotated "EA" exist. Published by La Societe d'Editions d'Art Les Heures Claires, Paris under rights granted to Giuseppe Albaretto by Salvador Dalí.

The Lions
(Les lions)
(Leoni)
(FO 273) .... **pg 276**
1975, 21½" x 16 1/4"
Lithograph in color. Signed in pencil and annotated. An edition of 195 examples numbered in Arabic and an eprueve d'artiste (artist proof) edition and annotated "EA" exist. Published by La Societe d'Editions d'Art Les Heures Claires, Paris under rights granted to Giuseppe Albaretto by Salvador Dalí.

Love Affairs
(Liasons d'amour)
(Liaisons d'amour)
(FO 274) .... **pg 276**
1974, 21¼" x 16"
Lithograph in color. Signed in pencil and annotated. An edition of 245 examples numbered in Arabic and an eprueve d'artiste (artist proof) edition and annotated "EA" exist. Published by La Societe d'Editions d'Art Les Heures Claires, Paris under rights granted to Giuseppe Albaretto by Salvador Dalí.

Mayflower
(Mayflower)
(FO 275) .... **pg 277**
1974, 19¼" x 13½"
Lithograph in color. Signed in pencil and annotated. An edition of 245 examples numbered in Arabic and an eprueve d'artiste (artist proof) edition and annotated "EA" exist. Published by La Societe d'Editions d'Art Les Heures Claires, Paris under rights granted to Giuseppe Albaretto by Salvador Dalí.

Orient
(Orient)
(Oriente)
(FO 276) .... **pg 277**
1974, 19" x 14"
Lithograph in color. Signed in pencil and annotated. An edition of 245 examples numbered in Arabic and an eprueve d'artiste (artist proof) edition and annotated "EA" exist. Published by La Societe d'Editions d'Art Les Heures Claires, Paris under rights granted to Giuseppe Albaretto by Salvador Dalí.

Sinbad the Sailor
(Sindbad le marin)
(Sindbad il marinaio)
(FO 277) .... **pg 277**
1978, 21¾" x 15¾"
Lithograph in color. Signed in pencil and annotated. An edition of 195 examples numbered in Arabic and an eprueve d'artiste (artist proof) edition and annotated "EA" exist. Published by La Societe d'Editions d'Art Les Heures Claires, Paris under rights granted to Giuseppe Albaretto by Salvador Dalí.

ABOUT THE AUTHOR

Eduard Fornés
AUTHOR

Eduard Fornés has authored, edited and – including this book – has now published 20 books on Salvador Dalí, and is unquestionably the most prolific authority on the artist. His publications on Dalí have been translated into multiple languages including English, French, German, Italian, Japanese, Spanish and Catalan.

Fornés began his writing and publishing projects with Dalí in 1977. In 1982, Dalí asked him to personally take on the responsibility of making the Surrealist master known as a writer. "Do you know that I was born to be a writer?" the artist asked him at the time. Fornés' 20th book, *Dalí Illustrator* (2016), took over 20 years to complete due to its exhaustive research. Dr. A. Reynolds Morse, founder of the Salvador Dalí Museum in St. Petersburg, Florida, authored the book's introduction in 1991.

Fornés maintained his relationship with Dalí until the artist's death in 1989. He accompanied the artist's cousin, Montserrat, to Dalí's funeral. His project, *Dalí and His Books: Dalí the Writer, Dalí the Illustrator* (1982) was the origin of 34 major exhibitions that toured for 12 years and visited museums in 11 countries, including Dalí's own museum in Figueres.

Eduard Fornés was born in 1940 and is eldest of three children. His father worked in the wine business in Barcelona. Called at just 13 years of age to the Catholic Church, he began his seminary studies in 1953. He became a priest and remained devoted to his first calling until 1967 when he became disillusioned with the oppressive regime of Franco's fascist dictatorship and observed firsthand the influence it exerted on his beloved Church.

That year, while witnessing a brutal attack by police on a group of festival goers, Fornés opened the doors of his church to shelter the crowd and provide safe sanctuary from the police who surrounded the building with guard dogs at the ready. The next day, the bishop, whom Fornés had believed would laud his efforts to protect the innocent, allowed the police to enter the church and arrest the crowd. Fornés and his fellow priests were also arrested. Tried in a closed-door session in Madrid, Fornés was sentenced by the presiding fascist-leaning judge to two years in a prison in Zamora reserved for anti-fascist clergy. He served a six-month incarceration and upon release — exhausted, malnourished and disillusioned — left the Church to pursue his other passions, writing and publishing.

In 1968, he took his first position in the field as the editorial coordinator for NOVA TERRA, publishing many books and periodicals, many in the Catalan language which was forbidden by the regime. Several of his Catalan publications were directed to the clergy, and he was able to continue these risky projects only through the Church's protection. Today, Fornés retains his friendships with many of the clergy brethren of his youth, and enjoys widespread respect from the contemporary Catalan clergy due to his extraordinary and heroic efforts during the Franco years.

The year 1975 brought Fornés back into the dangerous world of political turmoil in Spain. He was appointed general secretary of the Christian Democratic Party by Mr. Anton Canellas, its president. Through his efforts in this role, he successfully organized his party and brought about the first democratic election campaigns in Spain after the end of the dictatorship in 1977. Upon seeing the elections completed and his political goals for a democratic monarchy achieved, he returned to his writing and publishing.

In 1977, the same year he met Salvador Dalí, he joined the prestigious firm Editorial Labor Book Publishing, assuming the post of director of production. Editorial Labor published art books, technical treatises, medical books, text books and a widely distributed encyclopedia. Fornés also became president of the large printing facility, Iberamerican Graphic Producers Association. These positions were instrumental in the development of Fornés' expertise and preparedness for his work with the demanding and unpredictable Salvador Dalí, and the comprehensive body of work he would produce on the subjects of both Dalí's visual and written works.

After working with Dalí on projects for two years, in 1979, Fornés founded his own publishing company, L'Editorial Meditereanea. Under his direction in 1980, the company published the first collaboration with the artist, the deluxe limited edition *Museum Works*, which included the writings of the Catalan author, Josep Pla. Fornés retained ownership of his company for 31 years, publishing a substantial body of work. Among the 1,500 titles published by L'Editorial Meditereanea during Fornés' stewardship were: 420 titles on cultural subjects; 90 titles on artists (which in addition to his Dalí publications, included books on Gaudí, Subirachs, Abelló and others); 70 novels and poetry compilations; and 530 illustrated children's books. His book, *The Little Story of Dalí*, published in 1989, has sold over one million copies and been translated into 10 languages.

The year 1979 also brought Fornés the opportunity to personally catalog, inventory and assign values to each work included in the Dalí retrospective exhibition held at the Beaubourg (Museum of Modern Art, Paris). He took possession of Dalí's personal collection for this task. Fornés was also instrumental in arranging the presentation of the Gold Medal of the Generalitat of Catalonia to the artist by Catalonia's President, Jordi Pujol, in 1982.

Through L'Editorial Meditereanea, Fornés also founded Distribucions d'Art Surrealista, which held extensive licensing contracts for the creation, distribution and sale of Dalí imagery. Focusing on creating high quality collectibles, souvenirs and memorabilia on Dalí, Fornés' company established itself in the book shop of the Dalí Theater Museum of Figueres, which was conceived, designed and decorated by the artist himself. In 1997, Distribucions d'Art Surrealista was purchased by the Gala-Salvador Dalí Foundation.

In 2010, Fornés sold L'Editorial Meditereanea to the Spanish publishing company Ormograf, which continues to operate it under the original name.

Eduard Fornés lives with his wife, Maria Antonia, in Barcelona. They have three grown children and three grandchildren. He continues to write on topics of art, architecture, literature and the Church and he is active in organizing and cataloging international touring museum exhibitions.

ABOUT THE PUBLISHER

Les Heures Claires, Paris and Director Daniel David

Daniel David was born on July 5, 1946 in Paris, France. After receiving his degree in clinical psychology from the University of Paris, he worked as a teacher and consultant in this field, and in 1984, he created a publication that focused on human sciences. In 1964, he met Mr. Jean Estrade and developed a relationship with him. In 1989 Daniel David and Jean Estrade created the company Lignes et Formes and purchased the publishing houses of Les Heures Claires, Henry Piazza and La Belle Edition, and all of the rights that they possessed. Daniel David and Jean Estrade worked together in the further development of these internationally recognized publishing houses which were already known for the quality of their creations. In 1994, Daniel David and Jean Estrade opened a gallery on Rue de Grenelle in Paris. In 1996, they published *Les Amours de Ronsard*, illustrated by Yvonne Vaulpré Debeauvais and then published *Les Fables de La Fontaine* illustrated with wood engravings by Henry LeMarié in two volumes. In 2005, they published *Cyrano de Bergerac* by Edmond Rostand and illustrated by Vaulpré Debeauvais, which would be the last publication that they produced together. After the death of Jean Estrade in 2005, Daniel David completed a work that Jean Estrade began in 1945 by publishing *L'Aiglon* by Edmond Rostand and illustrated by Vaulpré Debeauvais. In 2008, Les Heures Claires published *Mirages,* which was based on 54 paintings by Etienne Dinet accompanied by 24 short written works of Slimane Ben Ibrahim.

1945 The art publishing house Les Heures Claires, one of the first modern French bibliophiles to receive international recognition, was founded in June, 1945 by Jean Estrade and Jean Rivière. Shortly thereafter, Mr. Estrade and Mr. Rivière were joined by Robert Blairon. Jean Estrade was the artistic and technical director as well as the editor for all of the publications of Les Heures Claires up until his death in 2005.

1947 Les Heures Claires focused its first publications on the best sellers of the period and published *Toi et Moi* by Paul Géraldy and *La Mousson* by Louis Bromfield. The company took on the task of developing young talent, particularly Grau Sala in 1947 and Fontanarosa in 1949.

1948 Starting in 1948, Les Heures Claires worked with the master printer and engraver Raymond Jacquet. The common concern of Jean Estrade and Jacquet for quality, and their passion for beautiful books, guided them in their search for excellence. This taste for excellence and the quality of their creations attracted the famous miniaturist artist Henry LeMarié in 1953.

Raymond Jacquet, who had studied as a wood engraver, picked up his chisel and created a new technique that would allow faithful engravings of the most rich, colorful and precise illustrated works.

At the same time that these wood engravings were produced, the art publishing house Les Heures Claires published many dry points by P.E. Bécat, Grau Sala, Charles Samson and others.

1957 Les Heures Claires established its bibliophile at 19 Rue Bonaparte in Paris and created an edition of *Don Quixote* illustrated by Henry LeMarié, the same artist who also illustrated *Les Fables de La Fontaine.* These works became important benchmarks in the history of illustrated books.

Les Heures Claires also purchased the highly respected art publishing house, H. Piazza, and continued the tradition of good taste and quality for which H. Piazza had become so well known. In 1958, Antoine Branducci joined Les Heures Claires as the commercial director and honorary administrator. He would stay until 1986.

1964 Les Heures Claires published what would become its most important work ever, *The Divine Comedy*. This project took thirteen years from inception to completion. Between 1951 and 1960, Dalí painted 100 watercolors which were to become the basis for 100 wood engravings to illustrate the famous *Divine Comedy* written by Dante Alighieri in the 14th century. Between 1960 and 1964, the extraordinary creation of the wood engravings for *The Divine Comedy* took place. This daring production, demanding four years of work, required the selection of 3,500 blocks, engraved by Raymond Jacquet and Jean Taricco. This achievement of Les Heures Claires was internationally acclaimed and *The Divine Comedy* is now recognized as having been one of the most remarkable achievements of the 20th century in the world of art and illustrated books.

It was during the creation of *The Divine Comedy,* that Jean Estrade began his relationship with Salvador Dalí. During the four-year period it took to create the engravings, Dalí and Estrade would meet often. Dalí personally supervised Jacquet, Taricco and Estrade during the creation of the 3,500 blocks which it would take to finally achieve *The Divine Comedy*. Jacquet and Taricco created the engravings under Dalí's supervision, while Estrade, in collaboration with Dalí, determined the size of the works, the selection of paper, the style of the text and all details regarding the editing of *The Divine Comedy*. Jean Estrade arranged directly with Dalí for Dalí to hand-sign numerous sets of *The Divine Comedy*.

1964 For the occasion of the commencement of the drilling of the Mont Blanc Tunnel, Edmond Giscard d'Estaing requested that the art publishing house Les Heures Claires create a prestigious work for him, *De la Savoie au Pays d'Aoste.*

1965 Jean Rivière decided to separate from his colleagues, and he left the art publishing house Les Heures Claires and continued the art editions of H. Piazza alone.

Les Heures Claires installed their own engraving and printing workshop directed by Jean Taricco, who would engrave the watercolors of Henry LeMarié for *Les Fables de La Fontaine,* while Raymond Jacquet engraved the illustrations of R.W. Thomas for the *Poésies Complètes by Verlaine*. In 1965, Les Heures Claires also created the first edition of the *Œuvres de Jules Verne* illustrated in color by contemporary painters, with Maurice Gonon. It is still the only modern illustrated color edition of that work. In that same year, a work appeared that is still extremely sought after today, *Peintres mes Amis,* illustrated by several of the most famous artists of the 20th century including Picasso, Dufy and Miró.

Between 1965 and 1966, Les Heures Claires discovered Pierre Ambrogiani and Bernard Gantner, two artists who were little known at the time, but whose fame was confirmed with time.

1968 Les Heures Claires published the *Bestiaire* by Guillaume Apollinaire, accompanied by engravings by Tavy Notton.

1968 Les Heures Claires also opened an art gallery at 19 Rue Bonaparte in Paris.

1969   From 1969 to 1972, Les Heures Claires published *Théâtre* by Shakespeare and *L'Imitation de Jésus Christ.* Raymond Jacquet engraved illustrations by Carzou, Léonor Fini, Brayer, Chapelain Midy and others for *Théâtre* by Shakespeare, while Jean Taricco engraved those of Yvonne Vaulpré Debeauvais for *L'Imitation de Jésus Christ.* In October, 1972, Jean Estrade and Robert Blairon presented *L'Imitation de Jésus Christ* to His Holiness Paul VI, who granted them an audience in Rome. Between 1971 and 1978, Jean Estrade was the editor for 67 editions of graphic works of Salvador Dalí that were printed by Les Heures Claires for Salvador Dali and Giuseppe Albaretto, who formed the company Les Heures Claires, Italy. Between 1960 and 1978 Jean Estrade edited 167 graphic editions of the artwork of Salvador Dalí and developed one of, if not the most, significant relationships of editor and artist that Dalí ever experienced. The 168 editions include the 100 wood-engravings from *The Divine Comedy* and 67 works published by Giuseppe Albaretto with his company Les Heures Claires, Italy, but printed by Les Heures Claires, Paris and edited by Jean Estrade.

1972   Les Heures Claires completed the publication of *Ouevres Completès de Molière*, directed by Jean Meyer and started by Maurice Gonon. Also, in 1972, the Biennial of International Graphic Art of Florence awarded the Gold Medal to Marc Dautry for *Les Sonnets de Michel-Ange* through a work created by Les Heures Claires.

1973   Les Heures Claires began distributing its illustrated books in Africa by publishing a bilingual edition of the *Koran* and the edition of *La Vie de Mohammed.* In 1977, Les Heures Claires also published, for distribution in Africa, *La Chronique de Tabari.*

An The French government recognized Les Heures Claires when the President of the Republic of France, Monsieur Valéry Giscard d'Estaing, presented his compliments to Jean Estrade and Robert Blairon and then received them for dinner at the Elysée.

1974   From 1974 to 1976, Jean Taricco engraved the illustrations of Yvonne Vaulpré Debeauvais for the *Oeuvres* of Villon. This work, which was considered among the greatest achievements of Les Heures Claires, was published in 1976.

1975   In December of 1975, Les Heures Claires purchased the publishing house La Belle Edition. In August 1980, Les Heures Claires purchased the publishing house H. Piazza.

1981   Les Heures Claires published *Lettres de mon Moulin,* illustrated by Henry LeMarié, as well as the first of four volumes of *Commentaire du Koran* by Tabari, and the volume *L'Alsace* illustrated by Jean Pierre Rémon. In 1982, Les Heures Claires published *Tristan et Iseult,* illustrated with wood engravings by Marc Dautry.

1989   In April 1989, Les Heures Claires was purchased by SARL Lignes et Formes, created by Jean Estrade and Daniel David.

1996   Les Heures Claires published *Les Amours de Ronsard,* illustrated by Yvonne Vaulpré Debeauvais.

1999 Les Heures Claires published *Les Fables de La Fontaine* in two volumes, illustrated with wood engravings by Henry LeMarié.

2001 For the 100th anniversary of the birth of Dalí, Les Heures Claires published *The Divine Comedy* as a collector's book, in six volumes. This edition was accompanied by reproductions of the original watercolors created by Dalí between 1951 and 1960 for *The Divine Comedy* project. The format of the reproductions was a substantially smaller size than *The Divine Comedy* wood engravings which were completed in 1964.

2005 Les Heures Claires published *Cyrano de Bergerac* by Edmond Rostand, illustrated by Yvonne Vaulpré Debeauvais.

2006 Les Heures Claires published *L'Aiglon* by Edmond Rostand, illustrated by Yvonne Vaulpré Debeauvais.

2008 Les Heures Claires published *Mirages,* which was based on 54 paintings by Etienne Dinet accompanied by 24 short written works of Slimane Ben Ibrahim.

2010 Les Heures Claires published *Le Jazz et la Java,* 30 songs Claude Nougaro illustrated with 30 drawings and 20 lithographs of his friend the painter Jean François Arrigoni Neri.

2012 Les Heures Claires published *12 Poemes des Fleurs du Mal de Charles Baudelaire,* illustrated with 13 lithographs and 48 drawings of Alain Bonnefit. In 2012, the book received the award Le Grand Prix du Jury.

2014 Les Heures Claires published *La Peregrination vers l'Oues de Wu Cheng'Hen,* illustrated with drawings and 17 lithographs by the French-Chinese artist Fanfan Li.

2016 Les Heures Claires published *Dalí Illustrator* by Eduard Fornés.

INDEX OF CONTENTS

GENERAL INDEX